P9-DET-993

UNNATURAL SELECTION

UNNATURAL SELECTION

CHOOSING BOYS OVER GIRLS,
AND THE CONSEQUENCES OF A
WORLD FULL OF MEN

MARA HVISTENDAHL

PUBLICAFFAIRS
New York

Designed by Trish Wilkinson
Text set in 11 point Minion Pro

Library of Congress Cataloging-in-Publication Data

Hvistendahl, Mara.
    Unnatural selection : choosing boys over girls, and the consequences of a world full of men / Mara Hvistendahl.
        p.   cm.
    ISBN 978-1-58648-850-5 (hardback)—ISBN 978-1-58648-991-5 (e-book edition)
    1. Demographic transition—China. 2. Sex determination—China. 3. Birth control—China. 4. Sex discrimination against women—China. I. Title.
HB1064.A3H87 2011
304.6'60951—dc22   2011004471

First Edition

10 9 8 7 6 5 4 3 2

To Mom,
and to moms

CONTENTS

CONTENTS

We will now discuss in a little more detail the Struggle for Existence.

—CHARLES DARWIN,
ON THE ORIGIN OF SPECIES

PROLOGUE

Mao Zedong once said that women hold up half the sky, and until I moved to China I believed it. My mother, a missionary's daughter with a decidedly agnostic bent, was the first to tell me that in the People's Republic men and women were equal. She had spent her teenage years in Asia before returning to the United States to study Chinese history, and when she informed me about Mao's famous fraction she probably took out a photo album and pointed to photos of sensible-looking women with hair cropped into practical bobs. I can't remember. In any case, the lifestyle she chose for us drove the lesson home.

When divorce left my mother with two young children and a mortgage, she took a Chinese friend into our Minneapolis home as a roommate. Hongyu was also recently divorced, and she had a son, who with my brother and me made three. Both Hongyu and my mother soon started graduate school, and they devised a strategy that might today be called coparenting. Back then it was called making do. They were something of an odd couple; my mother was happiest when dancing in a new outfit to Marvin Gaye albums, while Hongyu—who had grown up in Inner Mongolia during the Cultural Revolution—bought her clothes secondhand and could make a chicken last a week. But while they weren't life partners, they were partners in raising us, trading off cooking and child care and planning outings and vacations together.

We lived on discount real estate, in a small house adjacent to the Minneapolis-St. Paul airport. Several times a day airplanes roared overhead, cutting so close to the roof that they darkened the sky and rendered conversation all but impossible. Between the planes and three children stir-crazy from Minnesota winters, I am not sure how my mother and Hongyu ever managed to study. But what I remember most from that time is an impression of strength. In our house women held up all the sky—and took out the garbage.

That impression stayed with me as I grew up, started studying Chinese, and finally went to China. In the summer of 2000 I spent a few months in Beijing on a language course. I was twenty and in college and had seen very little of the world, but from what I could tell my childhood vision of gender equality was accurate. China had female tycoons, female scientists, female writers, and in some ways the lot of women—like that of men— was improving every day. The faces in the photos from my mother's 1980s albums had projected a sort of grim hopefulness. Back then women were so proud to own refrigerators that they crocheted dust covers for them and placed the appliances in the living room. (Then too most Chinese apartments had kitchens so small that refrigerators did not fit anywhere else.) By 2000 women were zipping across Beijing in Audis, dining at fancy restaurants, and stopping in for coffee afterward at Starbucks.

But there were also signs of trouble. Midway through the summer our teachers took us on a field trip to a kindergarten. Probably the goal was to have us talk with the one subset of Chinese people who shared our limited power of expression. What I remember, though, is the school's population. In the sea of tiny smiles that greeted us, boys outnumbered girls.

On the bus ride back to the university one of our instructors, an energetic, sturdy woman named Teacher Zhang, explained in slow, clearly enunciated Chinese. I couldn't have known the word for "ultrasound," which had been imported from the West so recently that it contained a piece of the Roman alphabet: B超. But somehow I understood: some women were going in for scans halfway through their pregnancies. If they discovered their fetus was female, they would abort.

I wish I could say that was my eureka moment, that I fast-forwarded to what it would mean for China as the boys in the kindergarten grew up—that I looked into the issue and realized boys were proliferating in India, Azerbaijan, Vietnam, South Korea, and Albania as well. But the truth is I didn't imagine the sex ratio imbalance could endure. While ultrasound technology was modern, like many people at the time I thought that using it for something as crass as sex selection had to be temporary: one last instance of sexist traditions rearing their ugly head.

It was only after I moved to China to work as a journalist four years later that I started to dwell on the societal implications of a population with tens of millions more men than women. The scene from the kindergarten repeated itself again and again. Once I journeyed to a small city in Shandong province to write an article on the solar heating system being installed in a school, and I found myself in another classroom full of smiling boys. I was tempted to abandon the solar power article and interview the teachers about the school's population. Being my mother's child, and being Hongyu's child, I didn't understand it. But it was clear the sky was sagging.

For as long as they have counted births, demographers have noted that on average 105 boys are born for every 100 girls. This is our natural sex ratio at birth. The ratio can vary slightly in certain conditions and from one geographic region to the next. More boys are born after wars. More girls are born around the equator, for reasons we don't yet understand.[1] But in general the sex ratio at birth hovers around 105.

So is our population male-dominated from the start? To the contrary: that more boys are born is itself a form of balance, neatly making up for the fact that males are more likely to die young. That extra 5 percent of boy babies compensates, as the German statistician Johann Peter Süssmilch observed in 1741, "for the higher male losses due to the recklessness of boys, to exhaustion, to dangerous tasks, to war, to sailing and emigration, thus maintaining the balance between the sexes so that everyone can find a spouse at the appropriate time of marriage."[2] While today males are less likely to die from sailing, exhaustion, or migration, they still account for the majority of soldiers throughout the world. They also disproportionately expose themselves to threats like smoking—a man's pursuit in many countries—or riding motorcycles without wearing a helmet. Boys outnumber girls at birth because men outnumber women in early deaths.

Süssmilch, who was also a priest, was an early proponent of intelligent design; he concluded this natural check was the work of a meticulous creator. (The book in which he put forth his theory was titled *The Divine Order as Derived from Demography*.)[3] When Charles Darwin looked into the sex ratio at birth a century later, he intuited that a balanced number of males and females instead connected somehow to evolution. Trends in human populations, Darwin noted, paralleled those found in the animal world.* But that raised a question: What then was the purpose of the intense battles for mates among many species? To witness "two males fighting for the possession of the female, or several male birds displaying their gorgeous plumage, and performing strange antics before an assembled body of females," as Darwin wrote in *The Descent of Man*, it was clear that a fierce evolutionary competition was at work.[4] This competition was perhaps most evident in the peacock's feathers: the colorful plumes would make sense if, as a rule, the sex ratio were skewed. If peahens were generally scarce, the male birds' adornment would be a feature they had developed over generations to boost their chances of passing on their genes. A balanced sex ratio meant even the ugliest and most pitiful peacock had hope of finding a peahen.

But after extensive correspondence with farmers, shepherds, and biologists—Darwin even dutifully tallied sex ratios among English racehorses—the naturalist determined most species were in fact balanced. "After investigating, as far as possible, the numerical proportion of the sexes," he wrote, "I do not believe that any great inequality in number commonly exists."[5]

Darwin went back and forth on exactly how a balanced sex ratio could be reconciled with his theory of natural selection, coming very close to a solution in the first edition of *The Descent of Man* and then retracting it in the second edition. "I now see that the whole problem is so intricate that it is safer to leave its solution for the future," he wrote.[6] And yet the naturalist surmised that balanced sex ratios were somehow critical to species survival.

---

*To Süssmilch's reasons for early male deaths Darwin added one gleaned from observing animals: males, he wrote, are "exposed to various dangers, whilst wandering about in eager search for the females."

In 1930 the English scientist Ronald A. Fisher arrived at the explanation that had eluded Darwin. Fisher's theory works like this in humans: if male births become less common, men have better mating prospects than women. People with an assumed genetic disposition to have boys then have an advantage in passing on their genes. Put more simply, parents of sons have more grandchildren than parents of daughters. As the overall sex ratio approaches equilibrium, however, the advantage of producing sons disappears, and the sex ratio at birth balances out. (Unfortunately, this mechanism does not work on skewed sex ratios of the sort seen in Asia today.) Fisher was also an enthusiastic eugenicist who believed in sterilizing the "unfit." With John Maynard Keynes, he was among the founding members of the Cambridge University Eugenics Society.[7] But he enshrined in evolutionary biology the notion that sex ratios are naturally balanced. Today a 1:1 sex ratio is called "Fisherian."

A balanced sex ratio is now considered healthy in most species, to the extent that conservation work often focuses on boosting the number of females. It isn't just that females are the ones who bear offspring, though of course that matters. In mammals who spend years rearing their young a skewed sex ratio can quickly veer out of control. If females are scarce, males may kill a female's existing offspring to maximize their chance at passing on their genes, inadvertently speeding up the species' path toward extinction. When the sex ratio of a group of brown bears living in the French Pyrenees recently skewed male, conservationists recommended a relocation program aimed at bringing males closer to potential mates. As one scientist put it, "Male bears need more females."[8]

But when it comes to our own species, we are considerably less attentive. While evolution encourages a balanced sex ratio, our large brains have always worked against one. For as long as we have documented reproduction, we have also sought ways to control it.

The ancient Greeks believed that when it came to procreation men's testicles had specific roles: the left testicle produced girls, while the right one yielded boys. Aristotle took this to its logical but painful conclusion, teaching that men should tie off their left testicle during intercourse if they wanted a son. Well into the eighteenth century European men continued to follow this line of thinking; some went so far as to cut off their left gonad.[9] But Aristotle also believed a baby's sex was determined by a number of other factors. Women, he advised, should help their suffering husbands by making an effort to "think male."[10] And he observed, based on interviews with farmers, that with livestock "more males are born if copulation takes place when north [rather] than when south winds are blowing."[11]

The Greeks were hardly alone in offering complicated prescriptions for sex control. The Talmud advised men to bring their wives to early orgasm in order to have a son, advice that may have ended up in more pregnancies but probably had little effect on the sex ratio.[12] And Indian ayurvedic texts outlined practices for manipulating the sex of a fetus—once it was in the mother's womb.[13]

But it is only in the past three decades that we have been able to control a baby's sex with certainty. Our new capabilities demand a reconsideration of Darwin's work. What does it mean to tinker with one of evolution's most fundamental balances? Do we have the hubris to assume that what disrupts the brown bear won't affect us? We still don't know the evolutionary effects of fundamentally altering the sex ratio at birth, but a cursory glance back at history suggests it is not a great idea to mess with something we don't understand.[14]

If anything, we are making more of a mess of our species than brown bears ever could of theirs. When I started thinking about this book, I pictured talking to parents, demographers, perhaps a few government officials. I did not imagine I was beginning a journey on which I'd encounter prostitutes and trafficked wives and mail-order brides, gun enthusiasts and militant nationalists and the proprietor of a *Fight Club*–like "anger bar," geneticists and AIDS researchers—and a lone U.S. military contractor. I did not know it would take me back in time to the American Wild West and into the future to the 2047 India that now preoccupies fans of science fiction. I did not picture villages in poor countries where most women have been sold or villages in rich countries where most have been bought. I had only the vague idea that a sharp decrease in women could not be good for the human race. And on that point I was proven sadly correct.

———— ✎ ————

On other assumptions I was wrong. I began reporting on the sex ratio imbalance by making a series of trips to a particularly skewed quarter of

China, a corner of Jiangsu province where the ratio of boys to girls born had reached 3 to 2. After the third trip I returned to Shanghai and read everything I could find on the topic. I had been assigned a long article for the *Virginia Quarterly Review*, a small literary magazine whose editor gives writers a rare degree of freedom, and as I sat down to write I decided it would be a story about gender discrimination and how it persisted as China developed. That wasn't just my own prejudice. As a science journalist I was used to relying on data, and that was what all the reports said. It was also what the parents I had interviewed told me.

That article ran to nineteen pages, but when I finished it I felt vaguely unfulfilled. I still didn't fully understand why girls were "missing" from China, as some had put it. The way I grew up and the degree of gender progress I witnessed in the few years I'd spent in China conflicted with the notion that entrenched discrimination was at play. Somewhere in the back of my mind lingered my mother's descriptions of equality, even as I recognized that on the most fundamental level men and women were no longer equal. Some reports I read traced the disappearance of girls to the one-child policy, to the fact that Chinese parents wanted to carry on the family line with their one chance to have a child. That made some sense. And yet the one-child policy did not explain why girls had gone missing from Albania or Azerbaijan. But as the article grew into a more ambitious undertaking I stuck to the gender discrimination explanation, for it was the only one I had. "The best way to convince more couples to have girls," I wrote in the proposal for this book, "is to improve the status of women by boosting opportunities for education and career advancement."

It was midway through a trip to India that I realized the reports I'd been reading were wrong. Two men I met there—a gynecologist and a public health worker—told me a very different tale. In their version of events, the sex ratio imbalance now sweeping through Asia and parts of Europe traces to elite institutions in the West.

At first I was skeptical: how had the reporters, demographers, and various activists who write about sex ratio imbalance missed such a critical link? But a little time wading through archives quickly cured me of disbelief. And that is how this became a book about information that some had hoped to keep hidden, about misguided theorists focused only on the big picture and scientists with tunnel vision, and about population, technology, and abortion.

A final word on this last point: not all sex selection involves abortion. Sophisticated technologies used with in-vitro fertilization or artificial insemination now allow parents to control the sex of a baby at the embryonic stage—in some cases even before conception. But outside of the United States those technologies are still nascent. Today in the developing world, abortion is most of the story. For now.

Abortion is also an issue with a long and fraught history in the United States. That history should not affect Americans' concern for what happens in China and India, but sadly it does. I inherited my mother's agnosticism, and I have always believed in a woman's right to terminate a pregnancy, but again and again over the course of reporting this book I ended up treading onto unexpected political ground. At moments I found myself perusing right-wing religious websites and agreeing with anti-abortion activists and corresponding with public relations officers whose voice mail messages ended with "God bless." At others I shook my head in dismay at deceptive reports put out by organizations whose dictums I had once accepted as fact. More frequently, I was disappointed at the degree to which domestic American politics prevented action on a problem of great importance shaping a large portion of the world's population—a fact for which both the right and the left bear responsibility.

The finer points of the abortion debate elude me. When does life begin? And what do we mean by life—a heartbeat, the ability to exist outside the womb with medical assistance, the ability (now something else entirely) to exist outside the womb without technology? These questions have always struck me as unanswerable, and my reporting only made them more muddled. The reality I know is too nuanced to support an absolute line. A zygote is different from a fetus at six months, and a fetus at six months is different from a baby. And any mother will tell you there are many gradations in between—the first bout of morning sickness, the first kick to the gut, the first secondhand hiccup.

Since I refuse to venture a guess at when life begins, this is not a book about death and killing. I do not talk about feticide or gendercide or genocide, though some of the people I interviewed use those terms. On the other hand, I don't believe the gradations in fetal development and the process by which life takes shape should be ignored, for they are what make widespread sex selection possible. Women who would never kill a newborn girl may abort on the basis of sex, and women who would never selectively abort may feel differently about eliminating embryos or sorting sperm. But in the end this is a book not about life and death but about the *potential* for life—and denying that potential to the very group responsible for perpetuating our beleaguered species.

PART ONE

"EVERYONE HAS BOYS NOW"

Chapter 1

THE DEMOGRAPHER

It is often said that women make up a majority of the world's population. They do not.

—AMARTYA SEN[1]

Midway through his career, Christophe Guilmoto stopped counting babies and started counting boys. A French demographer with a mathematician's love of numbers and an anthropologist's obsession with detail, he had attended graduate school in Paris in the 1980s, when babies had been the thing—the only thing, really. The field of demography had grown out of Thomas Malthus's eighteenth-century predictions of exponential population growth and had remained focused on fertility figures and total population counts straight through the 1970s, when books like *The Population Bomb* gripped the popular imagination. By the time Guilmoto started his PhD, birth rates had started falling around the world, but the populations of many developing nations were still growing, and it was hard to shake the idea that overpopulation was a grave threat. Like many of his contemporaries, he concentrated on studying the drop in fertility, searching for clues of what factors proved decisive in lowering a country's birth rate. He did his dissertation research in Tamil Nadu, a state in southwestern India where the birth rate had fallen to European levels even as income levels remained low, and as he graduated and started working as a

3

scholar he returned there many times. By 1998 he headed up the South India Fertility Project, a formal effort to catalog the successes of Tamil Nadu and surrounding states.[2] But over the course of working in India, he realized demography's big story had changed. People were not simply having fewer children. They were having fewer girls. Population growth had been slowed, in part, by reducing the number of daughters.

Guilmoto's first inkling that something was wrong came in 1992, when he interviewed village nurses in Tamil Nadu for a short research project. A wiry Frenchman with wide-set eyes rattling off questions in Tamil, he must have cut an odd profile, but when he explained that he wanted to understand the demographic history of the area, the nurses spoke frankly and openly. Several offered up the detail that villagers occasionally killed their daughters shortly after birth. The news shocked him—as a demographer, he was well aware that humans committed infanticide at various points throughout history, but in most cultures the practice had disappeared by the early twentieth century—and he made it his private mission to determine just how pervasive daughter killing was. Later he visited an orphanage, where he found an aging French volunteer who had lived in India so long that she no longer spoke French. In a mixture of Tamil and English, the woman explained that most of the babies abandoned in the area were female. "Look, in the orphanage we have mostly girls," she said. "What do you think?"

The encounters left a deep impression on Guilmoto, and he thought of them at the turn of the millennium, when Indian census figures showed 111 boys born for every 100 girls.[3] At first glance, the experiences of the village nurses and the orphanage worker helped explain the disparity, and indeed many foreign press reports blamed India's dearth of girls on infanticide and abandonment. Looking into the matter, however, he realized they were only a small part of the story. Outside of the pocket of rural Tamil Nadu where he had happened to do field research, Indians rarely killed infants. "Everybody talked about infanticide because it carried more emotional weight," he recalled. "But actually it was hardly in existence." Tamil Nadu was one of the states where girls in fact had a better prospect of survival, while the northwest, a wealthy region considered India's breadbasket, reported a regional sex ratio at birth of 126: 126 boys for every 100 girls.[4] The real cause for the gap, Guilmoto quickly learned, was that pregnant women were taking advantage of a cheap and pervasive sex determination technique—ultrasound—and aborting female fetuses.

The link to technology was alarming, for it meant that India's skewed sex ratio at birth was an outgrowth of economic progress, not backward traditions. And India was hardly alone in recently developing a sex ratio imbalance. As he expanded his focus from fertility rates to sex ratio at birth, Guilmoto found that several other Asian countries exceeded the biological upper limit of 106 boys born for every 100 girls.* In the 1980s, South Korea, Taiwan, and parts of Singapore registered sex ratios at birth of above 109.[5] China reported a sex ratio of 120. (Figures in both China and India have since risen to 112 in India and 121 in China.)[6] Humans, Guilmoto realized, were engineering what he calls "rampant demographic masculinization"—a change with potentially grave effects for future generations.[7] "It was very difficult," he said, "not to see it as a revolution." Within a few years, the revolution would spread to Western Asia and on to Eastern Europe.

And yet in the places where this sinister biological shift should have been front and center, it was noticeably absent. Reports on global gender issues omitted the imbalance entirely, copiously detailing the status of women and yet ignoring the blatant fact that their ranks were decreasing. The United Nations Population Fund (UNFPA), the agency that finances population initiatives in the developing world, had been largely silent on the issue. Sex ratio imbalance lacked attention from reproductive rights organizations or funding from major philanthropies. With the exception of a few impassioned doctors and public health workers in Asia, it lacked advocates, period.

For the past few years Guilmoto, now a senior fellow at the Institut de recherche pour le développement in Paris, has tried to fill that void by educating the world about the gravity of sex ratio imbalance. In 2005 he calculated that if Asia's sex ratio at birth had remained at its natural equilibrium of 105 over the past few decades, the continent would have an additional 163 million females.[8] The combination of ultrasound and

---

*While 105 is our natural sex ratio at birth, anything between 104 and 106 is considered acceptable.

abortion, in other words, has claimed over 160 million potential women and girls—in Asia alone. In the years he has spent studying the issue, the French scholar has noticed imbalanced sex ratios at birth crop up in unexpected places as economic development reaches new regions. And yet, because of other pressures on United Nations demographers, UN Population Division projections for the number of men and women who will inhabit the earth two, three, and five decades from now assume the sex ratio at birth has reached its highest level ever.[9] Guilmoto believes those projections give a dangerously optimistic picture of where we're headed. To him, gender imbalance resembles what demographers call a transitional phenomenon—a phase nations go through as they develop. That means it won't be around forever. But countries in Asia and Eastern Europe are developing quickly, and many more are on the brink of economic progress. Millions of households around the world will enter the middle class over the coming years. In the process of leveling out, the world's sex ratio imbalance will get a lot worse.

If 160 million women were missing from the U.S. population, you would notice—160 million is more than the entire female population of the United States.[10] Imagine America's women wiped out. Imagine the country's malls and supermarkets, its highways and hospitals, its boardrooms and classrooms exclusively filled with men. Imagine the bus or the subway or the car that takes you to work, then erase the females commuting alongside you. Erase your wife and your daughter. Or erase yourself. Imagine this and you come close to picturing the problem.

But women have not disappeared from North America. They have disappeared from Asia and Eastern Europe. And that is why if you have heard about the gender imbalance it probably came in the form of a short international news item. Gender imbalance has been treated as a local problem, as something that happens to other countries. It is not a local problem. China and India together account for one third of the global population.[11] Their lopsided birth totals have already skewed the sex ratio at birth of the entire world, which has risen from 105 to the biologically impossible 107.[12] Sex selection defies culture, nationality, and creed. Gender imbalance has hit Vietnam, which wasn't supposed to be patriarchal enough to avoid having girls. It has hit the Caucasus countries—Azerbaijan, Georgia, and Armenia—which no one had even contemplated as possible trouble zones. And it has hit the Balkans, that war-torn region a quick boat ride from Italy. Added up, these figures yield a gap in male and female births unrivaled in human history.[13] The gender imbalance is a local problem in the way a superpower's financial crisis is a local problem, in the way a neighboring country's war is a local problem. Sooner or later, it affects you.

If today's disproportionately male generation of young people—call them Generation XY—were small, the sex ratio imbalance would be easy to dismiss. We might make up for the lack of women later on. But because the reduction in the number of females in the population has paralleled a reduction in the global birth rate, this generation is the largest that will hit many developing countries for decades to come.[14] There are fewer potential mothers in China and India today, and tomorrow there will be even fewer daughters. Wang Feng, a demographer at the Brookings Institution who studies China's sex ratio imbalance, calls it a "double whammy."[15] Guilmoto, meanwhile, now disseminates a bleak set of predictions in an attempt to jolt the world to action. Even using the conservative UN population projections, which assume that couples soon start having boys and girls in equal numbers—a change that is highly unlikely—restoring the global balance of males and females will take until 2050.[16]

⸺⬥⸺

Development was not supposed to look like this. For as long as they have speculated about the status of women, social scientists have taken for granted that women's position improves as countries get richer. Economic growth means that more girls go to school, and that those girls have access to a broader array of job opportunities when they grow up. It means that health care improves, leading to a drop in the number of mothers who die during childbirth. And it means, in most cases, that women gain access to contraception, allowing them to have fewer children and in turn spend more time working outside the home.

The relationship between women's empowerment and development is so sacred that it clouded the perception of scholars in developing countries as sex selection spread throughout Asia. Even as they witnessed the introduction of cheap ultrasound machines, many downplayed the impact of sex selective abortion, thinking it would disappear as their countries grew wealthier. At the Korea Women's Development Institute in Seoul, sociologist Whasoon Byun confessed to thinking sex selection a distant threat when it hit South Korea in the 1980s. "My assumption was that if a woman was educated, then she would prefer a girl," she told me. "But my assumption was wrong. I thought my case was general. I was a bad sociologist." Instead, South Korea maintained a skewed sex ratio at birth straight through its entry to the elite club of nations that is the Organisation for Economic Co-operation and Development.[17]

Scholarly thinking began to change in 1990, when the Nobel Prize–winning economist Amartya Sen published a watershed essay in *The New York Review of Books* entitled "More Than 100 Million Women Are Missing." Social science theories had failed scholars, Sen wrote. Despite the economic progress that had swept Asia, at the level of raw numbers women and girls were worse off than ever before. "Economic development," he stated, "is quite often accompanied by a relative worsening in the rate of survival of women"—a fact that constituted "one of the more momentous, and neglected, problems facing the world today."[18]

Sen did not sufficiently explain why 100 million women were missing, but simply by pointing out the disparity he made an impact.* His essay was both a wakeup call and an embarrassment to scholars. Western anthropologists and sociologists realized that in their painstaking analyses of women's status across countries and cultures they had missed the big picture. Demographers saw they had been counting and projecting the wrong metric. Local scholars like Byun cast about for a new development theory that better explained their realities.

By the time Guilmoto turned his attention to the sex ratio imbalance, it had become fashionable to study Sen's missing women. But rather than illuminate the reasons behind the disturbing shortage of females, this boom in studies, and the press coverage that followed it, had the effect of further obscuring the issue. False accounts of female infanticide and

---

*Like the later foreign press reports, Sen blamed the gap on female infanticide combined with selective neglect of girls, not once mentioning sex selective abortion.

widespread abandonment of girls in India were just the beginning. Some scholars found the gap between boy and girl births so outrageous that they concluded it must be the result of girls going unregistered. In the interpretation that gained credence for a few years, females were not missing; they were *hidden.* Papers appeared with titles like "Manipulation of Statistical Records in Response to China's Population Policies" and "On the Trail of 'Missing' Indian Females."[19] Others dreamed up still more fanciful explanations. In 2005 University of Chicago economist Emily Oster wrote a paper claiming that the high rate of hepatitis B among Asians, which increases the probability a woman will give birth to a boy, was responsible for nearly half of Amartya Sen's 100 million missing women.[20] (Among other problems, Oster's analysis did not account for the fact that in countries with imbalances the sex ratio at birth jumps significantly for children born second or later, a phenomenon that can't be explained by disease. She later retracted her findings.)[21] Western scholars found comfort in numbers, which could be interrogated and turned around or explained away. To read the papers written during this time is to be pulled into a world where an explanation is judged by the elegance of its equations rather than by how accurately those equations represent what is actually happening in a region's villages and hospitals and classrooms. Asian scholars working on the ground, meanwhile, talked to average people extensively and then offered up narrow conclusions that explained sex selection as the product of local practices and traditions. In India they looked at the convention of dowry, which made daughters expensive; in China they focused on the one-child policy, which meant parents had limited chances to have a son.[22] Cultural and political constraints mattered, of course, but they did not explain why sex ratio imbalance had hit so many countries at the same time. The problem demanded a global theory.

A few years into researching gender imbalance, Guilmoto decided he would come up with one. "I was fed up with the local stories," he told me. "There is a general trend of son preference visible in many places, and that is what matters." As the number of missing females surged from 100 million to 160 million, he traveled the world, talking to government statisticians and hospital directors, touring cities and villages, and clipping newspaper reports. He combed through all the birth statistics he could find. He made digital sex ratio maps of Asia and Europe, shading danger zones in red. Then he started searching for patterns.

Initially his data raised more questions than it answered. At the time he sat down to analyze his maps, Asian countries with skewed sex ratios at birth could be divided into regional blocks—East Asia (China, Taiwan, Singapore, and Vietnam), South Asia (India and Pakistan), and West Asia (Armenia, Azerbaijan, and Georgia).[23] Beyond that, things got tricky. Sex selection happened among Hindus, Muslims, and Christians; among ethnic and political rivals; in economic powerhouses and in countries just on the cusp of development. Sexism might be an obvious culprit for imbalance if it weren't so universal. Parents in nearly all cultures say they prefer boys, and yet sex selection only strikes in part of the world.*

As Guilmoto continued to research the issue, however, he found some common threads that unite countries with gender imbalances. First, the countries where sex selection occurs are developing rapidly, and their health care systems have matured to the point where prenatal screening is widely available. Second, abortion is pervasive. China, Vietnam, and South Korea all have exceptionally high abortion rates, and a reliance on pregnancy termination as a contraception method is also common to the Caucasus countries, as former Soviet republics. The final commonality derived from his early work in India. Most affected countries have recently experienced a drop in fertility.

Over the past fifty years Asia has seen the most rapid decline in population growth of any continent in the history of the world. In the late 1960s, the average Asian woman had 5.7 children. In 2006 she had 2.3.[24] When it comes to sex selection, a drop in the total fertility rate to two children is something of a turning point. If parents have more than two children, they have a good chance of having a son by sheer chance, without technological intervention. If they have only two children, though, 24 percent will conceive only daughters—and 24 percent screening for sex and aborting is enough to seriously skew a country's sex ratio.[25] And yet in parts of East Asia parents rarely have even two children. In South Korea, Japan, Taiwan, Singapore, Hong Kong, and Macau, which together boast the lowest fertility rates in the world, parents are far more

---

*This was even true for the United States until recently.

likely to have one. Moving beyond the Asian tigers, the list of low fertility countries reads like a rundown of hot spots for missing girls. The
average Vietnamese woman has only 1.9 children. Her Chinese counterpart has 1.5. Georgians are at 1.4 children per couple, just behind Swit-
zerland. Armenians rank even further down the list, with just over 1.3, a
total fertility rate close to that of Italy. Azerbaijanis have fewer children
than Americans do.[26]

Examining geographical variations within countries with imbalances
yielded still more insights. By breaking down sex ratio at birth by city
and region and then comparing those figures against education and income levels, Guilmoto found sex selection typically starts with the urban,
well educated stratum of society. Elites are the first to gain access to a
new technology, whether MRI scanners, smart phones—or ultrasound
machines. In South Korea the first parents to selectively abort were urbanites in Seoul. In Azerbaijan they were residents of Baku, the capital.[27]
According to India's 2001 census, women with high school diplomas and
above who gave birth over the previous year had 114 boys for every 100
girls. Among illiterate women, by contrast, the sex ratio for recent births
was just over 108—still skewed, but much closer to normal.[28] This holds
true for fathers' education too: Indian households in which the head—
and in India the father is almost always the head—has at least a high
school diploma are 25 percent more likely to have a boy than those where
the head has minimal schooling.[29]

But like any new technology, sex selection does not remain the domain of the elite. Women whisper to each other about the new technique
over tea, neighbors copy neighbors, and the middle class emulates the
rich. By the time the technology reaches the lower classes, the elite is often ready to move on to the next big thing. But a technology that shapes
human reproduction is by its nature more significant than a cell phone,
and it takes longer to disseminate. From start to finish, thirty years might
elapse—enough to indelibly mark two generations.

If gender imbalance is a transitional phase, as Guilmoto believes, then
the phase is over in South Korea, which after decades of rampant sex
selection now has a normal sex ratio at birth. The wealthier parts of
China and India have hit their peak; their sex ratios at birth are still
shockingly high but show a slight decline.[30] In regions and countries that

were touched by economic development later, however, the phase is just beginning. In Vietnam, for example, sex selective abortion is mainly practiced by middle- and upper-class people in and around Hanoi. Guilmoto fears the poor could soon embrace it. Other places still have normal sex ratios at birth, but their proximity to countries or regions where sex selection is rampant suggest they will be the next to develop imbalances: southern and eastern India, western China, Nepal, and Bangladesh.* "Masculinization" is not something demographers have encountered before—not on this scale, at least. And yet, as Guilmoto crunched numbers and searched for patterns, he realized it had a parallel. In the manner in which it diffused through populations, gender imbalance looked eerily like an epidemic.

⸺⸭⸺

I meet Guilmoto in his office at the Institut de recherche pour le développement, which is situated on a broad thoroughfare lined with cafés and shops in Paris's twentieth arrondissement, one steamy day in August. Most Parisians have fled the city for the beaches of the south, and even on a Tuesday the institute is deserted, its corridors dark and stuffy. The only other person on the floor where Guilmoto sits, working straight through the vacation in a small office decorated with colorful batik prints, is a janitor. Today, like every other time I meet or speak with the demographer over the coming year, his behavior conveys the sense that time is running out.

When I arrive, Guilmoto's computer screen is filled with a cluttered spreadsheet. He has been scanning Vietnamese birth registration statistics in search of abnormalities. A skewed sex ratio at birth has been found in some northern Vietnamese provinces, but others are, for now, unscathed, and it is these areas he is monitoring closely. Early changes in policy have been shown to lessen the impact of sex selection, and if sex ratio imbalance can be caught sooner, Guilmoto believes, governments may be convinced to take action. "When I have free time I scan

---

*Pregnant women from Nepal's Terai region have already started crossing into India for ultrasound examinations.

data," he explains, as if poring over spreadsheets were a common hobby. He abandons the monitor and rises to shake my hand. "Any language I can handle. Recently I tried scanning data for Tunisia in Arabic. I had to give up."

But the exercise isn't always futile. It was precisely this sort of analysis that led to the discovery of sex ratio imbalance in the Caucasus countries. No one had thought to look for missing girls in Azerbaijan, Armenia, and Georgia. The three small countries sandwiched between the Black and Caspian seas have far more in common with Europe, after all, than with China or South Korea. Guilmoto takes our interview into CEPED's kitchen, where he makes himself a double espresso as he explains that the Caucasus countries also have very little in common with each other: "One is Muslim, one is Orthodox Christian, and one is Armenian Christian. They have three different religious groups, and they are at war with each other on a regular basis." Geography, he adds, is about all they share.

Then one day Guilmoto's friend France Meslé, who works down the street from him at the National Institute of Demographic Studies, was analyzing birth and death statistics in former Soviet countries when she noticed a striking gap between the numbers of male and female infants born in the Caucasus region. Meslé was initially skeptical that sex selection could have caused the gap. The number of female births had begun dropping after the fall of the Soviet Union, as bureaucracy weakened and the quality of government records deteriorated, and like scholars confronted with large imbalances in China and India in the 1990s, she reasoned that maybe families in the three countries had simply stopped bothering to register their daughters.[31] "There are a lot of problems with data quality now," she told me. "And I was very surprised" by the Caucasus figures.

To double-check the figures, she enlisted two other scholars, and together they contacted every county in the region to collect records at the district level. When they compared these numbers against countrywide totals for sex ratio at birth, the national data turned out to disturbingly accurate—with the exception of Armenia, where the actual sex ratio at birth was even more extreme than national records had indicated. All told, the Caucasus countries' gender imbalance rivaled that of China and India. The sex ratio at birth in Azerbaijan was 115. In Georgia it was 118. In Armenia, it was a whopping 120.[32]

Meslé's research, which Guilmoto included in *Watering the Neighbour's Garden,* an edited volume he and a colleague recently compiled on sex ratio imbalance, was important to his own work. It meant that sex selection defied geographic as well as religious and ethnic stereotyping: it happened in Central, South, and East Asia. And it meant that the "masculinization" that had struck him, back in India, as a revolution was spreading around the globe.

But even with Meslé's study to point to, he has encountered stiff resistance in trying to convince policymakers that the sex ratio at birth in the Caucasus countries is truly askew. He recalls meeting an Armenian statistician working for the Armenian UNFPA office at a conference in New York several years after the incriminating data had been published. When Guilmoto brought up Armenia's skewed sex ratio at birth, the man gave him a blank look. "The guy had no clue about it!" the French demographer recalls. "He said, 'That's very interesting, what you're saying. How do you know?' I said, 'Well, Armenian data.' He said, 'Oh really, is that so?' Then he said something stupid like, 'Maybe we should work on it.' And I said, 'Yeah, I think it's high time!'"

We return to his office, where we are interrupted from time to time by the hum of a vacuum cleaner coming from the hall. Guilmoto simply talks over it. The newest area to show a sex ratio imbalance, he says, is Europe. He ticks off a list of suspected candidates in the Balkans: "There is definitely something in Albania. Might be something in Bosnia, might be something in Serbia—not very clear. Probably something in Montenegro, in Kosovo, and in Macedonia."

Just keeping track of new hot spots would be a full-time job. But recently Guilmoto has become preoccupied with another issue, and as a result he has less and less time for scanning birth statistics. He now worries about the tens of millions of bachelors due to come of age in the next few decades.

Demographers call them "surplus men": the ones left over in an imagined world in which everyone who can marry does so. Men doomed to a life of singledom. Overstock. But the loneliness that accompanies bachelorhood is in fact the least of Asia's problems. Surplus men have been going to great lengths to find women—and in many cases succeeding. As the first generation touched by sex ratio imbalance grows up, the silent biological discrimination that is sex selection has been exacerbated by more visible threats to women, including sex trafficking, bride buying, and forced marriages. In South Korea and Taiwan, surplus men obtain wives on one-week "marriage tours" of Vietnam. In wealthy parts of China and India, men buy women from poorer regions, working through shady brokers who may or may not bother to secure the women's consent. In poorer parts of China and India, they visit brothels staffed by prostitutes who have often been forced into sex work.

As Generation XY matures in other parts of the gender-imbalanced world, moreover, even such crude tactics will not be an option. Men in western China, eastern India, Vietnam, Georgia, Albania, and other countries with recent or looming sex ratio imbalances will not be able to import women because at some point in the near future the supply of women will dry up. "The idea of importing brides to solve the shortage in women may work in countries with lower populations, but in a huge country like China they are just a drop in the ocean," China Population Association deputy director Tian Xueyuan recently told the *China Daily*, as if diminishing numbers were the only problem with bringing in boatloads of bought foreign women. "It's not a realistic solution."[33]

Lately, Guilmoto has dedicated himself to calculating precisely how bad the male surplus will be by, as he puts it, "trying to marry these guys off." The outlook, he says, is grim. "It's not sustainable. It's not such a great idea to have children of only one gender. At the beginning it's a dream—I call it a male utopia." He smiles slightly. "But if you start imagining that the neighbors are going to do the same, then these good-looking boys will face trouble in the marriage market. The surplus will pile up."

And it won't just be forlorn single men who will suffer in 2020s Asia and 2030s Eastern Europe. Other scholars have begun to calculate the impact tens of millions of surplus men will have on everything from health care to crime. Historically, societies in which men substantially outnumber women are not nice places to live. Often they are unstable. Sometimes they are violent.

Which brings us back to Guilmoto's contention that gender imbalance resembles an epidemic. In the number of lives it has touched, he says, sex selection merits comparison with AIDS. In the introduction to

Watering the Neighbour's Garden, he and colleague Isabelle Attané point out that AIDS has claimed an estimated 25 million people worldwide—a mere fraction of the number of missing females. "Suffice to compare" the two issues, they write, "to gauge the relative lack of interest that the female deficit has attracted."[34] In 2008, the HIV virus commanded fully one-fourth of global spending on health.[35] AIDS has the attention of nongovernmental organizations, policymakers, and schoolchildren around the world. It boasts its own United Nations agency. Sex selection remains mostly invisible, however, a more pervasive and yet quieter epidemic, observed only by demographers scrutinizing birth registration records years after the fact—and, of course, by the hundreds of millions of people who live or will live in communities where women are scarce.

Chapter 2

The Parent

Money often costs too much.
—RALPH WALDO EMERSON

The county of Suining sits halfway between Shanghai and Beijing in northern Jiangsu province's Huai valley, the agricultural plain that is something like China's heartland. For centuries, it was nothing more than that: an area notable only for its ordinariness. The people of Suining eat food that's a little spicy, a little salty, a little sweet. They speak a dialect that's close to Mandarin and intelligible to most outsiders. The most famous person to come from the area was the emperor Gaozu, who ruled in the third century BC, and even he was of humble peasant origins. Today, though, Suining is developing—and fast. If you have read about China's boom, you probably know about Shanghai's whimsical skyscrapers, about the billions Beijing spent on the 2008 Olympics, about the luxury malls and car dealerships and yacht clubs of the country's leading cities. But economic progress is in many ways more visible in places like Suining, where the change wrought is more stark, its impact on local psychology more extreme.

Suining's version of the boom started in the 1990s, when residents took the overnight bus to Shanghai and the wealthy cities around it and found jobs constructing skyscrapers, laboring in factories, and diapering the babies of China's nouveau riche. A few paychecks later, they began sending back money, thousands of wire transfers all directed to Suining's Agricultural Bank. Suining's towns and villages swelled in every direction at once. For years the county seat—a settlement of a few hundred thousand people also called Suining—had been a place for the farmers who worked the surrounding wheat fields and rice paddies to sell their harvest and buy supplies. Now its meager grid of roads expanded outward in ever larger squares. Tall apartment buildings outfitted with Roman columns, rooftop pagodas, and bubblegum pink facades sprouted out of nowhere, colonizing whole blocks. The larger housing developments could accommodate thousands of residents. Supermarkets that sold jewelry and watches as well as vegetables and rice opened to fireworks and ribbon-cutting ceremonies, and suddenly every other storefront, it seemed, was a real estate agency. Advertisements for life insurance, heretofore a foreign concept, appeared on billboards. For decades the only hotel was a state-owned institution called The East Is Red. Now it was joined by the Suining International Hotel and the U.S.-China Friendship Hotel. A savvy entrepreneur looking to cash in on a new market, meanwhile, opened The East Is Red Appliances.[1]

On the outskirts of the town, factories set up shop. They were small operations at first, Chinese-owned, but the change they brought to Suining was big. The Suining Meat Products Company built a boxy brown building and surrounded it with sod, yielding a vast, aggressively green lawn. The chemical industry followed, and a blanket of smog settled over the land, permanent and yet subtle; after a while, residents only registered its presence through the way their lungs expanded as soon as they cleared the county limits. Suining's wheat fields and rice paddies endured, but the factories needed roads, so the government paved over the dirt paths on which peasants had once found their way into town. The grid grew even larger.

The boom overwhelmed the very people who started it. Returning from their stints in Shanghai, the migrant workers had trouble finding their way home through the maze of new streets and buildings. Then again, even homes were no longer static; everyone talked constantly of upgrading. The men took to smoking Sequoia cigarettes, while the women turned to exotic new media like Korean soap operas. Teenagers went online for the first time. But no change was so great that the people of Suining could not adapt. As farmers continued to sow their fields, they discovered that freshly built highways make excellent platforms for drying wheat. Show up in late spring, and you can see evidence of this new art everywhere, the major roads filled not with cars but with enormous circles fashioned from tiny tan grains, like offerings to giant bird gods.

The last pivotal change to hit the population was, in the midst of such constant flux, almost invisible, a change that only became apparent if you zoomed out to look at whole blocks or whole neighborhoods. In 2007, according to National Population and Family Planning Commission data, Suining's mothers gave birth to 152 boys for every 100 girls. But zooming out can also confuse the matter, since you may miss the fact that this demographic shift has occurred in tandem with Suining's economic shift—that girls have gone missing in the midst of immense progress. From afar Suining looks poor. But from inside the boom things have never been better.

———— ⁕ ————

Wu Pingzhang was among the first to profit.* As the people of Suining bought new homes, they furnished them with appliances they had little experience operating. An air conditioner repairman with two cell phones he kept on day and night, Wu was soon in great demand. He amassed a modest savings, and before long he had enough to rent an apartment for himself and his wife in town, away from his ancestral village. The apartment sat on the second story of a cement block building, above a portrait studio called Flying on the Wind, and consisted of a large room looking out on a spacious balcony. To turn the one room into two, Wu affixed hooks to the ceiling and hung from them an airbrushed canvas backdrop lent to him by the proprietors of Flying on the Wind—a vista of clean white windows opening onto a flawless blue sky. He then arranged his own appliances, bought from customers secondhand, in front of the backdrop like a set in a play: a Wanbao refrigerator, a Midea microwave, a PANDA color television. The centerpiece was an upright air conditioner that stretched from the cement floor to near the ceiling. Wu and his wife

---

*This name, like the name of other residents of Suining I interviewed, has been changed. Many of the parents I spoke with had violated the one-child policy or other Chinese family planning regulations.

started eating more meat, and he started drinking beer. Against one wall he stockpiled cases of Yincheng beer, signaling to guests that in his house there was always more to drink. He bought a small motorcycle. His ascent into the middle class even came with a small indulgence: a collection of Cultural Revolution–era Mao pins he picked up at flea markets and bought from friends. He felt entitled to a son. "It's a question of fate," he told me. Having a boy was, he felt, his destiny.

Wu Pingzhang wasn't the only one thinking about heirs. Across town his cousin Wu Bing was enjoying a more modest success. After stints as a migrant worker in Shanghai and Nanjing, Wu also rented an apartment in town, in a maze of alleys near an elementary school. He bought a cell phone and a television. He too started drinking beer; his brand was Pengjing. His wife joined the Protestant church, and he began giving her ¥1,000 ($150) a year to tithe, and a little more to buy clothes for herself. His view on children was less grand than Wu Pingzhang's but no less urgent: what good is material wealth if you don't have a son to inherit it?

The cousins are, to some degree, foils. Wu Pingzhang is plump and gregarious, with a wide, impish smile and a fondness for one-liners, while Wu Bing is slight and timid, with delicate cheekbones, a pencil-thin mustache, and a hunch that makes him appear even smaller than he is. Liu Mei, Wu Pingzhang's wife, is also plump, a physique she blames on her love of cooking. Liao Li, Wu Bing's wife, is pious and serious and interested most of all in prayer. But in the 1990s, when the two cousins started their families, their lives unfolded in parallel.

A generation earlier, Suining's children were not planned; they just happened. And since men and women married young, never used contraception, and needed labor to help out on the farm, they happened again and again. People who wanted a son—and most wanted a son—simply had sex and left the outcome to chance. If a son didn't come on the first or second try, they tried again, and chance almost always worked in their favor. In any human population, 88 percent of couples have at least one son after three births.[2] After six births the odds of having a son jump to 99 percent.* Six children is exactly how many children Wu Pingzhang's

---

*There are, of course, exceptions to this rule. One woman I met in Suining had between ten and fourteen daughters—neighbors give a different account than she does—before finally giving birth to the son she coveted.

mother had—he was the youngest—and she got the son she wanted without having to tamper with nature. For Wu, however, nature was not good enough.

The one-child policy had arrived in 1980, and mass-produced ultrasound machines in 1982. The machines' appearance, so soon after the introduction of birth targets, was greeted as a stroke of serendipity. For parents, the technology provided a way to have fewer children and yet beat the odds.* For local government officials who had been given unattainable birth targets, meanwhile, ultrasound held out the possibility of meeting their quotas without forcing mothers to abort.

Compared with the alternative of having additional children, sex selection was also cheap. Sex determination is illegal in China, but because local officials do not have much incentive to crack down on it, a red envelope full of money or a carton of prized Chunghwa cigarettes can go a long way. At the time I visited Suining, a sex determination test reportedly cost around ¥1,000 ($150) in bribes to ultrasound technicians. The fine for having a child without a birth permit, by comparison, was ten times that.[3] The parents I met who selected for sex were far from the poorest residents, and indeed across China, according to one anthropologist, the first to seek sex selective abortions were the "early birds who are gaining from economic reform."[4] But the economic incentive, at a time when everyone had gone a little money crazy, made sex selection even more attractive.

The first time around the Wu cousins both had girls. Wu Bing's daughter was born in 1993, and Wu Pingzhang's in 1998. Both couples made the decision, then fairly common in China, to have another child outside the policy. And both began screening for sex.

The second time Wu Bing's wife Liao Li got pregnant, it was a girl. She aborted. The third pregnancy, also a girl, she carried to term. It is unclear why she and Wu Bing decided to have a second daughter, though Liao Li's discomfort with abortion may have played a role. Her pastor disapproves of abortion, she tells me, and she only mentions the procedures

---

*Many provinces in China later adopted a gender-based exception to the one-child policy, a caveat often called the "1.5-child policy." Under this exception, a first daughter becomes a sort of childbearing trial run allowing you to try again for a boy. Jiangsu province has no such provision, though.

once, after a few glasses of warm Pengjing beer. Another factor in her decision to keep the girl may have been that only about a year had elapsed
since her last abortion, which, like most sex selective abortions in China,
had been performed after twenty weeks. In any case, Liao Li and Wu Bing
named this second daughter Panpan, for *panwang*, which means "hope,"
in the hope she would augur a son the third time around. The portentous
name didn't work, though, for the fourth fetus to appear in Liao Li's
womb was a girl too. She had another abortion.

When at last a boy came, he was Liao Li's fifth pregnancy and third
child. She and Wu Bing called him Maodan, which means Fertilized Egg.
The right egg had dropped into Liao Li's uterus, and they were elated.
That bit of genetic providence, coming as it did after years of bad luck,
was especially sweet. To them the boy's nickname, Liao Li explained,
symbolized a sort of victory—and indeed they had conquered biology.
Fertilized Egg, she said, "means something like Treasure."

Across town Wu Pingzhang was busy engineering his own family.
After the birth of their first daughter, he and Liu Mei didn't want to risk
having another girl. It wasn't that they couldn't afford the fine; he was
making ¥30,000 ($4,600) a year, over four times China's household per
capita income at the time.[5] It was that they didn't see the point in having
another daughter, not when Liu Mei already had her hands full with one
child. After that first birth, seven years elapsed—a sign, say doctors who
work in China and India, that Liu Mei probably had a few abortions.
Then one year Wu Pingzhang took her in for an ultrasound examination at five months of pregnancy and was overjoyed at what popped up
on the monitor screen.

To ensure that family planning workers wouldn't foil his plans to
have a son, he sent his daughter to live with his parents, rented a small
apartment in Nanjing, Jiangsu's provincial capital, and installed Liu Mei
there as her stomach ballooned. By roaming the city on bicycle, sometimes logging fifty or sixty miles a day, he patched together a living doing odd jobs. At night he returned to Liu Mei and the small apartment,
and together they eagerly awaited the birth.

The precaution of staying in Nanjing paid off, and a few months later
Wu Pingzhang and Liu Mei returned to Suining the proud parents of
identical twin boys.[6] He easily picked up air conditioner repair work

again, and soon he had enough to buy the boys identical outfits, identical plastic trucks, and identical toy guns. As often as he could he walked around the neighborhood, a twin on each shoulder, smiling his wide smile. He was, he thought, the luckiest father around. "Not everyone has twin boys!" he told me. It was only later that he started to think about the fact that there are some problems even technology can't solve.

One afternoon I stand outside the elementary school near Wu Bing's apartment just before classes let out. The school is a long whitewashed building surrounded by a gated asphalt courtyard and bordered by shops selling penny candy and toys, and I stand near the shops with parents waiting for their children. Then a bell rings, and strings of children headed by smiling young teachers flood into the courtyard. The teachers lead their tiny charges toward us in two straight lines, one pair after the other, like the young characters in the children's book Madeleine. Except for one major difference, which becomes painfully apparent as I fix my gaze on a point just inside the gate and count. Boy-boy, boy-girl, boy-girl, boy-boy, boy-girl, boy-girl: the sex ratio at the school is two to one.

I repeat this exercise in Lianyungang, a city northeast of Suining with an even more severe gender imbalance; there government statisticians have found 163 boys for every 100 girls under age five.[7] One sunny Saturday morning at verdant Cangwu Park, I count six boys and three girls bouncing on an inflatable castle. Near the ice-cream stand a dozen sticky-faced kids, seven boys and five girls, feed pigeons. The children running after kites in a grassy field: three and two. The drivers of the cheerful little tanks circling an electric track: three and one.[8] But I could have extended the experiment to any of several dozen towns in eastern China. In Yichun, Jiangxi, there are 137 boys for every 100 girls under age four. In Fangchenggang, Guangxi, the number jumps to 153. And in Tianmen, Hubei, 176.[9]

It seems so basic: you cannot have all boys, all the time, and expect your society to get very far. And yet for the parents who select for sex, gender imbalance is easy to dismiss as someone else's problem. Most parents wait, as the Wu cousins did, until they already have one or two daughters before resorting to sex selective abortion; very few abort be-cause of the fetus's sex during the first pregnancy. We know this because around the world the sex ratio at birth jumps abruptly with birth order. In 1989, at the height of South Korea's sex selection binge, the country's sex ratio for first births was 104—just about normal. For second births it was 113, for third births it was 185, and for fourth births it was 209—putting the odds of a couple having a boy over a girl at over two to one.[10] Today China, India, and other countries with serious sex ratio imbal-ances show similar trends. And if couples already have one or two girls, they may believe that by insisting on a boy the next time around they are simply balancing out their families. If you aren't the sort of parent who sits around thinking about evolution in your spare time, it may be hard to fathom that in taking pains to have children of more than one sex you are harming your community.

The other effect of parents having a few girls before they select for boys is that they don't personally suffer from the skewed sex ratio. As their girls grow up and start searching for partners, they aren't so bad off. Wu Bing's two daughters will not have a problem finding husbands, and if their son remains single and dependent on him and Liao Li the daughters' marriages will lessen the pressure somewhat. It is, paradoxi-cally, the parents who have a son on the first try out of sheer fifty-fifty chance—the parents who do not abort female fetuses—who suffer the most as they struggle to marry off that son in a society in which their neighbors have engineered their reproductive lot.[11]

A final factor behind sex selection's ubiquity has to do with de-velopment, and in this regard sex selective abortion looks a lot like any other major technological change. When many aspects of life are in tran-sition, people simply focus on navigating those changes as effortlessly as possible, and a new technology can quickly come to feel almost natural. During the weeks I spend interviewing residents in Suining, the ones who see the seeds of misfortune in the community's transformation are mainly elderly. They are people like Wang Xiucong, a wiry grandfather I find sitting with a group of older men inside a village mud-walled house, playing cards and drinking one hundred–proof grain alcohol. He is jovial, already drunk at noon, and excited to meet a foreigner. But his mood dips when I bring up the sex ratio at birth. "There are boys everywhere," he says, shaking his head glumly. "Everyone has boys now. Take this child"—he continues, gesturing to a toddler waddling through the door. "He will have trouble finding a wife when he grows up."

This is not to say that Suining's young parents don't notice the preponderance of boys. They see the sex ratio imbalance manifest around them. They note the disparity when they pick up their children at school. They notice that older siblings are always girls, and notice, perhaps, that there are often suspiciously large gaps between these girls and their brothers.* But they register these details and then, like the owner of a single-occupancy SUV who convinces himself his environmental impact isn't really that bad, they tell themselves others will pick up the slack.

The sex ratio imbalance is "obvious," demographer Shuzhuo Li tells me as he shows me around a high sex ratio community in central China one day. "The *laobaixing,* the average people, they all know about it. *Everyone* knows about it. But they all think they can invest a lot in their son and have him grow up well and find a nice daughter-in-law. Other people's sons aren't their business. They know individual choice affects social benefit, but still they want choice." And why shouldn't parents have faith that their own sons will be fine? The story of contemporary China has been one of relentless progress. To believe sex selection is anything more than a minor problem is to stop believing in the country's economic miracle.

But some parents do worry. Wu Pingzhang insists his twin boys will have to get married. "Not getting married, not having children—not possible!" he tells me. And yet as proud as he is of them, he sometimes worries that they won't be able to find wives. He can't help but notice that his block of cement-walled apartments exudes testosterone. The owners of Flying on the Wind have a boy. The jolly bakers from Hunan province who hawk saccharin cookies from a streetside folding table have a boy. The woman who sells five-cent ice-cream bars, mostly to

---

*The fact that couples mostly try for sons after they already have one or two daughters means girls are typically born into larger families, a fact that—in the developing world, at least—diminishes their chances for success throughout life. Older sisters often end up raising their much younger brothers; one Indian doctor tells me the girls are turned into "minimothers."

boys, from a cooler farther down also has a boy. When all of these boys reach adulthood together, Wu sees that things could get dicey, and he has therefore devised a plan. In China, a man's marriage prospects often come down to how much capital his parents can amass to attract a potential bride, and in this area Wu believes his collection of Mao pins will give his sons an edge. In twenty years' time, he wagers, Chinese collectors will feel real nostalgia for the Cultural Revolution and will pay top dollar for a little piece of history. Wu will then funnel that money into cars and houses to make his sons good catches. It is with the twins in mind that he keeps the pins in a drawer away from the light, sheathed in a folder lined with red velvet.

<hr />

And what of the women who abort? Reproductive rights activists often blame men for sex selection. Men, after all, perpetuate sexism, and they uphold the economic and social inequalities that make women see daughters as liabilities. But often these organizations point to more overt oppression, to husbands and fathers who bully women into abortions. "In Gujarat, women do not decide whether they will have male children or female children," the leader of an Indian feminist group has said. "To be frank, she is never consulted on whether she will go to bed with the man. So there is no freedom of decision . . . So many women die or commit suicide because they give birth to daughters. Husbands torturing wives because of the birth of a daughter is not unique."[12]

In reality, however, such cases account for only a small portion of Asia's sex selective abortions. Across China and India, across South Korea and Vietnam and Azerbaijan, the decision to abort is most often made by a woman—either the pregnant woman herself or her mother-in-law, who has a vested interest in her son's offspring. A report by the Indian NGO Center for Women's Development Studies describes a woman who concealed two abortions from her husband. After he forbade her to abort the female fetuses she was carrying, she hid out at her parents' place, both times returning home to her husband only after she had gone through with the procedure.[13] Sex selection happens, after all, in an atmosphere in which everyone is trying to get ahead, and women are hardly immune from a craving for status, even if it comes at the expense of their own kind. A recent paper in the journal *Reproductive Health Matters* states, "For women attempting to have a son and experiencing pressure to fulfil their 'womanly duty' by having a male child, sex-selective abortion can be extremely empowering."[14] The other, more tragic factor—and here a Suining woman has a lot in common with the African grandmother who holds down a teenage girl while her clitoris is sliced off—is that women know best just how difficult it is to be female.

Liao Li, for example, calls the shots in her relationship with Wu Bing. A sturdy woman with an undefined waist and hair cropped into a wispy bob, she keeps his cell phone when he is away on jobs, leaving him to venture out from the worker's dormitory and use a pay phone every time he wants to make a call. Throughout my visits, Wu Bing is largely silent, speaking up only to round out his wife's answers. Liao Li also tells me she prefers daughters. "Girls are very good," she says. "They're soft. And they can take care of you when you're older." But she aborted two female fetuses, she intimates, because having a son is crucial to keeping up appearances: "If you don't have a boy, you lose face."

Women have become, in a sense, their own worst enemies. Development, remember, was supposed to improve the lot of women—and in many areas it does. But when it comes to reproduction, the opposite happens: women use their increased autonomy to select for sons. Liao Li openly acknowledges that contradiction. Submitting one's body to multiple late-term abortions out of a craving for status is "stupid thinking," she says, "when one is, after all, oneself a woman." And yet she almost always speaks in third person, as if Suining's imbalance were something other people caused.[15]

One morning I accompany Liao Li to church. She worships at the Three Self church, the only state-sponsored Protestant denomination in China. (Three Self's membership has swelled with economic growth, as the Chinese attempt to make sense of the constant change around them.) The church is housed in an old warehouse on one of Suining's few remaining dirt roads, next to a billboard advertising a coming resort. We arrive a bit before 6:00 AM to find the red benches lined with people, their backs straight and faces turned expectantly toward a glittery gold cardboard cross mounted on a platform at the front of the church. The congregants are almost all female. Over several trips to Suining this is the only time I see so many women in one place.

The assistant minister stands front and center. Sturdy and middle-aged, she is wearing large thick-framed glasses and a brown polyester jacket. She picks up a piece of chalk, strides over to a blackboard positioned behind the cardboard cross, and scrawls the numbers 36:10–12 on it, denoting a passage from the book of Job in which Job deliberates the meaning of suffering with four friends. Three of the friends interpret misfortune as divine punishment. The fourth friend, Elihu, says there is righteousness in suffering, that God often intends hardship to teach humans lessons. It is Elihu's words to which the minister directs us. Liao Li pulls out a small notebook and carefully copies out the numbers.

"Do you want to be a *small person*?" the minister booms through the microphone, her voice low and rumbling. A small person, she says, is one who covets too much, who doesn't see what Elihu explains as the virtue in suffering, who can't understand the lessons to be learned in not getting everything she wants. The minister gives a few examples—a woman who treats people differently depending on their background, a woman who puts on airs and loses sight of her own origins—before mentioning a woman who pressures others to have sons. "Do *you* have to raise [your neighbor's] son?" comes the minister's voice through the microphone. "Do *you* have to care for him when he grows up?"[16]

It is a small moment in a long sermon, but it stays with me long after I leave.

Outside Suining is waking up. Construction workers head to work, newly minted consumers stroll down the town's shopping streets, and appliances start humming. Somewhere a migrant worker sets off for Shanghai to make still more money to pump back into the local economy. But inside the sparely furnished church the women stop for a brief moment of reflection. The minister gives a signal and the worshipers drop to their knees, turn so they are facing the back of the church, and rest their foreheads on the pews. A few curl up on the floor. Then they cry, loudly and in unison, in waves of long, tearless wails.

Chapter 3

THE ECONOMIST

*I turned away and, despite myself, the tears came, tears
of weakness and disappointment; for what woman
wants a girl for her first-born? They took the child from
me. Kali said: "Never mind. There will be many later
on. You have plenty of time."*

—KAMALA MARKANDAYA,
NECTAR IN A SIEVE

Bookstores these days are filled with works detailing the rise of Asia. If
you are looking for a title on economic growth in China and India, for
example, you can choose from among *Chindia, Chindia Rising, Making
Sense of Chindia, The Elephant and the Dragon,* and—as if one weren't
enough—*The Dragon and the Elephant.* But while Asia's boom can be
overhyped, it is, at least at the level of basic economic gains, entirely real.
The people of Suining, who in one generation have transitioned from
poor peasants to semiurban consumers, are hardly exceptional. Across
the continent poverty rates are falling.[1] Families are sending their children to high school, and often on to college, for the first time. A middle
class is emerging in countries where there was once only the very rich
and the very poor, and as the members of that middle class watch their
economies steam ahead at unprecedented growth rates, they are mainly

optimistic. China, a retired teacher in Beijing once told me, is enacting its own version of the American 1950s.

In addition to economic progress, many Asians have witnessed more social and political change in the past thirty years than most Americans register in a lifetime. Vietnam, Armenia, Azerbaijan, Georgia, and Nepal have all seen major political upheaval in the past few decades. A portion of the Indian economy is driven by people who adopt names like Trisha and John and sleep during the day so they can spend their nights fielding complaints from consumers in Alabama. Koreans complain of a "hurry-hurry" culture, a rat race so fierce and sudden that it leaves its competitors disoriented, while malls in Seoul stay open until 4:00 AM to accommodate workaholics. China is changing with a speed comparable to, if not surpassing, the West during the Industrial Revolution. These are not countries where life continues as it always did, and change has seeped into the very term we use to describe them. They are no longer frozen into one suffering bloc called the Third World. They are developing.

To an extent, development has raised the status of women, much as social science theories predicted it would. Take the case of India. "Women shoot past men across the spectrum," declared a 2009 article in the Indian paper *Economic Times*. The occasion was that the top finishers in the country's civil service exam that year were female. But advancement isn't limited to test scores, the article noted: "On several platforms, the fairer sex is doing better than men."[2] Indeed, that same year the Indian parliament elected its first female speaker, Meira Kumar, a lawyer who is, remarkably, Dalit, a member of the low-ranking caste formerly known as Untouchables. Not content with that breakthrough, feminists now lobby for a bill that would reserve one-third to one-half of parliament seats for women—a level of affirmative action unthinkable in the United States.[3] Similar changes are afoot in China. "[Women] know so much more about their rights," Guo Jianmei, director of the Beijing Zhongze Women's Legal Counseling and Service Center, recently told the *New York Times*. "They are better educated. For those with a competitive spirit, there's a world of opportunity here now, whether they are businesswomen, scientists, farmers or even political leaders. There really have been huge changes."[4]

And yet the proportion of women and girls in the overall population has decreased over the exact same period in which women's economic and political rights have improved. It might be argued that Indian feminists are asking for more than their fair share in parliament, since women no longer make up 50 percent of India's population. "It is a paradox," says T. V. Sekher, a demographer I meet at the International Institute for Population Studies in Mumbai. "On the one side India is shining. We have 8 percent, 9 percent growth. We have all these developments, India becoming a superpower, all of that. More and more girls are going to school and getting educated. More and more women are getting employment. More and more women's participation in political affairs. These are all very progressive developments. But on the one side you have all these developments and on the other side you have this kind of thing happening—killing the fetus just because she is a girl."

It isn't just foreigners like Christophe Guilmoto who marvel over the fact that highly educated couples are more prone to abort a female fetus than couples with lower levels of education; the contradiction shocks Indian scholars as well. Nor is education the only marker of progress that correlates with an increased prevalence of sex selection. Economist Sakthivel Selvaraj, a fellow at the Public Health Foundation of India, says income and caste also predict whether an Indian woman will abort a female fetus. "Take any socioeconomic indicator," he says, "and it correlates with [skewed] sex ratios." The women who select for sex in India include lawyers and doctors and businesspeople.

But on closer inspection it is no coincidence that sex ratios spike as countries get rich. As Guilmoto found around the turn of the millennium, sex selection is a byproduct of a sudden drop in fertility. And for at least the last sixty years, sudden drops in fertility have been inextricably tied up with development.

The Malthusian projections that shaped demography up until the late 1970s also gave rise to population control and family planning programs around the world, many of them paid for with Western money. In India and Tunisia and Taiwan alike, these programs were founded on an economic promise: staving off overpopulation is good not only for the planet but also for growth. As the agricultural era gave way to the industrial one, large families were no longer an asset, and by the mid-twentieth century wealthier countries were ones in which people had fewer children. President Lyndon B. Johnson made this link explicit in a speech at a 1965 San Francisco event held to mark the twentieth anniversary of the United Nations. "Less than five dollars invested in population control," Johnson said, "is worth a hundred dollars invested in economic growth."[5]

There was a certain urgency to Johnson's message. In the 1950s, demographers who studied global population trends had reliable statistics for the first time, and the prognosis was not good. Projections released by the UN Population Division in 1951 suggested rapid population growth was on the horizon, particularly in the developing world. It wasn't that people were having more babies but that breakthroughs in science and medicine were allowing everyone to live longer than ever before. Advances in public health meant fewer died of diseases like malaria and tuberculosis and more survived to a healthy old age.[6] But while death rates had fallen in many countries, birth rates had not caught up, and women had the same number of children they always had. The world now had what Western population activists dubbed "death control."[7] It needed birth control.

It was true that unfettered population growth would almost certainly strain developing countries' resources and deepen poverty. Privately, however, Western donors worried less about poverty than they did about the global balance of power and specifically about what they believed to be one of poverty's effects: communism. The population control movement arose at the precise moment that Western powers were losing their grip over Asia, Africa, and Latin America. Around the world, colonies were gaining independence, with Cold War tensions replacing imperialism. Many early population activists thus belonged to the U.S. business and political elite. Big names included Hugh Moore, the millionaire inventor of the Dixie Cup; John D. Rockefeller III, heir to the Rockefeller family fortune; Lewis Strauss, head of the U.S. Atomic Energy Commission; and Will Clayton, former undersecretary of state. Rising birth rates, as this group saw it, would make countries more susceptible to communism at a time when the United States urgently needed allies in Asia and Latin America. "We are not primarily interested in the sociological or humanitarian aspects of birth control," Moore and Clayton once confided to Rockefeller. "We are interested in the use which Communists make of hungry people in their drive to conquer the earth."[8]

The movement coalesced in 1952, when Rockefeller gathered a group of influential Americans at the Conference on Population Problems in Colonial Williamsburg.[9] When everyone had arrived at the Williamsburg Inn to discuss the possibility of exporting population control to poor growing countries, economist Isador Lubin voiced their collective fears. They mostly centered on Asian countries, which because of their large, young populations were prime targets for Western organizations, and particularly on China and India. "Almost everybody who spoke this morning talked about India," Lubin said. "What is there about India that makes this situation so acute? And I think unconsciously we are scared, and I think we have a right to be."[10]

On the heels of the meeting Rockefeller founded the Population Council. Moore went on to found the Population Crisis Committee. These two organizations, together with the Ford Foundation, the World Bank, the United Nations Population Fund (UNFPA), the U.S. Agency for International Development (USAID), and the International Planned Parenthood Federation (IPPF), helped sell Asian nations on population control, primarily by spreading the logic that lower birth rates lead to richer people.[11] Between 1965 and 1976, money spent on research and development for contraceptive methods around the world more than doubled. Developing countries received the lion's share of that money while contributing less than 3 percent of it.[12] The most funding came from the United States.

At times, Western donors made the link between wealth and small families strikingly explicit by making other types of aid contingent on the adoption of population control targets. In 1966 President Johnson signed the Food for Peace Act, which required USAID officers "to exert the maximum leverage and influence" to guarantee that famine-stricken areas accepting food aid also take steps to control their populations.[13] In 1969 World Bank president and former U.S. secretary of defense Robert McNamara explained to his advisory council that he didn't want to fund public health work "unless it was very strictly related to population control, because usually health facilities contributed to the decline of the death rate, and thereby to the population explosion."[14] According to a

history of the World Bank's population program, the mood in Washington at the time was that "no organization concerned with economic development could ignore the implications of accelerating rates of population
growth."[15]

Concern soon heightened into frenzy. In 1968 Paul Ehrlich published
the bestseller *The Population Bomb*, which predicted widespread poverty,
ecological destruction, and war. That was followed by *A Blueprint for Survival*, a tract warning of the imminent "breakdown of society and the irre-
versible disruption of the life-support systems on this planet, possibly by
the end of the century."[16] Finally in 1972 the Club of Rome, an international group of scientists, released *The Limits to Growth*, a report forecast-
ing the toll exponential population growth would take over the next few
decades. The report contained serious inaccuracies and famously predicting that existing oil reserves would be exhausted within twenty years.[17] At
the time, however, the club's predictions worried many influential Western thinkers, who racked their brains for creative ways to staunch rising
birth rates.

Some of the strategies they came up with bordered on demeaning. In
1967 Disney produced a movie for the Population Council called *Family
Planning* that was translated into twenty-four languages.[18] The film de-
picted Donald Duck as the responsible father of a small family, wealthy
and surrounded by modern appliances. Without family planning, view-
ers were told, "the children will be sickly and unhappy, with little hope
for the future."[19] But in the end it was the influx of Western money that
did the trick, especially in Asia, where beginning in the 1950s countries
implemented comprehensive population control programs. In South
Korea, which following the Korean War remained under American influence, the ruling military regime embraced family planning as an integral
part of its economic development strategy, writing birth targets into its
five-year economic plans.[20] Extensive birth control measures were also
adopted in Taiwan, which like Korea received a steady flow of U.S. aid.
Singapore first moved ahead on family panning while a British colony;
later the dictator Lee Kuan Yew withheld tax and housing benefits from
couples who had three or more children and deemed fourth and fifth
children "antisocial acts."[21] And India, the country that economist Isador
Lubin had declared "makes this situation so acute," became the site of
ambitious, often draconian experiments directed at getting couples to

stick to two children, again funded by Western money. For a period Delhi was overrun with American population advisors, and for years afterward the Indian government continued to operate within "a paradigm where the entire problem was population," public health activist Sabu George told me. "Everything was oriented toward fertility. That was a national obsession."

Western organizations even had an impact on China, where their work culminated in the one-child policy. The Cultural Revolution started in 1966 and lasted ten lonely years. But as isolated as the country became in the 1960s and 1970s, China nonetheless remained the world's most populous country, and population control advocates never lost sight of it as a target. It is no coincidence that the country's birth planning policy took shape precisely as hysteria around overpopulation was mounting in the West.

For China's Communist Party, in fact, a strict population policy marked an abrupt ideological shift. Malthus had once been demonized as anti-Communist, and as late as 1974 China protested that the population crisis was a "false alarm" concocted as an excuse to deny developing countries aid.[22] But by then a significant ideological change was already under way. Before long party officials were quietly absorbing and repackaging ideas from *The Limits to Growth, A Blueprint for Survival,* and other Western texts.

Chinese officials began phasing in the "longer, later, fewer" policy—an emphasis on late marriage, small families, and spaced births—in the early 1970s. Social life in China was so highly regulated that state administration of women's reproductive cycles was not much of a stretch, and the policy yielded quick results: the birth rate plummeted.[23] But then cadres began worrying about the increasingly bleak projections coming from Europe and the United States, and in the late 1970s they pushed for China to take its birth policy one step further. "Developed countries spread Club of Rome thinking to the developing world," Liang Zhongtang, an economist at the Shanghai Academy of Social Sciences who participated in deliberations over the one-child policy, told me.[24] That thinking did not spread on its own, however. It had an ambassador in a state military scientist who had been spending time in Europe.

Song Jian had what in 1970s China passed as a charmed career. In 1946, at age fourteen, he left home to fight in the Communist revolution for the Eighth Route Army. When the Communists won control of China three years later, Song's army service helped him climb the ranks of the party. He soon passed a state examination that got him sent to the Soviet Union to train in cybernetics and military science, and upon returning to China in 1960 he became a protégé of Qian Xuesen, Mao Zedong's trusted science adviser.[25] Qian's support allowed Song to rise to an influential post in the Seventh Ministry of Machine Building in China's Ministry of National Defense, and when the Cultural Revolution broke out and anti-intellectual witch hunts consumed the country, Premier Zhou Enlai put him on the list of the few dozen scientists who were protected by the state. By surviving the Cultural Revolution with his career intact, Song became what anthropologist Susan Greenhalgh calls a "superscientist": one of a select group of Chinese scholars "who could speak with originality and authority on any subject and command attention."[26]

Song used that authority to pursue an interest in demography. The Seventh Ministry of Machine Building was not a likely entity for work on population, of course. But few other scientists in China at the time were qualified to work on the topic. The country's social scientists had not been as lucky as Song; most had been persecuted or otherwise ostracized in the Cultural Revolution. In 1970s China missile science was all there was.[27]

In 1975 Song's research took a new turn when he joined a Chinese government delegation to the Netherlands. At the Twente University of Technology in Enschede, a small town on the German border, Geert Jan Olsder, a thirty-one-year-old assistant professor, was assigned to show him around. A modest, unassuming man who loved formulas and hiking above all else, the Dutch scholar was an unusual host for a senior Communist Party official. But Olsder did not realize Song's power, or even have a clear idea of what he worked on. "We were called from the main office of the university and told, 'Hey, we have a couple of Chinese here. Can you entertain them for the afternoon?'" Olsder recalled. All he knew was that Song spoke decent English.

Olsder took Song out for beers at a local café. He made small talk about the university, reviewing the size of the faculty and student body. Song, he said, was friendly and easygoing, and feeling comfortable around him, Olsder decided to tell the Chinese missile scientist about his work. The Dutch scholar was a theoretical mathematician who focused on game theory and other entirely conjectural problems: the probability two ships sailing on intersecting paths will collide, the probability a monster will find a princess stranded on an island, and so forth. But he and a few other mathematicians at Twente University of Technology had, as it happened, recently developed a series of equations dealing with population control after reading *The Limits to Growth*. It was this work he mentioned to Song.[28]

Their equations were designed to limit the population on a fictional island, Olsder explained to Song, and the key variable was number of births. "He immediately became enthusiastic," Olsder said.[29] Song corroborated this in a 1986 account in which he credited the work of "some Dutch scientists" along with *A Blueprint for Survival* with influencing his thoughts about population. Returning to China, he wrote, "I was extremely excited about these documents and determined to try the method of demography."[30]

Olsder had mailed a copy of his paper "Population Planning: a Distributed Time Optimal Control Problem" to an address Song gave him in China, and the Chinese scientist soon got to work.[31] A good deal was apparently lost in translation: Olsder's equations were not intended to be applied to real populations, let alone populations of over 1 billion. But since the same Club of Rome report that had inspired Olsder to create the equations had convinced Chinese leaders that they needed to take drastic measures to reduce China's birth rate, Song decided to put Olsder's equations to practical use.

In the years that followed he and colleagues in the Seventh Ministry of Machine Building used the Dutch mathematician's methods, along with those of other European scholars, to come up with formulas for controlling China's population. The ministry was one of the few places with computers, and Song's projections wowed Communist Party leaders. Song also repackaged ideas from Western texts on overpopulation into a series of essays that he distributed among cadres and published in Chinese journals.[32]*

---

*Song was certainly not the only conduit of information from the West. The Population Crisis Committee, IPPF, and UNFPA made overtures to the Chinese government throughout the 1970s. But the Chinese government did not accept overt foreign involvement until 1979, on the eve of the one-child policy's unveiling.

The economic argument for reducing population growth, in particular, captured cadres' attention. Cutting the birth rate, Chinese officials deduced, was a crude way of boosting per capita gross domestic product. While increasing productivity was complicated, reducing the number of people who share in its spoils was, they believed, attainable.[33] According to Greenhalgh, the anthropologist, stricter population targets were also a way for China to earn respect abroad by addressing an issue perceived as critical in the West. "By arresting the fierce growth of its human numbers, China could accelerate its own modernization and at the same time help to alleviate a global crisis," Greenhalgh writes. "From a shameful contributor to the world's problems, China would become a proud solver of these problems."[34]

From its unveiling on September 25, 1980, then, the one-child policy was designed to propel China into the ranks of developed countries. In a sense, it succeeded. China's growth rate over the past few decades is unparalleled in modern history. But the policy—and the policies that other countries adopted at the urging of Western advisers—may not have been all that necessary. China's shrinking birth rate coincided with a rapid drop in fertility rates in countries that did not implement such extreme population control measures. From 1970 to 1990, as China's fertility rate fell from 5.5 to 2.3, Thailand's dropped from 5.6 to 2.1, and Brazil's from 5.0 to 2.8.[35] It turns out the link between economic development and declining fertility holds true in reverse. While fertility decline can spur development, economic progress can also prompt people to have fewer children.

Total fertility rates do not, as some 1950s analysts assumed, continue to rise indefinitely. A country's death rate may drop, but—provided the country can be set on a path toward development—at some point its birth rate catches up. With development comes urbanization, and with urbanization come significant lifestyle changes. As more children live to adulthood, parents no longer feel the need to have six or seven children. Access to contraception is critical, since it allows residents to avoid unwanted pregnancies, but ultimately in this scenario a low fertility rate is the result not of draconian birth targets and coercive population control but, as one public health textbook puts it, a "rational response to parents' knowledge that their children are likely to survive into adulthood."[36] Even in countries with strict population control policies, the wealthy are the first to have smaller families—a sign that self-interest is more powerful than concern for government targets.[37] And in countries with no population targets, other strategies of boosting development—spending heavily on education, for example, or investing in work opportunities for women—have been shown to naturally result in a lower birth rate.*

Some variation of this occurred in the former Soviet republics and in parts of Eastern Europe. As the Iron Curtain fell and the Eastern Bloc stumbled through economic restructuring, people had fewer children or held off from marriage out of fear of the future. For the most part, they prevented births through abortion, which in parts of Eastern Europe was newly legal and in the former Soviet republics had long been both legal and widely available.[38] But even as the region's economy began to recover and living standards improved in the late 1990s, its birth rate continued to decline. People took jobs in offices, factories, or small businesses, and they married later, this time propelled by modernization rather than fear. Parents who might have once had five or six children held themselves to one or two. Ultimately, development yielded what one geographer calls "precipitous declines in fertility" across the region.[39] Today Eastern Europe and the onetime Soviet republics are among the few developing countries in the world whose populations appear to be shrinking.[40]

Economic development, along with the urbanization, education, and new job opportunities it brings, may well make parents less sexist. But because development is accompanied by plummeting birth rates, it raises the stakes for each birth, increasing the chances parents will abort a female fetus. This triangle of concurrent trends—development, falling

---

*This is the approach Bangladeshi economist Muhammad Yunus follows with his renowned Grameen Bank, which gives microcredit loans to women in developing countries. Raising the status of women, Yunus has written, has "more impact on curbing population growth than the current system of 'encouraging' family planning practices through intimidation tactics."

fertility, and sex selection—is alarming because it means sex selection won't simply disappear. It also does not bode well for places like Afghanistan or the Middle East, where couples have a long-standing preference for boys and fertility is, at least for now, still high. If access to abortion improves and the birth rate falls in the Middle East, some scholars believe it will be the next region to develop a gender imbalance.[41] And in places where sex selection has already hit, its link to development makes it a thorny issue. Just as some of Suining's parents ignore the sex ratio imbalance as a shameful blip in their otherwise rosy ascent to the middle class, so too do governments see it as an unpleasant side effect of progress—and one better denied.

———✦———

"Really, China and Albania?" Flora Ismaili is offended. We are in Tirana, Albania's capital, in the United Nations Population Fund office where Ismaili works as a program officer. A thin, severe-looking woman, she has been assigned by her supervisor to talk to me about sex selection, but now she seems upset at my suggestion that Albania and China share a common problem. "There is no comparison."

In the years since the fall of communism, Tirana has acquired a bright veneer. The UNFPA office sits down the street from a gleaming shopping mall. The surrounding neighborhood is dotted with upscale restaurants, spas, and boutiques. An ambitious mayor even ordered the capital's grim cement block apartment buildings painted over, so that their exteriors are now a joyous mélange of color. Albania remains poorer than its Western neighbors, but it is casting its lot with Europe. Perhaps that is why Ismaili is miffed. "To compare India and China and Albania is not a very good approach in my opinion," she continues. "Are you getting this? We have completely different policies. We have completely different cultures."

I say that a skewed sex ratio at birth is not a question of culture or policy. China's culture and government differ hugely from India's too. But the real problem seems to be that the Albanian government considers itself to be in a separate category altogether. The last of the Eastern European countries to implement economic reforms, Albania has nonetheless seen remarkable growth in the past few years, with its gross domestic product increasing by an average of 6 percent a year from 2004 to 2009.[42] Inflation is low, and foreign investment is starting to trickle in. That is apparently why, even as evidence of sex selective abortion in the country mounts, the Albanian Ministry of Health—and UNFPA, whose agenda must be approved by the government—maintains that everything is fine.

Everything is not fine. Even as the local office denies the problem, an internal memo issued by UNFPA's global headquarters puts Albania on the short list of countries with a sex ratio at birth of 115 or higher.[43] Government birth registration statistics, meanwhile, give the sex ratio at birth at 114 in 2007, while a preliminary analysis by one economist based on a detailed household survey found over 120 boys for every 100 girls under age five in Albania.[44] Even the lowest estimate I could find, which is the result of rounding out health survey data for the years 2005 through 2009, indicates a sex ratio at birth of 110.[45] But Albania's skewed sex ratio at birth, Ismaili says, "is not a Ministry of Health concern, so we cannot say that it is a concern." When I press, she flips open her cell phone and dials an official at the ministry. A conversation in muted Albanian ensues during which I make out only the English phrase "sex selection." Snapping the phone shut again, Ismaili summarizes: "She said it's not a problem here. It never came out as a problem. So they don't discuss it."

Ismaili is not the only one caught off guard by Albania's skewed sex ratio at birth. Christophe Guilmoto, the first demographer to call attention to the country's problem, initially found it surprising as well. "Albania was mostly Muslim, but then it was under a socialist regime," Guilmoto said. "And *then* there are a couple of Christians who are mostly Orthodox or Catholics. Within Albania we have some information on where the Catholics are—north central. They shouldn't rely on abortion [as contraception]. These guys have a moral problem with abortion. Well, doesn't match." But then he examined the country more closely. Albania turned out to be a classic candidate for sex selection, adhering closely to the pattern found in other countries with gender imbalances. The country's abortion rate is quite high; when Albania was under Soviet rule, an estimated one-half of all pregnancies ended in abortion, and today only 11 percent of Albanians report using modern contraception methods like condoms or birth control pills, a figure that suggests many births are still avoided through abortion.[46] Ultrasound became available in the 1990s, and by 2010 the price of a scan had come down to 1,000 leke—around $10. Most urban Albanian women now have at least one exam during their pregnancy.[47] Finally, as the country has grown richer its fertility rate, like the fertility rates of many Eastern European countries, has plummeted. In 1990 the average Albanian woman had 3.2 children.[48] By 2010 she had 1.5.

But Guilmoto simply adjusted his thinking, added Albania to his list of hot spots, and moved on. Ismaili's office, on the other hand, went so far as to protest the country's high sex ratio at birth totals. In February 2010, Manuela Bello, Ismaili's boss, sent an email to Trevor Croft, the head of data processing at Macro International, a Washington, DC–based research firm that implements the demographic surveys on which UNFPA bases its figures, to dispute Albania's gender imbalance. "As per the UNFPA guidance on [sex selection]," Bello wrote, referring to the internal memo sent out by global headquarters, "Albania has been 'classified' under countries that are recently facing the problem. To my knowledge, this is not [an] evidence based statement. . . . Your assistance asap would be highly appreciated."[49] (It is unclear whether this yielded any action. Croft did not reply to my emails.) Throughout our interview, Ismaili uses the rounded health survey data, which was the lowest sex ratio at birth total I could find. To one decimal point, that number is 109.9. But Ismaili rounds it down to 109, which she asserts is "not a big difference" from the biological norm.*

At the end of our interview, she concedes she has heard of sex selective abortion occurring in northern Albania. "But," she adds, "really I am a data person. When I don't have evidence I cannot say yes"—she can't comment on whether sex selection is widespread. "I say these are the data, and we have to go in deeper and see what's behind them." UNFPA plans to do a more detailed analysis of the country's sex ratio at birth once the results from the next demographic and health survey come in, she adds. I ask when that will be. "After five years," she says.

---

*Demographers consider this a big difference. Since 106 is the upper limit of a biologically possible sex ratio at birth, anything above it is deemed suspect.

It doesn't take a government concealing a sex ratio imbalance to miss its existence. In 2008 a study in the *Proceedings of the National Academy of the Sciences* revealed that sex selective abortion is disturbingly common among certain Asian groups in America—and had been for some time. Using results from the census conducted a full eight years earlier, economists Lena Edlund and Douglas Almond parsed sex ratios for babies born to couples of Chinese, Korean, and Indian descent. A husband and wife team then at Columbia University, the two sketched a portrait of sex selection that was strikingly similar to the one found in Asia. For first births, the sex ratio was close to normal. But for couples who already had a girl, the sex ratio for second births was 117. For those who had two girls, the chance the third child would be a boy jumped to three to two: a ratio of 151. Breaking down this data a little further to account for immigration status produced other interesting nuggets. In America, as in Asia, high social standing did not diminish the chance a woman would abort. Whether a mother gave birth to a boy could not be predicted by her immigration status, Edlund and Almond found. If anything, mothers who were U.S. citizens were slightly more likely to have sons. Sex selection, in other words, is not a tradition from the old country that easily dies out.[50]

The census study only indicated widespread abuse among Chinese, Indian, and Korean Americans, who make up less than 2 percent of the U.S. population.[51] But when Almond first told his wife about the abnormal sex ratio at birth figures, which he stumbled upon while examining census data for another paper, she insisted the world needed to know. Edlund was born in South Korea before the advent of cheap ultrasound and put up for adoption because, she thinks, she was a girl. After being raised by Swedish parents, she became curious about her origins. That curiosity sparked a lifelong quest to research the discrimination that presumably prompted her abandonment.

I first encounter Edlund in New York, outside her office in Columbia University's School of International and Public Affairs building, where she stands in the hallway, gripping a double stroller. A petite woman, she has tousled shoulder-length hair and small, intent eyes. She looks harried. She apologizes, explaining she is running late after a red-eye flight the night before and hasn't had time to drop off her kids (both girls) at day care. I accompany her down Amsterdam Avenue to the Columbia nursery, watching her expertly maneuver the clunky stroller over the narrow sidewalk as she launches into an explanation of her research.

Like many economists, Edlund has broad interests: since arriving in the United States in 1996 she has tackled subjects ranging from prostitution to hermaphrodites.* Before we have gone two blocks she has demonstrated an impressive command of both religious history and evolutionary biology. For the most part, though, she has made a career out of debunking accepted theories on missing girls.

Anti-abortion activists had already begun spinning Edlund's *Proceedings of the National Academy of the Sciences* study for their own benefit. But she maintains her study actually reveals more about the rest of the world than it does about America. The fact that sex selection occurs in the United States, she tells me, shows that it does not disappear as people move up the socioeconomic ladder or into different political systems. "There is social security here," she says, referencing the lack of adequate pensions that is sometimes said to fuel Chinese couples' desires for sons. "There's no one-child policy. And *still* there's a sex ratio at birth problem." By showing that Asian immigrants continue to select for boys in a new environment, even as they earn more money and become U.S. citizens, Edlund and her husband have come up with compelling evidence that what Christophe Guilmoto dubbed "local stories" simply don't work.

So what explains America's pockets of sex selection? Considering how close to home this latest rash of gender imbalance is, it is poorly understood. We do have a few clues, though. The fertility rate among Asian Americans is among the lowest of any minority group in the United States, at 1.9 children per women.[52] According to the magazine *Hyphen*, meanwhile, 35 percent of Asian American pregnancies end in abortion, almost twice the abortion rate among whites.[53] These conditions remain essentially the same as in Asia. But the last ingredient, the equipment necessary to scan fetal sex, is entirely American.

---

*This last paper, written for the *Journal of Theoretical Biology*, is called "Hermaphrodism: What's Not to Like?"

Chapter 4

THE DOCTOR

*Most prospective couples in quest of a male child, as the
social set up in India demands, keep on giving birth to
a number of female children, which in a way not only
enhances the increasing population but also leads to a
chain reaction of many social, economical and mental
stresses on these families. Amniocentesis and Antenatal
sex determination has come to our rescue and can help
in keeping some check over the accelerating population
as well as give relief to the couple requiring male child.*

—NEW BHANDARI HOSPITAL, INDIA, 1984[1]

For Dr. Puneet Bedi, the intensive care unit in Apollo Hospital's maternity ward is a source of both pride and shame. The unit's technology is
among the best in Delhi—among the best, for that matter, in all India.
The technology is one of the reasons he chose to take his gynecology
practice here. But as a specialist in high-risk births he works hard so
that babies can be born, and the fact that the unit's technology also contributes to India's skewed sex ratio at birth gnaws at him. Seven out of
ten babies born in the maternity ward, Bedi says, are male. He delivers
those boys knowing many of them are replacements for aborted girls.

He supports abortion for medical reasons, along with early-term abortion obtained after some deliberation. He performs abortions himself. For sex selection, however, he reserves a contempt bordering on fury. To have his work negated by something as trifling as sex preference—by *any* preference—feels like a targeted insult. "You can choose whether to be a parent," he says. "But once you choose to be a parent you cannot choose whether it's a boy or girl, black or white, tall or short."

He stands in the intensive care unit now, gazing through a thick glass wall into a sealed, shadowless, temperature-controlled room lined with rows of cribs. The cribs are outfitted with tiny plastic orbs, and inside each orb is a tiny sleeping baby. Next to Bedi in the control room, seated in ergonomically correct chairs and clad in stiff white coats, are three technicians, their hands darting soundlessly back and forth along a table outfitted with various slides and buttons. The rest of the space is taken up by equipment: the telemetry system, the respiratory monitor, the central nervous system monitor.

For the infants in the incubators this is the last stop in what have been, from the start, highly monitored pregnancies. An infant ends up in the ward only after being carefully checked. Delhi's mothers know that ultrasound scans can yield incorrect determinations of fetal sex, and so they often check three times, with three different doctors. The babies who make it to the cribs in the sealed room are healthy, undeformed, and male. True, they came a little early. But then science has not yet come up with a cure for prematurity.

Bedi says sex selective abortion—which he, like many Indians, calls "female feticide"—has caught on in Delhi precisely because it bears the imprint of a scientific advance. "It's sanitized," he says. The fact that sex selection is a medical act, he adds, neatly divides the moral burden between two parties: parents tell themselves their doctor knows best, while doctors point to overwhelming patient demand for the procedure. "There is a complete lack of shame on behalf of the parents and doctors who do it."

A tall, broad-shouldered man with a disarmingly gentle voice, Bedi has an immaculate British accent that hints at years spent studying at King's College in London. The accent helps in this part of the world, where breeding can trump all else. His patients live in spacious homes tended by gardeners, belong to bucolic country clubs, and send their children to study in the United States. They want doctors who have been educated abroad as well, and they choose Delhi's Apollo Hospital, which opened thirteen years ago as development was bringing improvements in health care to India's middle and upper classes, because of its prestige. (The hospital, part of a prodigious health care chain that conducts clinical trials for Pfizer Inc. and Eli Lilly & Co, is accredited by the American health care certifier Joint Commission International.)[2] On the day I visit, the parking lot is packed with gleaming Benzes and BMWs, and the first floor waiting room is filled with polished, well-heeled people. One couple strides through the room with such entitlement that they nearly bump into me. The man is clad in khaki pants and a pressed polo shirt, while the woman is a blur of black hair and black silk, her mane deeply conditioned, her *salwar kameez* studded with rhinestones. At the doorway, glaring at any visitors who look out of place, are two giant Sikh doormen in spotless turbans and tasseled white suits.*

Several floors up in the intensive care unit, Bedi is getting worked up. "I am so emotionally involved in the subject," he says, his voice wavering, "that it's difficult for me to be very articulate." Sex selection, he says, is "probably the single most important issue in the next fifty years that this country and China are going to face. If you're going to wipe out 20 percent of your population, nature is not going to sit by and watch." But hospitals have little incentive to do anything about the problem because maternity wards bring in substantial business. At Apollo, a deluxe delivery suite outfitted with a bathtub, track lighting, a flat screen television, and a large window looking out onto landscaped grounds runs to $200 a night. Although India outlawed fetal sex determination and sex selective abortion in 1994, the law is poorly enforced, and as sex selection is an easy procedure in high demand, doctors continue to openly perform it. Bedi says he makes less money than many Delhi gynecologists simply because he refuses to abort female fetuses. Some of his patients, he says, are "extremely disappointed when I do ultrasounds. They think it's just a waste of time and money if you don't even know whether it's a boy or a girl."

Indeed, some of India's top physicians help patients scan for fetal sex. A notorious case in Delhi is that of Mangala Telang, a Harvard-educated

---

*A flourish introduced in the 1940s by tycoon Mohan Singh Oberoi at his line of luxury hotels, the giant Sikh doorman—usually over six feet tall—is a mark of institutional distinction in India.

physician who is something like gynecologist to the stars. Telang's patients range from wealthy foreigners—both the American and British embassies recommend her to citizens living in Delhi—to India's Bollywood glitterati. In 2007 a pregnant British reporter of South Asian descent sent undercover by the BBC's Asian Network caught Telang ordering an ultrasound scan for sex determination and assuring the reporter she could recommend an abortionist if the fetus turned out to be female.[3] (Bedi appears in the segment, commenting dryly, "I'm not surprised at all.") After the show aired, the health ministry suspended Telang's license, but at the time of my visit to Delhi she was practicing again. The BBC reporter, moreover, found three other doctors in South Delhi willing to identify the sex of her baby. One didn't even bother to mention that sex selection was illegal—and then, smelling British money, charged the reporter twice the going rate. "When you confront the medical profession, there is a cowardly refusal to accept blame," Bedi tells me. "They say, 'We are doctors; it's a noble profession.' This is bullshit." Later he adds: "When it comes to issues like ethics and morality you can have an opinion, but there is a line which you do not cross. Everybody who does it knows it's unethical. It's a mass medical crime."

⸺∞⸺

Signs that trouble was brewing in Asian hospitals and clinics appeared as early as 1975. That was the year Delhi's government hospitals first began offering amniocentesis, which entails inserting a needle through a pregnant women's abdomen into the amniotic sac surrounding the fetus and removing a small amount of protective amniotic fluid, a substance rich with fetal cells. Within a few years, the technology was commercialized and made available at private clinics. Amniocentesis had been developed to diagnose fetal abnormalities, but by the early 1980s it was so commonly used for sex identification that Indians popularly referred to it simply as the "sex test."*[4] Still, amniocentesis was a relatively invasive procedure that carried a risk of miscarriage, and it lacked mass appeal.

---

*Similar trends were shaping other Asian countries. In 1984, according to the Korean press, 90 percent of amniocentesis tests were used for sex determination. In China, meanwhile, pregnant women started to use the word "examine" to mean determining a fetus's sex, as if there were nothing else worth checking.

Other technologies were on the way, however. In 1982 a report issued by the U.S. Office of Technology Assessment warned of new sex selection methods whose "probable impacts . . . could be highly disruptive and contrary to rising expectations of sexual equality" in the developing world. "It seems likely that a simple, effective technology for sex selection would be widely used," the report's authors concluded.[5] Almost on cue, high-quality second trimester ultrasound arrived.

By the mid-1980s scores of clinics in Delhi were offering prenatal ultrasound examinations. The technology also disseminated quickly in South Korea, Taiwan, Singapore, and China—so quickly, in fact, that scholars would later marvel over the speed with which sex selection caught on. "The sudden increases in sex ratios in East Asian countries are impressive," wrote demographers Chai Bin Park and Nam-Hoon Cho in 1995. "In each country, within a single year the sex ratio has jumped to a high level that has subsequently been sustained. This suggests that people have been anxiously awaiting the availability of sex-control technology."[6]

Indian clinics made sure consumers knew about sex determination tests through crass advertisements touting their economic benefits. "Better 500 rupees now than 500,000 later," read an ad that appeared throughout Mumbai.[7] Indians knew what that meant: thanks to a cheap technology, daughters, and the expensive dowries that accompanied them, were now avoidable. Other clinics maintained they were fending off population growth by helping parents meet government targets. One Mumbai hospital distributed fliers calling amniocentesis "humane and beneficial." "In developing countries like India," one advertisement read, "as the parents are encouraged to limit their family to two offspring, they will have a right to quality in these two"—*quality* was a favorite word of population control activists, but in this case it doubled as a euphemism for male—"as far as can be assured. Amniocentesis provides help in this direction."[8]

The new prenatal diagnostic methods arrived at a fortuitous time. After decades of strict population targets, Indians were having fewer children. Salaries had begun to rise, meanwhile, and Delhiites had become infatuated with technology. When a photojournalist I met in South Delhi got pregnant in 1986 and refused to have an ultrasound scan, she was already far outside the norm. She and her husband were artists, nonconformists who preferred ayurvedic medicine to Western drugs. "People have had babies without ultrasound for thousands of years," she told me.

In 1986 Delhi, however, having a baby without ultrasound was almost a political statement. When the baby was born and the couple rejoiced to learn it was a daughter, they became even greater oddities in their neighborhood. Her husband remembers sitting in the hospital waiting room after the birth, eager for a report on how it went, and then listening to the obstetrician—a woman—deliver the news as if it were a calamity. "You have a *daugh*-ter." The doctor's voice fell when she said the word. The subtext was that India had procedures to protect against such disappointments. (Today their daughter is an accomplished woman in her twenties training for a position in international hotel management. Contrary to the suggestions of Mumbai's tasteless 1980s ads, she may actually prove a financial asset.)

Sex determination technology reached Asia as many countries were building their economies around manufacturing, and it was commercialized and distributed throughout the continent, in part, by companies like Korea's Kum Sung Ultrasonic and China's Mindray Medical International. But Western firms got in on the market as well. General Electric's first joint venture in China was a factory it established in the early 1990s to produce ultrasound machines for the local market.[9] GE executives had identified significant demand for the technology; in a recent article for *Harvard Business Review* CEO Jeffrey R. Immelt recalls that "by the late 1980s it had become clear that a new technology—ultrasound—had a bright future" in Asia.[10]

In 2007, after GE's market share in China dropped, the multinational introduced a low-end, compact ultrasound machine that could be hooked up to a PC—at one-sixth the cost of a conventional device. The compact machine, Immelt writes, was "a hit in rural clinics . . . Today the portable machine is the growth engine of GE's ultrasound business in China."[11] In India, meanwhile, GE cornered the ultrasound market in a joint venture with the Indian conglomerate Wipro.[12] In 2006 Wipro GE Medical Systems did $250 million in sales in ultrasound and other diagnostic equipment. As in China, the company has helped sex selection reach new parts of the country by marketing cheap machines to small-time doctors in remote areas. "During the last decade," says T. V. Sekher, the demographer in Mumbai, "sex selection technology and sex selective abortion facilities have become very common, easily available, and cheaply available, even in the remotest rural areas."

A second trimester ultrasound is called a fetal anatomy survey. It is meant for checking fetal growth, a metric that can be used to calculate fetal age as well as identify abnormalities. But for many parents the fetal anatomy survey, which is typically done at twenty weeks of gestation, also imbues a pregnancy with newfound magic. The survey struck me, the two times I observed one, as akin to snorkeling in a still lake at night. As the wet transducer passes over the mother's belly, first you see an expanse of black, cloudy and indeterminably deep. Then, out of nowhere shapes pop into view, amazingly clear. More sophisticated machines can detect a remarkable range of characteristics, zeroing in one by one on the fetus's forearm and hand, its stomach and umbilical cord, its lips and nose. The machines introduce you to each individual toe and each individual finger, to two small but defined ears, to a tiny button nose. You see the diaphragm, the kidneys, the brain. A beating heart pops on screen, slippery and quivering gently. Zooming in, the transducer can detect the atria, the ventricles, and the valves.

But most ultrasound technicians in Asia learn only to identify sex, which is one of the easier characteristics to find. With some training, even people with no medical background can locate fetal genitalia, which typically show up white against the gray backdrop of the monitor screen. Perhaps this is why when it comes to sex determination ultrasound technicians use terms that are almost comically informal. Around the world, the small sprout of a penis peeking out from between the testes of a male fetus on the ultrasound monitor is known as "the turtle," and indeed it does look like a turtle's head emerging from its shell. In Asia and Europe, the three tiny parallel lines that form the fetal labia and clitoris are called "the sandwich." If you are American, you may hear them called "the hamburger."[13]

After a basic introduction to the turtle and the sandwich, technicians know enough to determine sex anywhere—and many test the limits of acceptable clinical settings. Some administer the exam out of the back of their cars. Mindray, the Chinese company, manufactures a handheld ultrasound machine that makes drive-by sex determination tests possible.[14] Sex determination is not entirely foolproof, though. Penises, in particular, can hide during examinations, and technicians sometimes mistake boys for girls. Christophe Guilmoto remembers meeting an Indian woman who was livid because she had accidentally aborted a boy

after a doctor misdiagnosed the fetus's sex. It stands to reason that the
technician who administers examinations in the daytime glare of a parking lot is especially prone to mistakes. But for the most part, as Asia's lopsided sex ratio at birth attests, the technology works.

Fetal sex determination is not just illegal in India. China and South
Korea also outlawed it early on, and governments in all three countries
have launched sporadic sting operations. As a result, technicians often
avoid announcing a fetus's sex outright in an effort to protect themselves
from possible hidden recorders. And yet the behaviors they substitute are
only legal in the most literal interpretation of the law. They make pointed
remarks: "Time to decorate the baby room in pink" or "You're going to
have a fine footballer."[15] Or they complete the exam professionally, with
no references to girls or boys, vaginas or penises, pink or blue—and then
hand the departing mother an image of the fetus's genitalia, circled and
annotated for easy comprehension.

Under pressure from Indian activists, Wipro GE has taken some measures to tone down its ultrasound push. The company now requires that
clinics sign an affidavit pledging they will not use the company's equipment for sex selection.[16] But the essential problem, GE representatives
maintain, lies with demand. They just provide the technology; if people
misuse it, that has nothing to do with them. Former Wipro GE executive
Vivek Paul said to the *Wall Street Journal*: "If someone drives a car through
a crowded market and kills people, do you blame the car maker?"[17]

Ultrasound manufacturing executives are not the only ones who blame
sex selection on public demand. Cho Young-Youl, a gynecologist in the
Seoul suburbs who performed sex selective abortions in the 1980s and
1990s, also considers himself powerless. An affable man with a hearty
laugh and a square jaw, Cho graduated from medical school and opened a
clinic in a suburb called Guri in 1983, the same year Kum Sung Ultrasonic
released ultrasound machines in South Korea for the mass market.[18] His
practice quickly boomed. He started out by doing all sorts of gynecological procedures—routine checkups as well as births and abortions—but
demand for the latter two was particularly high, and within a few years he

had opened a second facility exclusively devoted to obstetrics. The new branch grew into the largest obstetrics clinic in Guri.

Cho says he stumbled into a world in which it was out of the question for a doctor to refuse to identify a fetus's sex, let alone refuse to abort if the fetus turned out to be female. Pregnant women showed up for second trimester checkups eager to learn whether they were carrying a boy or a girl. "Almost all the patients wanted to know the sex," he says. "If you didn't tell the mother, she would go elsewhere. Pregnant women were desperate enough to go around to different hospitals looking for places where they could find out." Cho disliked the gender discrimination underlying sex selection, and he worried about the possible health effects of multiple late term abortions. But still he told the women the sex.

The reaction to his disclosure varied little from one patient to the next. "If it was a boy," Cho continues, "the woman would be overjoyed. If it was a girl, she would start thinking about what to do—about whether to have the baby or get an abortion." The women who were carrying girls rarely consulted him on the matter then and there, but Cho knows his diagnoses threw them into uncertainty because he could see it on their faces—and because many of them corralled the clinic nurses on their way out, seeking advice. He heard about the conversations later. "The nurses would ask the women why they wanted the abortion," he recalls. "They would ask if they really needed to have an abortion. But they didn't talk the women out of it. Instead they would try to figure out which direction they were leaning." As Cho describes it, a nurse's role when faced with a pregnant woman deliberating over whether to abort a female fetus is to access the woman's innermost yearnings, much as a psychologist might guide an indecisive patient through a tumultuous relationship.

Once a woman decided she wanted an abortion, she returned to the clinic, and Cho would explain the health risks of second trimester abortion. Like the nurses, he wouldn't try to argue with the woman. Just as there wasn't any point in refusing to identify the sex, he felt, there wasn't any point in refusing to abort. "They had already decided what they wanted," he says. So he performed the abortion.

Throughout the 1990s Cho split his time between his two clinics, seeing women for routine checkups at one and then delivering their infants, their boys and less frequently their girls, at the other. He took special pride in delivering babies, installing pink and blue neon lights in the waiting room and wiring them to buttons in the delivery room so a nurse could broadcast the sex of each newborn, adding a technological flourish to what had been an engineered process from the beginning. But by 2004, Korea's birth rate had plunged, and Cho discontinued his obstetrics practice and closed his second clinic. Today the remaining clinic stands in stripped-down form, above a Pizza Hut in a Guri strip mall, framed by a simple pink sign that reads Woman's Clinic.

Cho is in his fifties now, with deep spokes radiating out from his eyes. On the day we meet he is wearing a blue lab coat over a V-neck sweater. He has a lively manner of storytelling: at some moments he smiles sardonically, while at others he strikes a philosophical tone. Several times he calls something a "social issue," and he is deeply involved in his Christian church. It is only when discussing his contribution to South Korea's sex ratio imbalance that his tone turns indifferent.

⣿⣿⣿

Critics say that viewpoint has become pervasive throughout the medical establishment, both in Asia and elsewhere. Sunita Puri, a young American doctor who has done extensive research into sex selection among South Asians in the Bay Area, says she sees physicians' willingness to comply with sex determination requests as symptomatic of a broader trend toward patient-driven care. "The patient is a consumer now," she says. A doctor, in turn, has "become more of a dispensary of medicine rather than someone who gets to know the patients. But," she adds, "there *is* something called critical decision making." Sekher, the demographer in Mumbai, agrees. "If doctors were quite serious about this kind of large-scale distortion and elimination," he says, "it would never happen."

Determined medical professionals can in fact play an important role in identifying sex selection early on, before a country's sex ratio at birth skews. Unlike sociologists and anthropologists, they don't have social science theories standing in their way: they simply open their eyes to what's happening with their patients. Years before demographers learned about Albania's imbalance, for example, Rubena Moisiu helped reveal the existence of sex selective abortion at the hospital she directs—and might have prevented its spread had anyone in the government listened.

In 2002 Moisiu began suspecting that women were coming to Tirana's No. 2 University Hospital of Ob-Gyn, the large public hospital she oversees, to abort female fetuses. Years of observing deliveries had impressed on her that couples wanted boys very badly. She had seen women who gave birth to successive daughters—six, seven, eight girls—in attempts to have a son, and she had seen fathers get angry when their newborns turned out to be female. Once or twice, a man stood in the hospital's waiting room as his wife languished in the recovery room, yelling for all the nurses and patients to hear, "I'll be back in a year with a boy!" Then suddenly the strings of daughters decreased. With the abortion rate high and prenatal ultrasound examinations increasingly prevalent, Moisiu guessed some couples were taking advantage of what was the obvious shortcut to getting a son. She decided to find out.

During the first trimester, Albanian women can abort in small private clinics, but after twelve weeks the law requires them to visit a hospital for the procedure. Since ultrasound technology available in the country at the time could not identify the sex of a fetus until thirteen weeks, that requirement meant that, in theory at least, hospital physicians handled all terminations done for reasons of sex selection.[19] Moisiu hoped No. 2 University Hospital, as one of the country's two major maternity hospitals, might reveal just how common those were. For a full year, she instructed doctors to quiz all the women who came in for second trimester pregnancy terminations on their reasons for seeking an abortion—not to intervene in any way, but simply to try and understand why they wanted to abort.

When the results were tallied, the desire to have a son was the second most popular reason for aborting that year, after women who said they had gotten pregnant unintentionally. All told, around a fifth of the women had sought abortions because the fetus they were carrying was female. Moisiu says she informed UNFPA of the results; Flora Ismaili, the UNFPA representative I met, said she had never heard of the survey. In any case, in the absence of government or UNFPA action on sex selection, nothing happened. Moisiu told her staff that she would not tolerate sex selective abortion at No. 2 University Hospital from then on and turned her attention to other issues, though from time to time she would stop to worry about Albania's future. Sex selection, she tells me, "means females are underestimated from the time they are in the mother's womb. It's a kind of gender denigration."

But Moisiu's concern puts her in the minority among hospital ad-ministrators. The money sex selective abortions bring in is simply too great, says Bedi. "Almost a third of Indian gynecologists' income comes from abortion," he tells me. "Among those who do female feticide, 90 percent comes from abortion. Who the hell is going to stop it?" Sekher agrees. "The doctors are very greedy," he says. "They are behind the money. It has become a big business, this business of sex selection."

For the most part, the task of monitoring the medical industry falls to people like Indian public health activist Sabu George, a soft-spoken and compact man who cares so deeply about India's sex ratio imbalance that he roams the country with few possessions, staying with friends and liv-ing off donations. More than one person I spoke with compared him to Gandhi, and the analogy is probably apt; as with India's earlier crusader, his placid exterior belies a fierce and at turns inflexible morality.

George was instrumental in convincing GE to assume more responsi-bility for its ultrasound business. He has also fought Yahoo, Microsoft and Google, threatening legal action if the Internet giants did not remove sponsored links for terms like "gender selection" from their Indian search engines. Following a 2008 request by the Indian Supreme Court on his be-half, many of the ads disappeared.[20] (Global engines like Google.com con-tinue to allow sponsored links for sex selection, however, so he has yet to declare victory.) Lately George has turned his attention to mail-order blood tests that purport to determine gender as early as five weeks—a dangerous innovation, he believes, since early testing would allow women to abort female fetuses well before their pregnancies are apparent to the outside world.

In 2005 the Massachusetts-based company Acu-Gen Biolab introduced a $275 kit called Baby Gender Mentor, billing it as "99.99 percent accurate" at predicting sex at five weeks.[21] The kit, which debuted to effusive cover-age on the *Today* show, relies on the idea that a pregnant woman's blood contains a small amount of fetal DNA. To access that DNA, a woman pricks her finger and sends a drop of blood into the lab. Within days, she has a diagnosis—or so the company promises. In reality both consumers and scientists have raised questions about Baby Gender Mentor's accu-racy.[22] In 2006 dozens of disappointed parents filed a U.S. class-action suit against Acu-Gen after the kits they ordered incorrectly predicted the sex of their babies, alleging the company did not furnish a promised 200 percent refund. Acu-Gen subsequently filed for bankruptcy.[23] But more sophisticated fetal DNA tests are now under development, and George worries that Baby Gender Mentor sets a disturbing precedent. "If these people create new markets for products, we're lost," he says when we meet for lunch at a vegetarian restaurant in Delhi.

More broadly, he hopes to impress on American companies the fact that their technologies have a deep impact elsewhere in the world. "There is a global responsibility for this problem," he tells me. But he also realizes the prospects for sudden acknowledgement of that duty are dim. Westerners have been ignoring their responsibility for Asia's sex ratio imbalance, after all, for hundreds of years.

Chapter 5

THE IMPERIALIST

*What experience and history teach us is this, that
nations and governments have never learned anything
from history.*

—GEORG WILHELM FRIEDRICH HEGEL

In 1789, when Jonathan Duncan was dispatched by the English East
India Company to see how tax collection was progressing in the Indian
interior, he represented a new breed of colonial officer. The joint-stock
company had been siphoning resources out of India since 1600, when
the British crown granted it a monopoly on trade to Asia. But in its early
days the firm had paid its employees very little and attracted, accord-
ingly, a hodgepodge of adventure seekers and profiteers who devoted
much of their time to filling their pockets with bribes. News of misman-
agement had reached shareholders back home, and when the company's
profits began to falter, they insisted on better qualified employees. Under investor pressure, company directors sacked the corrupt old guard
and boosted pay and benefits in an effort to attract job candidates with
knowledge of Indian culture and history. At the same time, the executives took the opportunity to rework their company's image. The new
employees were, they declared, part of an identity based on bringing education and Western gentility to the uncouth natives. Education itself

was a good investment, as it ensured the stability of the East India Company's power in India. "Every accumulation of knowledge," one company governor-general explained in 1784 to investors, " . . . lessens the weight of the chain by which the natives are held in subjection."[1]

The new recruits came to be known as Orientalists (it would be two centuries before Edward Said gave the term a negative connotation), and Duncan, who spoke Persian and Bengali, was fairly representative. A meticulous man, he dressed in white silk stockings and stiff breeches that fastened below the knee, powdered his hair bright white, and had a reputation for being incorruptible.[2] Duncan was posted to Benares, the sacred city now known as Varanasi. Arriving in the illustrious city, a nineteenth-century historian writes, he "regarded the people around him, from the highest to the lowest, with deep paternal interest."[3] This too was typical of the new wave of officers. While they quoted freely from Indian texts and eagerly perfected their knowledge of local customs, they did so paternalistically, as tyrannical fathers searching for shortcomings in wayward children. For the East India Company, the arrival of the Orientalists marked the transition toward colonialist logic in India, toward the cloaking of unfair economic domination in moral and religious reasoning. And so after visiting members of the Rajkumar caste on his 1789 tax collection visit, Duncan dutifully noted that they killed their female children.

The dominant group in their area, the Rajkumars reigned over forty-two villages. They formed a subcaste within the larger Rajput caste, a group of powerful landholders critical to maintaining British rule in Benares and therefore a constant source of worry. Perhaps this is why upon returning to his office that October, Duncan sat down to write Lord Charles Cornwallis, the East India Company governor-general, about his discovery. He wrote, with no small amount of fanfare, "I am well assured, and it is, indeed, here generally believed (and being so, it is my duty not to keep such enormities, however sanctioned by usage, from the knowledge of Government), that it is no unfrequent practice among the tribe of Rajkoomar to destroy their daughters, by causing their mothers to refuse them nurture."[4] Duncan's enthusiasm for the topic of daughter killing was, it turned out, boundless. The letter continued for pages, detailing the social conditions under which he believed infanticide occurred as well as its effects. (One of the effects he listed was that Rajput men had a tough time finding women from their caste to marry.) A British historian would later call female infanticide Duncan's "private war."[5]

Duncan did not tell Lord Cornwallis how he discovered that the Rajkumars killed their daughters. Probably he simply stumbled on a village with no girls; that is how later inspectors registered the problem. In any case, he speculated that female infanticide had something to do with the Rajkumars' hunger for status. Female infanticide, Duncan wrote Cornwallis, was founded in the "extravagant desire of independency entertained by this race."[6] By killing their daughters, the officer surmised, the Rajkumars avoided marrying women into lower caste families—and maintained the local power that the East India Company found so troubling. Two months after writing Lord Cornwallis, Duncan forced Rajkumar leaders to sign a covenant under which they admitted to centuries of wickedness and pledged to change their ways by expelling any member who killed a girl. "We do ourselves acknowledge," the document read, that "murderous practices" are " . . . customary among us."[7] Duncan sent the signed covenant on to Lord Cornwallis, satisfied that the problem had been solved—or so it seemed.

Then in 1795 Lord Cornwallis transferred Duncan to Bombay, over nine hundred miles to the south, and promoted him to governor of that city. Duncan now administered a region that included a large section of western India, and he traveled more widely. Reports quickly reached him of female infanticide happening in other areas. In what is now Gujarat, he learned, one caste marked the birth of a girl by digging a hole in the ground, filling it with milk, and dropping her in.[8] After a few such accounts he commissioned a subordinate to write a report on the topic. The results were alarming. In one settlement of 1.2 million people, an estimated 20,000 female infants died every year.[9]

⸺⬡⸺

Thus began a century of copious documentation. The British administrators were enthusiastic record keepers, and reports compiled over the coming decades regularly enumerated instances of female infanticide, along with human sacrifice and *sati,* or bride burning, juxtaposing dry tables and figures with histrionic commentary. "Sentiments of nature and humanity have no influence with the Jareejahs," noted one report.[10] Indians engaged in the "shedding of innocent blood warm from the womb," observed another.[11] Female infanticide, the colonialists wrote, was "inhuman" and "barbarous."[12]

One account from this period is particularly notable. *The Administration of the East India Company: A History of Progress* is a breathy, unabashedly biased tract published in 1853 by British military historian John William Kaye, who succeeded John Stuart Mill as secretary of the East India Company Political and Secret Department. While Mill went on to an illustrious career as a political theorist, Kaye was a man of foiled ambition whose dreams of writing literature had come to nothing.[13] He had, however, infinite energy for detailing Indians' faults, and he devoted an entire chapter of his book to female infanticide. The existence of the practice, he wrote, proved that Indians were guilty of "grossness of ignorance, deadness of conscience—barbarism—devilry—what you will."[14] At moments, Kaye attempted something like balance. He conceded, awkwardly, that Indians could be good parents: "The tenderness with which strong bearded men devote themselves to the care of young children, is as touching as it is remarkable."[15] But such descriptions were overshadowed by a level of invective extreme even by colonial standards, mixed with gushing praise for men like Duncan who educated natives about the evils of infanticide. "They were," Kaye wrote of the company's officers, "the pioneers of humanity and civilization . . . and bravely they labored with axe and hatchet to clear away the dense jungle of barbarism that lay before them."[16]

Infanticide was, in fact, not unheard of in the West. Until the Middle Ages several European cultures held that life did not begin until days, or even months, after birth. Many early Europeans took that belief to its morbid conclusion, suffocating or exposing unwanted infants shortly after birth. By the nineteenth century, most Westerners considered infanticide morally unacceptable, but across Europe and colonial America parents continued to kill babies in secret, and in the mid-1800s England saw a spike in infant killings.* An article appearing in the *Journal of Social Science* at the time lamented that police "thought no more of finding the

---

*In 1864 infant deaths accounted for 61 percent of all murder cases in England.

dead body of a child in the street than picking up a dead dog or cat."[17] But England's imperialists took care to distinguish India's baby killings from the abuses that occurred on their own turf. "In this Christian country, it is to be feared that the dark crime of infanticide is painfully on the increase," Kaye wrote of England. "Still it is only a crime—incidental, exceptional. In some parts of India it has been, for many generations, a *custom*."[18] Helping Kaye make this case was the fact that Indians only killed girls. And sex selective killing, like sex selective abortion today, could be measured.

In 1858 the English crown assumed control of India from the East India Company, finally making the country an official colony, and a few decades later the colonial government conducted the first Indian census. In northwest and central India, British surveyors found populations that skewed significantly male. In the state of Gujarat, there were 954 females for every 1,000 males in the overall population. In Rajasthan, the sex ratio dropped to 905 females per 1,000 males, while in Punjab it was even worse, at 832 females per 1,000 males.*[19] The list of castes practicing infanticide, meanwhile, was extensive: along with the Rajputs, the group singled out by Duncan, girl killers included the northern warrior castes the Jats and Ahirs, the rebellious Gujjars, the mostly Sikh Mohyals, the largely Hindu Patidars, the Kanbis in Gujarat, and the Khatris in Punjab.[20]

That Indians practiced female infanticide in large numbers was now abundantly clear. The larger issue of why parents killed girls should have been a tricky one, however. Reliable population records might have shed light on whether in fact infanticide had been, as Kaye wrote, "for many generations a custom." But India lacked demographic records from the precolonial period. On other moral questions, the Orientalists looked to Hindu texts for evidence of depravity, but on this issue the scriptures were no help. Hindu tracts abhorred killing of all types, and of women and children in particular. The covenant Duncan forced on the Rajkumars had acknowledged this stance in vivid detail. "This is a great crime,

---

*Sex ratios in India are traditionally calculated as number of females per thousand males rather than as number of males per hundred females.

as mentioned in the *Brehma Bywant Purana*," the document read, "where it is said that killing even a foetus is as criminal as killing a Brahman; and that for killing a female or woman, the punishment is to suffer in the Naraka, or Hell called *Kat Shutala,* for as many years as there are hairs on the female's body, and that afterwards such person shall be born again, and successively become a leper."[21] Even Kaye, the East India Company historian, conceded in his curmudgeonly way that there was no link between infanticide and the Hindu faith: "It is almost the one exceptional case of a barbarous custom, that has not the sanction expressed or implied, by precept or example, of the monstrous faith which these people profess."[22]

But if religion didn't cause the practice, what did? How could men like Duncan and Kaye know whether the infanticide noted by colonialist surveyors represented some deep-seated cultural practice, or whether it was a phenomenon that had flared up more recently in response to social and economic changes? Indeed, some surveyors suggested female infanticide might be linked to the distribution of wealth. The castes that killed girls were invariably land-owning groups, and even within those castes the families that killed the most girls tended to be wealthier. Others had noted that the lower castes that practiced infanticide seemed to be simply copying the Rajputs—that the practice had never been a part of their particular group's history.[23] Of course, a group that systematically destroys its girls cannot survive for millennia. But the British didn't belabor these points. Instead, they singled out hypergamous marriage—the expectation, common throughout much of India, that women marry up—as infanticide's ultimate cause.[24]

Hypergamous marriage worked well for members of lower castes, who could raise their status by marrying a daughter into a more prestigious family. The issue, the colonialists noted, was that it left upper-class women with nowhere to go. With no castes above theirs, they could not marry up. Nor, according to most caste rules, could they marry someone of the same group. Rather than raise daughters who would remain unmarried, then, upper-class parents simply killed girls—and, the British believed, they had always done so. Marriage practices change over time, of course. Bride-price and dowry have long fluctuated with economic cycles. But the colonial surveyors treated the Indian marital practices they encountered as if they were static, drawing up detailed tables that divided marriage expenses into highly specific categories like "expenses on food for persons and animals who came with the groom" and "Cash payment to son-in-law when he visited his wife's parents for second time" under the illusion that understanding marriage practices might somehow help them stamp out infanticide.[25] As time went on, the idea that some castes and tribes had always killed girls evolved into doctrine. The report that accompanied the 1901 census, which found continued evidence of girl killing, explained that some castes had a tradition of female infanticide dating to "olden times." The 1921 census went one step further, classifying India's castes into those that killed their daughters and those that didn't.[26]

The British colonialists' reading of centuries of continuous history into conditions they found on arrival fit snugly with trends under way elsewhere in the imperial world. Across Asia, Africa, and the New World, Western officials, philosophers, and writers were swept up in a search for proof that the darker, southern inhabitants of the world needed to be civilized. The demand for cultural arcana drove the development of anthropology and archaeology, leading to detailed ethnographies replete with diagrams and field sketches. No custom was too obscure, no native crime too sensational. The census was a common classification tool that also served as a self-fulfilling prophecy. Imprecise and wrong-headed categories became exact and prescient with time, so that in places where ethnicity and caste had once been fluid, people freshly divided into categories began to act out their new identities. Rwanda existed for centuries as one cohesive nation until Belgian rulers classified the population into Hutus and Tutsis, setting up the country for later strife.[27] Elsewhere in Africa, in countries as diverse as Cameroon, Nigeria, the Congo, South Africa, and Egypt, censuses documented sex ratios that tilted toward females, and an excess of women too was found to be a marker of barbarity. Colonial scientists speculated that Africa's sex ratio—which was only slightly more female than Europe's—was caused by what they deemed excessive racial intermixing.[28]

The prescription for these societal ills was, almost without fail, intervention. Kaye, the East Indian Company historian, held that nothing short of political upheaval—and an upheaval that looked distinctly like colonialism—could cure India of female infanticide. Since the killing of girls was "an abomination propped up and sustained by feelings deeply implanted within men's hearts," he wrote, it was "not to be eradicated without . . . rendings and revulsions of the whole social and domestic system."[29] By the late nineteenth century, the white man sagged under his burden.*

One of the more imaginative pieces of colonial demography came from an officer posted in India named Colonel William Elliot Marshall. When Marshall began working on the Nilgiri plateau, Charles Darwin's theory of natural selection had just been published, revolutionizing how Europeans conceived of human origins. Marshall apparently had the theory in the back of his mind when he began conducting experiments in phrenology, the pseudoscience of determining personality from skull measurements, on the Toda, a pastoral tribe living on the plateau. In an account of these experiments, Marshall noted that the Toda counted 133 men for every 100 women.[30] Since the group numbered under a thousand people and rarely ventured beyond the plateau, Marshall hypothesized that perhaps their high sex ratio could be explained by natural selection. If the Toda ancestors had murdered their daughters, it would have meant that parents who produced boys had more opportunity to pass on their genes, leaving nineteenth-century tribe members, centuries later, prone to have sons. In other words, Indians had killed girls for so long that a tendency to produce boys was inscribed in their genes.

In the 1870s, Colonel Marshall's theory came to Darwin's attention as he sat down to revise *The Descent of Man*. In the second edition of the book, Darwin devoted a passage to the question of whether some cultures were predestined to have boys because of the sins of their ancestors.[31] He weighed Colonel Marshall's inquiry respectfully, at one point declaring his analysis "ingenious." Ultimately, however, science won out. Darwin was unsure whether a tendency to produce children of a certain sex was a heritable trait, but he concluded, in any case, that there is not "any necessary connection between savage life and a marked excess of males."[32] The imbalance among the Toda, he decided, was the result

---

*Flabby analysis of subcontinent history persisted well into the twentieth century. According to the historians Barbara and Thomas Metcalf, the idea that "because India was 'timeless,' the village and caste organization of colonial or even contemporary India was a guide to its historical past" remains one of the central misperceptions in histories of India.

of human behavior, not bad genes. The tribe, it turned out, did not have a skewed sex ratio because they killed girls centuries ago. Instead they killed girls in contemporary times, under English rule.

—∞∞∞—

When India gained independence in 1947, the British colonialists fled for Britain, abandoning their meticulous records in archives in Delhi and Mumbai. A few years later, two Indian sociologists visited one such archive and stumbled across reams of documents detailing female infanticide. They copied the records, but neither scholar found the time to go through them, and finally they passed on the collection to L. S. Vishwanath, one of their students, who was looking for a dissertation topic. By the time Vishwanath had completed his PhD, he had turned the conventional understanding of female infanticide in India on its head. What he found was no less than remarkable: the British tax collection drive that occasioned Jonathan Duncan's discovery of female infanticide had actually helped cause the crime.

When the first East India Company traders arrived in India in the seventeenth century, the country was flourishing. In addition to the largest economy in the world, it boasted a vibrant tradition of architecture, a sophisticated medical system, and a population of well over 100 million.[33] The trade relationship the company brokered with this booming empire was, from the beginning, tenuous. The foreign traders were primarily interested in purchasing textiles such as calico and muslin, which were in great demand back in England. But they had little to offer in return; there was little interest in woolen goods, one of England's big products, on the tropical subcontinent. The company tried exporting large amounts of English gold to pay for Indian fabrics. But by 1773, when the company required a bailout, King George III was fed up with the outward flow of precious metals, and at the crown's request the shareholders came up with a new approach. They would tax the natives and use the tax revenue to pay for Indian goods—essentially, use Indian money to buy Indian products.

Before the British arrived, land rights under India's Mughal rulers were dispersed and decentralized, held jointly by peasants, the government, and a class of tax collectors called zamindars. The Mughals were master bureaucrats, and they crafted a complex administrative system in which

caste mattered less than loyalty to the emperor. The zamindars, who received a share of the tax revenue they brought in, occupied an important
role in this system. In addition to collecting taxes, they exercised police,
judicial, and military duties. The Mughals supervised the zamindars
closely, a situation that both protected the zamindars from the whims of
greedy officials by keeping the revenue targets they were assigned constant and shielded average citizens by preventing the zamindars from
accumulating too much power.[34]

In 1793, as it consolidated its power in the interior, the East India
Company overhauled India's system of land administration, introducing
stricter, more delineated property rights. The new order was essentially
medieval feudalism transported to India, where such an arrangement
had never before existed. Women had once held property rights, but now
they were excluded from owning land.[35] The changes also hurt peasants,
who lost the right to the land they tilled. And for almost everyone, demands were more extensive than they had been under the Mughals. In
many cases tax collectors were required to turn over to the company one-
third of their region's harvest.[36]

For the most part, those collectors were the zamindars. Since the East
India Company was strapped for cash, its directors kept the old bureaucracy in place even as they upended the entire economic system. At the
same time, the English increased pressure on the zamindars by raising
taxes and hiking the penalties for poor performance. If the collectors
did not deliver their quota of revenue, their estates could be taken—and
the British made good on this threat again and again.[37] In Bengal, an estimated one-third of all estates went up for sale in the twenty years following land reforms.[38] This was hard on the zamindars, but supervision was
more lax than it had been under the Mughals, so many collectors simply
transferred their burden to the peasants living beneath them. In Benares,
under Duncan's watch, some collectors charged an 11 percent commission on taxes. Others beat peasants who refused to pay.

Then, just as Indians were adjusting to the changes and a handful of
zamandars had amassed small fortunes, the East India Company overhauled the revenue collection system again, this time in an effort to prevent abuses among collectors. Instead of reinstating the strict oversight
that had been a feature of Mughal rule, however, the British scrapped the
zamandars altogether, replacing them with appointees who had no con-

nection to the villages they administered. For the zamindars, this was devastating. The sudden loss in income squeezed whole castes, pushing them to come up with new strategies for maintaining their status and land. Among the qualities they reconsidered was family composition.

Sons inherited land, keeping it in the family. Daughters not only married out, they also required a hefty dowry, and with taxes higher than before, having a daughter could mean losing the family land. One way to safeguard their wealth, these parents reasoned, was to not have daughters in the first place. As the historian Bernard S. Cohn has written:

> By killing their daughters [families] did not have to enter into marriages with families and groups who were of lower status. Hence the question of distribution of infanticide must be tied to the question of economic resources and particularly of land resources.[39]

The choice these families made, to kill rather than accept diminished status, was hardly noble. It is important, however, to note that they made it in the face of rapid change—not because of tradition. Hypergamous marriage, it turns out, did play a role, but it was only after the practice was combined with unfair economic policies that Indians began killing girls in large numbers.

While the British publicly ignored any link between the new land policies and the dearth of girls, they could not have been oblivious to the connection. Combing over the infanticide archives years later, Vishwanath found many examples of Indians who had tried to bring the connection to the colonialists' attention. In 1849, for example, a man from the Lewa Patidar caste complained to the official J. Webb that as locals turned over larger and larger portions of their income as taxes they had little money for their daughters' dowries:

> Respectable persons give their daughters in marriage incurring the expenses according to their abilities, but amongst our people the expenses are daily increasing; whilst during the former administration, we used to obtain the management of the villages from the state on our own responsibility and therefore made the collections on our own authority, consequently our means were kept up; at present we have no such means.[40]

In 1847 other Patidars lodged similar complaints with a collector in Ahmedabad. A few years later, the officer W. R. Moore, who had been dispatched by the East India Company to conduct a detailed investigation into female infanticide in 1855–1856, wrote, "Among all tribes, the cause of the crime is said to be the same: the inability to expend such sums as they consider necessary. Their position and means are not what they once were, and they cannot afford, therefore, to contract such lofty marriages nor to spend such large sums."[41]

What Vishwanath believes happened is this: Jonathan Duncan's discovery, back in Benares in 1789, was genuine. Rajkumars—and other high-ranking Rajputs—did kill girls, and probably they had been doing so for years. But as the British tightened their control over India, female infanticide spread to other groups. First it worsened among the Rajputs, spreading from the top-ranking subcastes to less powerful ones. Then in 1795, when the first land reforms were introduced, the Rajputs lost 40 percent of their land. To make up for the loss they began demanding higher and higher dowries from the castes below them. Female infanticide then trickled down, catching on among lower castes as well.

In 1873 the British unveiled the Female Infanticide Act in an effort to abolish the practice they had unwittingly encouraged. Since hypergamous marriage had been singled out as the cause of female infanticide, the act attempted to cap dowry and other marriage expenses—a provision that some allege actually had the perverse effect of worsening infanticide in some areas.[42] But because the new law was supposed to mark the resolution of the problem, many officers thereafter steadfastly denied that girls were killed in their districts. "I am told by all I ask," wrote the officer H. R. Cooke, "that so far from now wishing evil to their female offspring and regarding their birth as a misfortune, [fathers] are only too glad to cherish and support them with care and affection."*[43]

When Vishwanath started poring over British archives, conventional wisdom held that the British had exposed and fought against female in-

---

*Elsewhere, Cooke conceded that to file a report describing anything but the enlightened treatment of girls would suggest a failure in British policy: "Let us while we can avoid so humiliating a position as to admit that such a foul crime can exist and prevail to any extent under our present police administration in Regulation Provinces without detection."

fanticide in India. What he found suggested exactly the opposite. "Unless female infanticide was almost whole scale or too blatant to be ignored," he observed, "the British turned a blind eye to it."[44] This abrupt switch—from descrying the barbarity of female infanticide at every turn to concealing its existence—was, to say the least, inopportune, because once set in motion a trend is not so easy to obliterate. By the time the colonialists began denying that Indians killed girls, infanticide had finally become a custom.

Today the logic put forth two hundred years ago by British imperialists in India is applied to sex selective abortion. If you have investigated Asia's gender imbalance, chances are you learned that cultural traditions are to blame.

One of the first works to address sex selection in the West was the 1991 book *May You Be the Mother of a Hundred Sons*, by Elisabeth Bumiller, then a reporter for *The Washington Post*. The book juxtaposed sex selective abortion among the wealthy in Mumbai with female infanticide in the poor Tamil Nadu villages where Christophe Guilmoto did his graduate research. Both infanticide and sex selective abortion, Bumiller concluded, grew out of the same root cause: India's entrenched gender discrimination. But portraying sex selective abortion as an updated form of infanticide disregards the fact that abortion is far more common than infanticide has ever been. (Indeed, several countries where sex selective abortion occurs have no history of female infanticide.)[45] It ignores the fact that no one wants the job of jamming rice chaff down a baby girl's throat, or feeding her the juice of poisonous weeds, or slipping her a liberal dose of sleeping pills—that Indians, like many people around the world, logically see abortion as cleaner and less ethically fraught than baby killing. But it is this explanation, this viewing the present through the abuses of a flatly drawn past, that has stuck.

Today the explanation comes from all camps. It comes from feminists. Underlying sex selective abortion, explains the women's organization Legal Voice on its blog, are "deeply-rooted cultural traditions."[46] It comes from organizations working on the ground. "At the heart of the matter," asserts a UNFPA India pamphlet urging artists and performers to join the fight against sex selection, "is the low status of women in society and the deep-rooted prejudices they face."[47] It comes from secretary of state Hillary Clinton, who recently called the abortion of female fetuses the result of "deeply set attitudes."[48] And it comes from the religious right. "A thousand years before the birth of Christ," reads a report on Catholic Online, "the Chinese were already prizing their sons—and scorning their daughters . . . The Hindus in India likewise regarded sons as treasures and daughters as expendable."[49] Even the Chinese government, which rarely sees eye-to-eye with the likes of Catholic Online, agrees on this point. Government reports on sex selection are peppered with terms like "backward" and "traditional thinking." Traditions, after all, are simply institutions that rigorous communist reforms have not yet obliterated.

Even parents themselves focus on tradition. Asked to explain why sex selective abortion has become pervasive, they talk about weddings and funerals, about ancestor rites, about the afterlife. In India, the son lights the funeral pyre. In Vietnam, he cares for a book containing the family tree, which shrivels if he is not born. In China, he cares for his ancestors. "You need someone to sweep your grave," Wu Pingzhang, the Suining man with twin boys, told me. Parents say there is no escaping the sexist past. "We farmers cannot get rid of this practice, it is so profound," forty-one-year-old Nguyen Thi Tham explained to sociologists in Vietnam after recounting how she and her husband used ultrasound to pinpoint the exact moment of ovulation at which she was most likely to conceive a boy. "This may illustrate how backward the rural areas are," she added.[50]

But tradition cannot be the whole explanation for a phenomenon that has only appeared in the past thirty years, of course, and so most works on sex selection also mention technology. Old traditions and new technologies are a nice pair, the sort of counterintuitive and yet simplistic duo that sells magazines and books. Bumiller called sex selection "a powerful example of what can happen when modern technology collides with the forces of a traditional society," and twenty years later the language is nearly identical. [51] A 2009 article in *The New York Times Magazine* maintained sex selection was a clash "between modern capabilities and old prejudices."[52] One recent UNFPA report explains, similarly, that "modern science tends to perpetuate traditional ideologies."[53] Or take

William Saletan, writing on Slate.com. The key thing to understand about sex selection, he says, is that "the new transforms the old."[54] Then there is the journalist Michelle Goldberg, who has written that sex selective abortion occurs because "social modernization has proven unable to catch up with technological progress," resulting in "a lag between social change and technological advancement."[55] But the technology portion of this opposition is typically sketched lightly. We are not told what brand of ultrasound machine is used, how sex determination tests were developed, or how abortion became so pervasive in Asia in the first place. Instead we get a black-and-white relief of Technology with a capital *t* plowing along inexorably, as if there is no such thing as bioethics and new developments are not first weighed and deliberated over for their possible effects on human populations, as if population changes themselves haven't been carefully studied for the past hundred years.

This explanation persists because blaming backward cultural traditions is simpler than the alternative of taking a hard look at how a particular phenomenon—including the technology that makes that phenomenon possible—came to exist. Just as discussing racism in the abstract is less painful than addressing the legacy of decades of slavery, talking about gender bias is easier than scrutinizing the spread of sex selection throughout Asia.

Analysts in the West are not alone in overemphasizing the role of culture. Two centuries after the British first blamed daughter killing on the pull of tradition, many Indian activists point to tradition as the cause of sex selective abortion. Instead of challenging India's history of population control or bringing entrenched interest groups like the medical lobby to task, these activists launch awareness campaigns directed at changing prejudices and societal mores. Positive reinforcement is a common theme in such campaigns. Daughters are portrayed as loving, intelligent, capable, fun—everything a parent could want in a child. There is the Save the Daughter Campaign, Shakti: the Initiative to Empower the Girl Child, the 50 Million Missing Campaign. There is even a "motorbike campaign against female foeticide," which involves politicians touring the country on motor scooters to preach the merits of having girls.[56] Organizations lead focus groups in remote villages. They hire television writers to pen soap operas showing women rejoicing over the birth of daughters. They enlist Bollywood stars to film public service announcements. They sponsor playwrights and hold art contests and develop school curriculums. An awareness campaign was the reason well-known Indian designers and models took time out from the shows during Delhi's 2009 Fashion Week to pose with children plucked off the street. "Through fashion," one celebrity told *ThaIndian News,* "we want to show that young icons of India are stepping forth to support the unborn girl child."[57] Even Apollo Hospital runs an awareness campaign staffed by employee volunteers at the hospital's Punjabi branch. As their coworkers stay back to help well-off urbanites abort girls, the volunteers disperse throughout poor villages to preach the merits of daughters.

To Puneet Bedi, the Apollo Hospital obstetrician, this approach is infuriating. "If people had a son simply because they want a son, girls would have disappeared from this country one thousand years ago," he says. The campaigns, he says, are an attempt to pawn off modern-day oppression on intransigent cultural mores. He believes it is time for India to start asking hard questions. What if the indiscriminate elimination of girls was planned—not by individual parents thinking only of themselves but by some larger force? And if the Indian and U.S. governments and leading Western organizations played a role in that planning? But Bedi leans toward scheming and subterfuge because back in the late 1970s, when he was still a wide-eyed medical student, that is what he saw unfold.

PART TWO

A GREAT IDEA

Chapter 6

THE STUDENT

*It is commonly said in the Orient that we want to cut
their population because we are afraid of them. . . . But
the program can be sold on the basis of the mother's
health and the health of the other children. . . . There
will be no trouble getting into foreign countries on
that basis.*

—WILLIAM VOGT, NATIONAL DIRECTOR OF
PLANNED PARENTHOOD FOUNDATION OF AMERICA,
SPEAKING IN COLONIAL WILLIAMSBURG IN 1952[1]

The subterfuge came to a head in 1978, on the first night of Bedi's first
rotation in medical school. He'd been lucky enough to gain admittance to
Maulana Azad Medical College, one of Delhi's top medical schools, which
meant access to the latest technology and leading professors. Bedi knew
that upon graduation he could expect a nice salary and a secure position
among the country's elite. Rather than imparting confidence, however,
that distinction scared him. Like most Indian medical students, he had
entered medical school at eighteen, after graduating from high school. He
was now halfway through his study at age twenty. As he walked with a
classmate to Lok Nayak Jayaprakash Narayan Hospital, the government
institution on the edge of campus where he was assigned to carry out his
rotation, his spirits sagged with the thought that in just two short years

he'd be a practicing physician responsible for human life—and yet until now medical school had consisted of long hours in the library. Tonight would mark his first time interacting with patients.

He'd had all day to think about what the rotation would be like. When he and his classmate arrived at the obstetrics ward that morning, a doctor had turned them away, explaining there were already too many student interns on duty, and asked them to return at 9:00 PM. The two students didn't feel like returning to campus to study, so to kill time they went to see a movie, then walked around Delhi, sweating in the oppressive early summer heat. Back then the city was a sensory overload, with creaky rickshaws, improvised food stalls, and limbless beggars thronging its streets, its air redolent of sizzling oil and fiery spices and decaying garbage. But this backdrop hardly existed for the young students, whose minds were elsewhere as they walked. Bedi thought about the coming night shift, feeling nervous and excited all at once. Lok Nayak Jayaprakash Narayan Hospital, which Delhiites simply called LNJP, boasted thousands of patients a year. Its doctors delivered between six and eight hundred babies a month.[2] He hoped he would get to witness a birth.

What Bedi had not considered, what he would come to reflect upon only later, was that simply by attending medical school in 1970s India he had stumbled into a world in which learning was tangled up in geopolitics. He was vaguely aware that population control had become a critical priority for the Indian government. Under Prime Minister Indira Gandhi, 59 percent of the Indian Health Ministry budget went toward family planning, and even as a student he could sense that level of investment.[3] "Between the 1950s and the 1980s," he recalls, "all public health meant was family planning. There was nothing else done. There wasn't malaria or tuberculosis. You would go to a hospital and all you'd see were advertisements for birth control, IUDs, and sterilizations." But he did not yet fully understand the reasons behind this push. Nor could he know that in the West India represented the holy grail of population control.

Following the 1952 Conference on Population Problems in Colonial Williamsburg, Western activists had seized on the idea that if a family planning approach worked in India, with its mushrooming, impoverished population, it might work anywhere in the world. One group of Harvard researchers charged with researching birth control use among Indian villagers went so far as to call the country "the cauldron in which mankind will be tested."[4] As Western advisers flooded into Delhi in the 1960s, they backed major surveys, paid for training India's first demographers, and wooed doctors over to their cause. Medical schools became an important source of potential recruits. A degree from Maulana Azad at this moment in Indian history, then, entailed much more than routine medical training.

Finally the moment Bedi and his classmate had been anticipating arrived. At exactly 9:00 PM they reached LNJP and found their way to the obstetrics ward. As he walked down the hall toward the labor room to which he'd been assigned, he may have mentally replayed the instructions his professors had given him. Or perhaps he reviewed the textbook passages he had read on childbirth in anticipation of the real thing. Three decades later, Bedi can't remember exactly what he was thinking as he neared the entrance to the labor room because what happened next overwhelmed all other memories. A moment after he stepped into the doorframe and caught his first glimpse of the labor room, he says, a cat bounded past him with a bloody blob dangling from its mouth.

Stray cats and dogs were not unusual in Delhi hospitals at the time.[5] But what was that thing—wet with blood, mangled, about the size of Bedi's fist—in the cat's mouth? Bedi entered the labor room to find a woman recovering in a hospital gown and doctors and nurses shouting harried instructions. As he began his shift, he searched for clues. Before long it struck him. Near the bed, in a tray normally reserved for disposing of used instruments, lay a fetus of five or six months, soaking in a pool of blood.

He told a nurse, then a doctor. Or maybe it was a doctor, then a nurse. *I saw a cat eat a fetus.* Nobody on duty seemed concerned, however, and finally he got on with his post. He couldn't escape the feeling that something was amiss, though. That night, Bedi witnessed more abortions than births, and all of the abortions, from what he could tell, were performed on women who were at least twenty weeks pregnant. Several of the fetuses Bedi glimpsed were at six or seven months of gestation. He didn't believe they constituted life, but he had to concede they looked like "minibabies," he recalled years later. With each procedure, moreover, the fetus was discarded in an uncovered tray, not autopsied and studied, as he had read was the protocol in high-risk pregnancies ending in late termination.

The doctors and nurses in the delivery room appeared unemotional, and Bedi briefly worried that he was being overly sensitive, that perhaps he couldn't handle the intensity of actual medical practice. But then finally he worked up the nerve to approach the head doctor with the mystery. Why had he seen a cat run off with what looked like fetal matter? And why had the fetus not been disposed of more carefully? Bedi says the nurse's explanation came out cold, her voice matter-of-fact. "Because it was a girl," she said.

———— ∞ ————

While Bedi and his classmates spent their days holed up in the library, blissfully unaware of the procedures their professors were overseeing, it had become open knowledge among Delhi's elite that government hospitals were performing sex selective abortions and had been for years. In 1975 the All-India Institute of Medical Sciences, the country's most prestigious medical school, unveiled India's first amniocentesis tests at its government teaching hospital. AIIMS officially introduced the test for identifying fetal abnormalities. But almost from the start doctors used it to pinpoint fetal sex. Before long, other government hospitals—among them LNJP—were offering the test as well.

In contrast to today's India, where a woman seeking a sex selective abortion may have to shuttle among multiple physicians, hinting at what she wants, the early procedures were performed openly at government-funded institutions. Doctors helpfully identified fetal sex. Then if a woman learned she was carrying a girl and wanted to abort, the doctors helped with that as well. In some cases, physicians may have even encouraged women to abort female fetuses; population control was deemed so urgent that they routinely encouraged women to abort healthy fetuses in other situations.[6]

Government hospitals in India serve poor and indigent patients, who receive care free of charge with the trade-off that it may be performed by a medical student. But as word of the "sex test" spread through the middle and upper classes, increasing numbers of well-heeled women showed up in government obstetrical wards, braving the austere conditions and inexperienced doctors in exchange for access to the new technology. A

little hardship was a worthy price to pay for avoiding the birth of an unwanted daughter.

In their remarkable openness about the tests, it wasn't simply that the
physicians neglected to consider the ethics of sex selection in the face of
widespread patient demand. No: not only did the doctors believe sex selection acceptable, they believed that by culling female fetuses they were
making the world a better place. Shortly after the amniocentesis tests began, several AIIMS doctors published a paper in the journal *Indian Pediatrics* explaining the project as an experimental trial with potential to be
introduced on a larger scale. Indian couples clearly desired sex selection,
wrote Dr. I. C. Verma and colleagues. And that interest, if tapped more
widely, could be a boon for India—and the world:

> In India cultural and economic factors make the parents desire a son,
> and in many instances the couple keeps on reproducing just to have a
> son. Prenatal determination of sex would put an end to this unnecessary
> fecundity. There is of course the tendency to abort the fetus if it is fe-
> male. This may not be acceptable to persons in the West but in our pa-
> tients this plan of action was followed in seven of eight patients who had
> the test carried out primarily for the determination of sex of the fetus.
> The parents elected for abortion without any undue anxiety.[7]

While the doctors defended their actions with cultural relativism—
"This may not be acceptable to persons in the West"—their logic was a
variation on Malthusianism, which India inherited from Europe. Verma
and his colleagues aborted female fetuses in the name of population
control.

Western money had backed the creation of an extensive network of
community family planning advisers in India, and as amniocentesis spread
from AIIMS to other government hospitals, these advisers encouraged
women to go in for the test, which the hospitals provided, like other services, free of cost.[8] Finally in the late 1970s, when sex selective abortions
showed no sign of abating, Indian feminists organized. India had a fledgling but vibrant culture of activism, and the noise women's groups made
marked the first anti–sex selection campaign in the world. In late 1978,
shortly after Bedi watched a cat trot down the hospital hall with a female

fetus dangling from its mouth, the health minister responded to the protests by barring government hospitals from performing sex determination.

By then, however, the hospitals had already done substantial damage. At AIIMS alone, doctors had aborted an estimated one thousand female fetuses.[9] Verma and his colleagues had also presented their research at a national conference, arguing before pediatricians from around India that sex selection was an effective and ethical method of population control.[10] For physicians from rural areas who sat in on that session, sex selective abortion must have seemed a breakthrough in family planning, coming as it did from researchers at India's top medical school. How many returned home to put it into practice is impossible to tell. In Delhi, meanwhile, the ban had the paradoxical effect of increasing the number of places a woman could go to abort a girl. For with government hospitals out of the market, private clinics stepped in.

Feminist outcry over the amniocentesis trials focused on the fact that Indian government money had been used to fund sex selective abortions. Though privately Indians speculated about a link to the Western foundation money that had been flowing in to Delhi for population control, no one succeeded in proving any connection. "I believe it was both the Population Council and International Planned Parenthood Federation—but mainly the Ford Foundation," Bedi speculated years later, when asked which organizations might have backed the trials. But "everyone is very tight-lipped about it." By the late 1970s most Western advisers had left, and the details of their activities in India remained opaque, sealed away in dusty boxes in office storage rooms or in closed archives on American benefactors' estates. Recently, however, IPPF and the Rockefeller Foundation opened up their early files, revealing reams of documents that, like the records the British kept in their quest to stop infanticide, are impressive in their detail. The intricacies of the organizations' work in India finally became clear. In the story told by those documents, the AIIMS experiments trace back to the West.

⸻ ∞ ⸻

The story begins in the mid-1960s, when Sheldon Segal, head of the Population Council's biomedical division, headed to Delhi for an overseas post. This was not a casual placement, for Segal was no middling figure within the population control movement. The success of the Population Council and similar organizations depended on the development of cheaper and more advanced contraceptives, and Segal was one of the scientists who were critical to that quest. In 1956, not long after Segal graduated from the University of Iowa with a doctorate in embryology and biochemistry, John D. Rockefeller III hired him as assistant medical director of the Population Council, a position from which he oversaw the council's research laboratories.[11] Shortly before his departure to India, Rockefeller promoted Segal to director of that same division. As one of the more senior members of the council, then, with coveted access to Rockefeller and other power brokers and an assignment in a country that had come to represent everything for the population control movement, Segal was poised to make decisions affecting tens of millions of lives. The Ford Foundation underwrote the cost of posting him to Delhi.[12]

Over his two years in India, Segal performed several roles. One of the most important was to serve as personal adviser to Lieutenant Colonel B. L. Raina, the former Army Medical Corps officer who had become India's director of family planning. Before Segal arrived, Raina had been responsible for both population control and maternal and child health. That soon changed. Segal sat on a three-person World Bank committee that scrapped Raina's job description—the World Bank wielded so much power in India that it could determine the duties of Indian government cabinet members—and recommended that the colonel give up the maternal health focus and make population issues his "unconditional first priority."[13]

Another of Segal's tasks was to oversee trials for some of the world's early birth control methods. India was an ideal place for such tests, since informed consent was a luxury there. At one point, Segal infuriated the Indian health minister by smuggling in experimental intrauterine devices in his luggage, claiming they were Christmas tree ornaments.[14] He also worked closely with Christopher Tietze, a U.S. State Department researcher and Austrian medical expert who wrote widely about abortion's utility in controlling population growth.[15] But Segal's primary assignment while in Delhi was to found the department of reproductive physiology at the All-India Institute of Medical Sciences.[16]

When Segal touched down at Delhi's Palam Airport, India was already overrun with foreign population workers. Personnel at the Ford Foundation alone numbered in the hundreds, putting the organization's staff on par with that of the U.S. embassy.[17] The Rockefeller Foundation, meanwhile, had twenty-four people in Delhi, its largest staff outside New York.[18] The web of advisers was incestuous, with substantial overlap in priorities and funding. The Population Council, for example, was miniscule in comparison to the Rockefeller and Ford Foundations, but most of its money came from these two groups, and Segal worked closely with colleagues at both organizations. To Indian government leaders trying to make sense of the influx, this interconnectedness was formidable. Early on, a senior government official admitted he was "watching with anxiety the increasing penetration and power of foundations like the Ford [and] Rockefeller . . . in governmental spheres."[19]

But there was little any single politician could do to slow this accumulation of power. By the 1960s, the U.S. government, UNFPA, the Ford Foundation, and the World Bank together accounted for most of the $1.5 billion India received in annual aid. Of these, the World Bank—which, recall, made loans for food and public health projects conditional on population control—had special influence. India was its biggest debtor.[20] Anxiety among Western advisers that no strings attached aid was a bad idea was particularly acute when it came to India. At the 1952 Colonial Williamsburg meeting, Rockefeller Foundation representative Warren Weaver had cautioned that India was in danger of becoming "nigger rich." He had explained: "A man who finds out that he has a little income . . . just stops working four days or a week, and he just sits there. I do not think that is what we want to bring to India."[21]

And many in the Indian elite did not want that, either. The racism and eugenic logic of the population control movement resonated with India's upper classes, who feared a high birth rate among the poor.* With support from wealthy Indians, Western organizations unveiled measures aimed at the lower classes, bankrolling sterilization campaigns that paid men in famine-stricken areas to undergo vasectomies.[22] It didn't hurt that the West courted the elite by funding university departments and

---

*The Indian population debate also cut across religious lines, with Hindus quick to point out that Muslims were overtaking them.

doling out research grants. The Population Council set up India's first demography center, the International Institute for Population Sciences in Mumbai, with United Nations money in 1954.* But AIIMS was the biggest target: Western aid to India's health sector, wrote sociologist Roger Jeffery after wading through funding documents years later, concentrated on "'elite' colleges (notably AIIMS) and their hospitals."[23]

By maintaining a presence at the institution that trained India's leading physicians and many of its public health officials, Western advisers ensured their access to both doctors and policymakers. The Rockefeller Foundation first posted an employee at AIIMS in 1958 as an adviser to the institute's director, and the foundation maintained a presence there throughout the 1960s. The Ford Foundation began backing the institution in 1962, giving it the lion's share of a $1.7 million grant for research in reproductive medicine at Indian universities.[24] Segal was the first adviser from the Population Council. His supervisors in New York likely had high hopes for what he might achieve there.

With sunken eyes and jet black hair that he slicked back every morning, Segal wore a perpetually weary expression on his face. His colleagues called him "Shelly," a playful nickname that belied a humorless industriousness. He worked tirelessly throughout his life, and when he died in 2009 he was eulogized as one of the giants of the birth control movement. (From India he went on to invent Norplant, the contraceptive implant that slowly releases progestin into a woman's arm.) Along with the administrative drudgework that came with setting up a department, Segal worked closely with medical students and doctors to get them up to speed on established Western techniques. It was in this role that he taught a group of AIIMS students how to determine sex in humans.

Years later, Segal recounted the training session in his memoir, *Under the Banyan Tree: A Population Scientist's Odyssey.* Sometime during his stay, he and Harold Klinger, a geneticist visiting Delhi from Albert Einstein Medical Center in New York, assembled a group of AIIMS pupils in a laboratory and instructed them on how to test human cells for XX and XY chromosome combinations. The procedure Segal and Klinger used involved taking smears from patients' cheeks and then analyzing them for

---

*Decades later, I journeyed to the institute's campus to interview demographer T. V. Sekher not about overpopulation but about India's skewed sex ratio at birth.

the presence of something called sex chromatin. The American scientists thought it important that Indian doctors learn the sex determination technique, Segal explained, "for its general usefulness in reproductive bio-medicine. It could help, for example, in clarifying a diagnosis in cases of intersexuality or infertility."[25] But helping infertile couples have children was the very opposite of what Segal had been assigned to do in India.

Segal intimated that it never occurred to him that introducing sex de-termination to India would lead to the abortion of female fetuses. Years before he and Klinger gathered the students in a Delhi laboratory, how-ever, scientists had applied sex chromatin testing to fetal cells, then used the results of their tests to perform sex selective abortions on women carrying sex-linked diseases. Segal was also almost certainly familiar with a 1950s family planning study carried out in Punjab with Rockefeller Foundation funding that had shown Indians prized sons.[26] And he may have read a paper entitled "Social and Cultural Factors Affecting Fertility in India" that a Delhi professor had presented at an IPPF conference in 1963.[27] (Christopher Tietze, the Austrian abortion expert working for the U.S. State Department, was present at the meeting and may have shared what he learned there.)[28] "[S]ome religious rites, especially those con-nected with the death of the parents, can be performed only by the male child," S. N. Agarwala of Delhi's Institute of Economic Growth had writ-ten. "Since the peace and salvation of the souls of the dead parents also depends on the proper and continuous performance of some religious rites by the male child, his importance in the family is great . . . [T]hose who have only daughters try their best to have at least one male child."[29]

Segal maintained in his memoir, however, that when he visited AIIMS a few years later and discovered his former students were using the tech-nique he taught them to eliminate female fetuses, he was shocked and upset. What he neglected to mention is that shortly after his stay in India he went on the record promoting sex determination as an effective method of population control.

———∞∞∞———

In the late 1960s Segal returned to New York, where he continued to rise through the ranks of the population control movement. Back in India, the links he had helped establish between East and West grew stronger, and Western money and expertise flowed into the new department of reproductive physiology at AIIMS. LeRoy R. Allen, a Rockefeller Foundation consultant posted at the medical school throughout the 1960s, brought Harvard scientists on board. In 1966 Allen oversaw a project that involved flying researchers from Cambridge to India for a two-year investigation, jointly conducted with AIIMS doctors, into barriers to population control in rural communities in northern India.[30] Working closely with village parents and interviewing them about their reasons for having more children, the American researchers would have received further proof of India's major family planning hurdle: that locals put great stock in having sons. In 1969, the year Segal took the podium at a national U.S. conference to advocate sex determination as a means of population control, the Ford Foundation allocated $63,563 for "research in reproductive biology" at AIIMS.[31] In 1972 students from the institute participated in an international seminar on the role doctors might play in ameliorating the population problem, and in 1974 the World Health Organization bankrolled a symposium at AIIMS on the latest developments in contraceptive technology.[32] But the most money came from the Rockefeller Foundation, which between 1950 and 1973 gave AIIMS $1.5 million that paid for everything from new buildings to fellowships for the institute's doctors. The bulk of that funding came between 1962 and 1974.[33]

Then things got dark. On June 25, 1975, as political unrest brewed across the country, Prime Minister Indira Gandhi drew on a little-known article of the Indian constitution to suspend democratic rule and invoke emergency powers. Over the next twenty-one months, she ruled by decree, stamping out freedom of speech and imprisoning her opponents. The Emergency, as the period came to be known, affected all areas of life in India, crippling the economy and scaling back civil liberties. But it was an especially bleak era for reproductive rights. Health officials in Gandhi's administration saw an opportunity to force drastic measures on Indians who had previously resisted birth control. The task of overseeing this gruesome campaign fell to Indira's son Sanjay Gandhi, who held no official political title.[34] He wasted little time in announcing a massive effort to sterilize poor men. Widespread sterilization was an idea that had been introduced to India by Western advisers, but Sanjay Gandhi ratcheted it up to an unprecedented scale. At first his mother's government rewarded men who consented to vasectomies. Before long, however, Sanjay Gandhi was issuing quotas so high that local officials could meet them only by dragging men to the operating room—typically a makeshift camp that had sprung up practically overnight. (Nearly two thousand men died from botched operations.)[35] In some areas, police surrounded villages in the middle of the night and apprehended all the men.[36] In others, they combined sterilization with slum clearance, razing whole neighborhoods and robbing men of both their reproductive ability and their homes at the same time. Protestors were killed.[37] The scale of the campaign, which was memorialized by Salman Rushdie in the novel *Midnight's Children*, is striking, given that many Americans today remain unaware of its existence. By the time democratic rule was restored, 6.2 million Indian men had been sterilized in just one year—fifteen times the number of people sterilized by the Nazis.[38]

Western experts later distanced themselves from the excesses of the Indian Emergency, but records from the time show that many advisers supported, if not cheered, India's fling with despotism. In September 1975, three months after the Emergency began, demographer Kingsley Davis considered the expansion of Asian slums in an article for the *Population Development Review,* a journal sponsored by the Population Council, and arrived at an endorsement of authoritarianism. Democracy, Davis concluded, was at odds with effective population control and stability in Asia; the only political system for the continent's mushrooming megacities was a "strong government that stands in contrast to the populace in skill as well as power . . . ruling a docile mass of semi-educated but thoroughly indoctrinated urbanities existing at a low level of consumption, working very hard, and accepting passively what is provided for them."[39] A World Bank official in Delhi at the time the Emergency began, meanwhile, returned to Washington to urge that the bank *increase* its support for India's family planning program. The Indian government asked for $26 million from the bank, explaining it would use a portion of the money to build sterilization camps in remote areas.[40] The committee that considered the proposal turned it down—not because committee members were alarmed at the human rights violations being perpetuated with World Bank money, but because $26 million was, as one employee wrote to a colleague in the bank's population division at the time, "disappointingly conservative."[41] Money came instead from UNFPA, which in 1974 had issued its largest grant yet to India, and the Swedish International Development Authority, which in 1976 contributed $60 million toward family planning in India.[42] And World Bank money continued to flow in as well. Between 1972 and 1980 the bank doled out $66 million in loans to the country for the express purpose of population control.[43]

A few months after the World Bank committee considered India's proposal, president Robert McNamara flew to India to make the bank's support for the Emergency overt. Arriving in Delhi as men were being forcibly rounded up for vasectomies, he met with health and family planning minister Karan Singh, who admitted the sterilization campaign had entailed a few abuses. Still, McNamara was apparently unfazed, writing in a summary of his trip: "At long last, India is moving to effectively address its population problem."[44]* When the archives of Western population control organizations were finally opened, the scholars who sifted through them might be forgiven for overlooking the role the organizations played in bringing sex selective abortion to India. At a time when the president of the World Bank endorsed the forced sterilization of millions of men, a few thousand voluntary abortions must have seemed like nothing. For it was in the peak of the Emergency that AIIMS launched its amniocentesis trials.

⸎

Bedi stayed at LNJP for twelve years, continuing as a doctor at the hospital after his graduation from medical school. Following that first harrowing night, his senses dulled. Nothing that happened afterward shocked him quite as much. The stream of late-term abortions continued for a while; as the young medical student worked the night shift, he witnessed numerous terminations that, like the ones he observed his

---

*The Indian elite was similarly pleased with the World Bank. When McNamara announced an increase in funding to Asia in 1977, the country's *Economic and Political Weekly* ran an article titled "Onward, World Bank Soldiers!" "As has become inevitable under Robert McNamara," the article raved, "[the 1977 report] discloses further progress in the operations of the Bank."

first night, involved fetuses at six or seven months of gestation. Then the government banned sex selection in government hospitals, LNJP ceased performing sex determination altogether, and Bedi watched as the practice migrated to private clinics. The first clinic to advertise sex determination was one in his native state of Punjab that began offering sex selection in 1979. The procedure quickly caught on in other states. Witnesses later testified at a government hearing on amniocentesis that between 1978 and 1983 an estimated 78,000 female fetuses were aborted in India.[45]

After the ban on sex determination in government hospitals, you might think it would have become more difficult for Indian doctors to argue they were performing a worthy service. But the logic planted by Western population control activists died hard, and the idea that sex selective abortion was a good method of population control endured. As late as 2001, the anthropologist Barbara Miller found that many Indian intellectuals remained loath to criticize sex selective abortion because "it serves as a quiet way to deal with 'overpopulation.'"[46]

Part of the problem is that population growth is in fact a threat in India. The country's birth rate has dropped by more than half in thirty-five years, from 5.7 children per woman in the mid-1960s to 2.7 in 2010.[47] But India is still growing, and it is set to overtake China as the world's most populous country by 2026.[48] Both the government in Delhi and Western family planning organizations—who are now back in India, though this time with less objectionable approaches—have retained an emphasis on small families. And yet in another regard the government has taken a step backward in how it frames family planning policy. The sterilizations of the Emergency period proved hugely unpopular, helping topple Indira Gandhi's government, and later leaders decided it was politically dangerous to target the reproductive ability of men.[49] Today in India, the onus is on women to control their fertility. Female politicians are disqualified from serving on the *panchayat*, the village councils that govern local life in much of the country, if they have more than two children.[50] And in a world where a woman is pressured both not to breed and to produce a son, sex selective abortion can seem like a windfall.

Still, uneasiness over what happened at Delhi's government hospitals in the 1970s lingers, and in some circles sex selection has been rightfully

stigmatized. Over the past few decades, the Indian intelligentsia has suc-
cumbed to bouts of tortured soul-searching over how the country got
itself into this mess. One such period came in 1982, when a collection of
women's groups held a meeting in Delhi to discuss the spread of sex
selective abortion. Feminist professor Vina Mazumdar, who chaired the
meeting, became increasingly agitated, until in her concluding remarks
she gave the proliferation of boys a sinister spin. "Hysteria about the
population crisis" was everywhere, she noted, and sex selective abortion
was turning out to be a very effective population control method. Could
it be that someone, somewhere, saw it as "a 'final solution' to the population question"?[51] Mazumdar later intimated that her reference to the
calculated genocide of the Holocaust had been excessive.[52] Who would
have dreamed up such a plot? But she didn't know the half of it.

Chapter 7

THE DOOMSAYER

*Countless millions of people would leap at the oppor-
tunity to breed male: no compulsion or even propaganda
would be needed to encourage its use.*

—MICROBIOLOGIST JOHN POSTGATE,
WRITING IN *NEW SCIENTIST* IN 1973[1]

On August 13, 1970, Americans watching Johnny Carson's *Tonight
Show* returned from a commercial break to find the iconic host promising
a debate on the future of the world. Holding court from behind a white
Formica desk, a young Carson laid out the terms: Paul Ehrlich, author of
The Population Bomb, would go head-to-head with Ben Wattenberg, a
critic who had dismissed Ehrlich's dire population growth forecasts in
a recent *New Republic* article, calling him a "prophet of doom." The discussion, Carson intimated, was sure to be an interesting one. "Would you
welcome, please," he announced, "Dr. Paul Ehrlich and Ben Wattenberg.
Gentlemen!"

The audience applauded, and the two men appeared at stage right. Almost from the start any pretense of equal standing dissolved. The tall,
gangly Ehrlich swaggered out first, grabbing the seat at Carson's side and
leaving Wattenberg the couch farther from the host. Ehrlich—then already something of a superstar—settled into his chair and crossed his legs

easily, while Wattenberg sat hunched over, his elbows propped on his knees, dwarfed next to Ehrlich's wiry frame. If this didn't look like much of a competition, though, such was the nature of demographic discourse in 1970s America. Since the days of the Colonial Williamsburg conference, concern about the coming population explosion had spread from business interests and McCarthyites to environmentalists, scientists, and a good number of concerned Americans. In the academy and the press as well as the World Bank, the idea that the world was on track for demographic disaster was now accepted at face value. The unresolved questions were when disaster would hit, how hard, and what humans might do, in the meantime, to mitigate its impact.

Carson let Ehrlich make his case first. The scientist began by laying out the terms of the explosion. "There are 3.6 billion people in the world today," he said, staring into the camera. "And that's too many. It's too many because we are getting desperately short of food. . . . We're in deep trouble."[2] Clad in a brown jacket, yellow shirt, and brown high-water pants that slid up to midcalf when he shifted his legs, his face accented by thick sideburns, Ehrlich looked the picture of 1970s fashion. But he was in fact an unlikely public figure, an entomologist specialized in the study of butterfly habitats who had spent much of his early career hunkered down in the biology department at Stanford. His fate had changed in 1968, when the executive director of the Sierra Club heard him speak charismatically on the radio and commissioned him to write *The Population Bomb*.[3] He had pounded out the work in a month, returning home from the university to spend evenings crafting breezy, novelistic passages with his wife, Anne.[4] (Ehrlich says the publisher refused to acknowledge her as the book's coauthor.)[5] The quirky, highly readable little book that resulted linked population growth to food prices, epidemic disease, and war, pummeling readers with frightening numbers, dystopic futuristic scenarios, and alarmist descriptions of foreign threats. It marked Ehrlich's transition from insects to populism.

The book begins with India. Ehrlich describes a trip he and Anne took to the country with their young daughter. "[O]ne stinking hot night in Delhi," he wrote, they rode back to their hotel in a flea-infested taxi. Along the way they passed through a slum, and he looked out the window. This is what he saw:

People eating, people washing, people sleeping. People visiting, arguing, and screaming. People thrusting their hands through the taxi window, begging. People defecating and urinating. People clinging to buses. People herding animals. People, people, people, people. As we moved slowly through the mob, hand horn squawking, the dust, noise, heat, and cooking fires gave the scene a hellish aspect. Would we ever get to our hotel? All three of us were, frankly, frightened.[6]

During that cab ride, population growth went from an intellectual to an emotional preoccupation for Ehrlich—and for his readers. Indians, he implied, were "multiplying like rabbits."[7] Once readers had the threat firmly in view, he reminded them that the United States shipped a sizable chunk of its wheat to India.* If Indians continued to reproduce, where else could they turn but to America's wealth?

The Population Bomb appeared at a time of rising inflation, mounting protests over the Vietnam War, and deepening civil rights fractures across the country. Difficult times make it easy to fear those different from ourselves, and the book preyed on this tendency. Ehrlich, the historian Matthew Connelly writes, "probably connected precisely with those readers who had imagined getting lost in a large city and ending up in the wrong neighborhood—not Delhi, but Harlem or Watts. Only Ehrlich invited readers not just to imagine a wrong turn, but to recognize that America—all of it—was turning into a bad neighborhood."[8] To be fair, *The Population Bomb*'s alarmism wasn't limited to poor developing nations. In later pages, Ehrlich urged action at home by imploring American couples to limit themselves to one child. But the book first and foremost evoked the specter of Asians overwhelming American shores. What in another era was called yellow peril Ehrlich repackaged as overpopulation.

Ehrlich was for the population problem what Al Gore would later become for climate change: a smart, passionate spokesman who disseminated

---

*The Indian masses were an old trope in population control manifestos. In the courses on political economy Thomas Malthus gave at Haileybury, a college set up by the British East India Company to train colonial officers, he taught students that aiding the starving during Indian famines would boost overpopulation.

concepts that had once been reserved for elites. Journalists and television personalities loved Ehrlich's charisma and energy, and Carson, in particular, couldn't get enough of him. The Stanford professor appeared on *The Tonight Show* several times, becoming the only writer ever interviewed for an entire hour.[9] His advocacy propelled the movement that had coalesced among wealthy industrialists and businessmen into the mainstream. By the time Ehrlich debated Wattenberg on national television, his little population tract had sold nearly a million copies. It had also moved a number of readers to action: Zero Population Growth, a group Ehrlich founded to lobby for population control around the world, counted tens of thousands of members in chapters across the country.[10] At Ehrlich's urging, ZPG members evangelized among friends and colleagues—my own mother was among those who limited herself to two children as a result of the group's work—and wrote members of Congress. A handy appendix in *The Population Bomb* contained sample letters.[11]

But in his eagerness to staunch population growth, Ehrlich and his followers backed extreme solutions that from the distance of history are blatantly wrong-headed. Among the policy prescriptions described in *The Population Bomb* was an increase in funding for sex determination research. "[I]f a simple method could be found to guarantee that first-born children were males," Ehrlich wrote, seven years before doctors at AIIMS introduced sex determination to India as a family planning tool, "then population control problems in many areas would be somewhat eased." Around the world, he continued, "couples with only female children 'keep trying' in hope of a son."[12]

As *The Tonight Show* episode wore on, Wattenberg vainly tried to point out that Ehrlich's predictions were off base. "Sooner or later," he said, "you suffer a credibility gap." But this did little to abate audience enthusiasm. The crowd applauded wildly every time Ehrlich made a new point. To Wattenberg, meanwhile, audience members were cold, bordering on derisive. When the demographer suggested the U.S. could remain a nice place to live with 300 million people—a number we reached in 2006—they broke into peals of mocking laughter.[13] A low point came when comedian Buddy Hackett, who had appeared earlier in the show, stumbled onstage in a dashiki, interrupting Wattenberg midsentence.

The episode helped boost sales of *The Population Bomb* to 2 million copies. The next year Milton S. Eisenhower, brother of President Dwight

Eisenhower, and former senator Joseph D. Tydings joined Zero Population Growth leaders in a coalition group that lobbied for population control.[14] And soon after the entomologist would see his policy prescription
become reality. As amniocentesis and ultrasound spread throughout
the developing world, they brought sex determination to countries with
rapidly growing populations. Looked at through a population control
lens, these technologies were undeniable in their success. Even Ehrlich
hadn't dared to dream about preventing 160 million births.

Paul Ehrlich helped popularize the idea that ensuring couples sons was
an effective means of curbing population growth. But he was not the first
to propose it, and he would certainly not be the last. Throughout the late
1960s and early 1970s a number of influential U.S. experts sounded their
approval for sex selection everywhere from the pages of major scientific
journals to the podiums at government-sponsored seminars. Many more
stood back and said nothing as their colleagues advocated a disturbed
sort of technological sexism, and then, decades later, pretended as if that
advocacy never happened.

The first time an American publicly espoused sex determination as a
method of population control seems to be in October 1967, one year before *The Population Bomb* hit bookstores. That month, the American Association for the Advancement of the Sciences and the National Institute
of Child Health and Human Development sponsored a conference in
Washington, DC, to explore cutting-edge research in family planning.
The event drew together journalists, scholars, and activists from a pan-
oply of respected institutions, including the American Newspaper Pub-
lishers Association, the National Institute of Mental Health, University of
California–Berkeley, Michigan State University, the Social Science Research Council of London, and Washington University in St. Louis. All
the major population control organizations sent representatives as well.

In the opening speech, Population Council president Bernard Berelson
noted approvingly that the study of human behavior had led to significant
advances in family planning. By enlisting the help of sociologists, anthropologists, and behavioral scientists like himself, he said, population control groups knew more than ever before about why people had children.

Knowing why they had children was critical to figuring out how to convince them not to have children, and so the new research, continued Berelson, who would later serve on a national population commission under President Richard Nixon, was translating into innovative solutions.[15] Then he handed the microphone over to Steven Polgar, head of research for Planned Parenthood Federation of America, to describe one such tool.[16]

An anthropologist who split his time between Planned Parenthood and Columbia University, Polgar had helped found the field of population anthropology, a distinction that put him on the front line of the group of academics Berelson described.[17] While sociologists might survey Asians or Africans on their attitudes toward childbearing, Polgar's work entailed mining cultural traditions for nuggets that could help population control organizations reduce the birth rate in various countries. Was it important to have a son to carry on the family line? What role, if any, did daughters play in performing ancestor rites? These are the sorts of questions Polgar would have asked. (He had good company in this quest. The legendary Margaret Mead was among the anthropologists who helped lay the groundwork for sex selection by lecturing population control activists on attitudes toward sons and daughters around the world; Mead herself reportedly supported sex selection on the grounds that it would reduce the number of unwanted girls born.[18]) Polgar had done his field work in Africa, not Asia, which remained the population control movement's major target.[19] But in his work with Planned Parenthood he would have become familiar with research from the region. Very likely, the continent flashed through his mind as he approached the podium and prepared to speak.

By the late 1960s, the link between the number of children a couple had and the sex of those children was well established, in Asia and elsewhere. The fact that couples kept having children until they had a son had a flip side, moreover: once they finally had a son, they stopped. What is known as the "stopping rule" was so pervasive around the world—in Asia, North Africa, the Middle East, Latin America—that demographers could predict whether a couple would have another child simply by looking at the gender of the couple's last child.[20] Even in the United States, women with only daughters were more likely to tell researchers they wanted another child than women who had at least one son.[21]

Planned Parenthood had amassed proof of the stopping rule at the household level. In Taiwan surveyors affiliated with IPPF had been passing along information on the sex composition of every family they visited in the form of worksheets that were filed away in the U.S. parent organization's archives.[22] Other studies, meanwhile, had made clear that parents in developing countries were more willing to accept contraception if they had sons. Research proving this first appeared in 1957.[23] When other studies corroborated that early finding, the connection between sex composition and birth rate became, in the words of Korean demographers Chai Bin Park and Nam-Hoon Cho, "a central concern of demographers and population planners."[24] (The connection also worried Chinese leaders, who beginning in the 1970s fretted that women's desire for sons was a major obstacle to slowing population growth in China.)[25]

In developing countries the population control movement faced an added challenge. Since death rates from disease had only recently begun to drop, the memory of harder times led many parents to doubt their children would live to adulthood, and as a result many wanted not one but two boys. In 1963 demographer Mindel Sheps calculated that if all families stopped after two sons, the average couple would have 3.88 children—far above the replacement level of 2.1 children population control advocates hoped for.[26] The task before the movement as Polgar took the stage in 1967, then, was to somehow enable couples in the developing world to have two children and yet feel satisfied with the sex of those children.

One obvious solution would have been to fight son preference by launching a campaign—in 1967 rather than 2007, as happened in much of Asia—promoting the value of daughters. Educational efforts meant a hefty outlay of time and money, and they yielded spotty results. But the population control movement was already backing foreign soap operas and informational films like Disney's *Family Planning* in an effort to change closely held notions about motherhood, femininity, and family size. A nod to gender equality would not have been a big stretch. And indeed a growing body of research suggested that investing in education and work for women propelled economic development and led to lower birth rates. Later in the 1967 meeting University of Chicago sociologist Philip Hauser alluded to this research when he asked the delegates: "Do we really know whether the classical approach of family planning propaganda and clinical services is more useful in reducing birth rates than the same effort spent on building a road into the village or constructing a soap factory where women can work or furthering education for girls?"[27] But population control activists tended to dismiss an emphasis on female workforce participation and education as a strategy dreamed up by unrealistic feminists.[28] And Polgar didn't mention the alternative approach from the podium. Instead, he gazed out at the delegates and, according to minutes from the meeting, "urged that sociologists stimulate biologists to find a method of sex determination, since some parents have additional children in order to get one of specified sex."[29]

The simplicity of Polgar's idea must have struck the delegates at once. If parents in South Korea or Bangladesh could be assured at least one son from the start, they would have fewer children voluntarily, without birth targets. The PPFA researcher left open, however, the questions of what method of sex determination biologists should focus their efforts on and how sex selection might work in practice. Making a baby in a dish, with presorted sperm? Selecting from among several embryos? Eliminating female fetuses? In 1967 sex determination in utero, which could only become selection through abortion, was the most advanced of any of these methods. But Polgar was also probably aware of a proposal from an Indian medical researcher that had landed on the desk of his boss at PPFA six months before the conference. In a long document pounded out on thin rice paper using an unruly typewriter, the American-educated Jaswant Raj Mathur had appealed to the organization for funding to back his research into sex determination. If only Planned Parenthood would fund him, he explained, he would get to work searching for a way "to control SEX in human reproduction."[30]

———— ∞ ————

Back then mass sex selection—or sex control, as Mathur and others had taken to calling it—was still not possible. Scientists had figured out how to identify a fetus's sex in the third trimester using amniocentesis, but the technology was neither widely available nor legal in most countries. That hadn't stopped groups like Planned Parenthood from looking into other ideas, however. Across the top of Mathur's proposal, Planned

Parenthood Federation of America director Alan Guttmacher—who also worked for IPPF—scrawled a comment that both suggested an interest in funding the Indian scientist's work and implied he had been trawling about for precisely this sort of research. In a hasty script rendered in red pencil, Guttmacher confessed to Dr. Richard L. Day, PPFA's national medical director, that the science outlined in the document eluded him. "It is beyond my feeble intelligence," Guttmacher wrote. He instructed Day to review whether the method described within was in fact "worth encouraging."

The Indian scientist's proposal, which relied on a link between sperm composition and blood type, was scientifically shaky. (From the start, Mathur didn't have much working in his favor beyond Guttmacher's apparent interest in sex determination. His tendency to refer to sperm as "sperms" might have set off alarm bells.) After reviewing the proposal, Day was hopeful that the research might pan out, however; the only problem, he wrote Guttmacher, was that the U.S. government had recently cut funding for fellowships to foreigners. He added that "as is suggested by his having received his Ph.D. at Ohio State and having done postdoctoral work at Boston University . . . this is probably quite a bright man" and recommended that Mathur apply for a fellowship from the Population Council, which after Sheldon Segal's stint at AIIMS evidently remained interested in sex determination research as well.[31] Guttmacher then personally wrote Dudley Kirk, director of the Population Council's demographic division, to suggest he fund Mathur's research.[32]

The Population Council declined to back the Indian scientist's work, but again only because of a bureaucratic technicality. (The organization exclusively funded Indians who had first been approved by a national committee in India.)[33] How much money IPPF and the Population Council spent on researching sex determination, or exactly where that money went, is uncertain. What is clear, however, is that Guttmacher wasn't alone among population control activists in finding sex determination intriguing. By the end of the decade, as *The Population Bomb* hit bookstores and widespread selective abortion finally looked possible, others chimed in their support for Planned Parenthood's big idea.

The endorsements came one after the other, in increasingly public outlets, and not just from employees of population control organizations; several advocates of sex selection were high up in the scientific establishment. In January 1969, William D. McElroy, head of the biology department at Johns Hopkins University, sounded his approval in the journal *BioScience*. "A type of research which would have a great effect on population control would be that related to the discovery of methods for sex determination," he wrote. "It has been suggested that if one could predetermine that the first offspring would be a male," McElroy continued, "it would have a great effect on the size of the family. In some, if not most societies, male babies are more desirable than females, and if the male was the first offspring, the motivation for having additional offspring would be reduced."[34]

Like Polgar, McElroy neglected to address an essential question: what then? If we allow people to choose the sex of their children, and if we know they will choose boys, what will be the effect on our society? Isn't a balanced number of men and women, an idea dating all the way back to the West's predominant creation myth, fundamental to the continuance of the human race? That question fell to Arno G. Motulsky, a geneticist at the University of Washington–Seattle, who became the next cheerleader for sex selection. In an article for *Science*, he conceded that a majority-male society would not be ideal, predicting that an excess of men would bring "significant long-term effects on society, such as an increase in homosexuality." But that was the only ostensible drawback Motulsky could come up with for the new technologies, and he noted, inaccurately, that a few extra men had not been known to cause trouble in the past. "It is of interest in this regard," he wrote, "that the state of Alaska already has an excess of males but has not encountered serious societal dislocations." Possible objections thus roundly dismissed, the geneticist concluded sex determination was a worthy cause: "such research should be encouraged, since the discovery of a simple method for choosing the sex of children would allow ideal family planning."[35]

Others displayed more foresight. In 1973 British microbiologist John Postgate predicted dire side effects, particularly for the women born into a society awash in testosterone, of widespread sex selection. "[I]t is probable that a form of *purdah* would become necessary," he wrote in the *New Scientist*, elaborating:

Women's right to work, even to travel alone freely, would probably be forgotten transiently. Polyandry might well become accepted in some societies; some might treat their women as queen ants, others as rewards for the most outstanding (or most determined) males.

The world, he continued, might soon resemble a "giant boy's public school or a huge male prison."

But Postgate was extraordinary not for his bleak predictions—many of which panned out—but for the recommendation he arrived at after considering sex selection's possible effects. Women might have to be locked up, or forced to marry multiple men, or traded like commodities, but sex selection was advisable, he suggested, for "the only really important problem facing humanity to-day is over-population," particularly in "under-developed unenlightened communities."[36]

Before long others began to argue that sex selection was not only an effective method of population control but also one of the most rational and ethical methods out there. In 1969 Berelson, the Population Council president who had chaired the 1967 National Institute of Child Health and Human Development meeting, penned an article for *Science* in which he ranked various family planning methods for feasibility and ethical acceptability. He labeled sex selection's ethical value as "high."[37] This analysis makes sense only if you consider that some of Berelson's other suggestions—introducing sterilizing agents to the food supply, the creation of a credit scheme for having children, and compulsory sterilization of men with three or more children—involved coercion.* Next to forcing men under the knife, reducing the number of girls and women seemed downright humane.

⁂

The late 1960s and early 1970s were a particularly strident era in population politics. As Paul Ehrlich made the rounds of talk shows, the Population Crisis Committee took out ads in the *New York Times* and *Washington Post* stressing the need for a "crash program" to combat growth in the developing world.[38] Others talked about the necessity of an Asian pregnancy

---

*Berelson also mentioned the participation of women in the workforce, since working women had been shown to have fewer children. But he gave it an Orwellian twist: female employment might need to be made compulsory.

police, foreshadowing China's system of birth permits under the one-child policy, and suggested flying planes over India once a year to spray it with a "contraceptive aerial mist."[39]* And the racist application of birth control was no longer confined to the developing world. In 1973 African American and Native American women across the American South and Southwest alleged in federal district court that they had been sterilized under threat of their welfare benefits being withdrawn. Gerhard Gesell, the judge who heard *Relf v. Weinberger*, concluded in his ruling that the women had been coerced. He estimated that between 100,000 and 150,000 poor American women had been sterilized under federal programs, adding, "the dividing line between family planning and eugenics is murky."[40]

But even the most diehard extremists believed that individual choice was the most feasible foundation for family planning. Ecologist Garrett Hardin summed up the views of this camp when he stated at a private meeting of scientists convened by the Population Council in 1970, as summarized in the minutes, "It would be much easier if we have a persuasive campaign first to prepare the way for coercion later."**[41] And so sex selection, which empowered parents to control their reproductive fate, gained credence: extremists saw it as a stepping-stone to coercion, and moderates saw it as less drastic way of achieving quick reductions in the birth rate.

Sex selection, moreover, had the added advantage of reducing the number of potential mothers—what the Chinese demographer Wang Feng would later call a "double whammy." And indeed the effects on population size of weeding out women are significant. At a 1970 meeting of the Population Association of America, Duke University demographers William J. Serow and V. Jeffrey Evans demonstrated this effect using the population of the United States as an example. Projecting growth rates over the coming 200 years, they showed that an imbalanced sex ratio at

---

*Today these strategies have their parallel in geoengineering strategies put forth as a cure for climate change. In both cases a legitimate and urgent problem has led to radical quick-fix solutions. Installing giant mirrors in space or dumping iron into our oceans sounds easier than doing the sustained belt-tightening necessary to mitigate centuries of abusing our environment.

**Hardin himself had four children.

birth could cause a drastic swing in numbers. If the portion of girls born increased by 20 percent, the U.S. population growth rate would jump to 2.4 percent, with fully 31 billion people crowded into America's borders in two centuries' time. If the number of males born increased by 20 percent, on the other hand, the growth rate would drop to 0.9 percent, and the population would increase to only two billion.[42]*

By August 1969, when the National Institute of Child Health and Human Development and the Population Council convened another workshop on population control, sex selection had become a pet scheme. Just two years earlier, Steven Polgar had proposed sex determination research offhandedly, as an idea that might be worth looking into. Now it was presented as one of twelve new strategies representing the future of global birth control.[43] This time the task of promoting sex selection fell to none other than Sheldon Segal, recently back from his stint at the All-India Institute of Medical Sciences in Delhi.[44] He now sat on the advisory committee for the National Institute of Child Health and Human Development's recently created Population Research Center, a think tank established by President Johnson in the wake of his Food for Peace Act and tasked with researching new population control methods.[45] Accompanying Segal at the podium was abortion expert Christopher Tietze, who had recently left his State Department post to work as associate director under Segal: one an enthusiast of sexist applications of technology, the other a believer in abortion's utility as a birth control method.[46]

Standing before the workshop participants, Segal and Tietze listed the twelve new birth control methods, explaining that they represented prospective breakthroughs in reproductive medicine. This time, sex selection appeared alongside more innocuous, woman-friendly forms of birth control, like the long-lasting implant, the morning-after pill, and low-dose oral contraceptives. To a modern eye, it stands out as the most alarming and unethical method in this group, an obvious candidate for interrogation when the floor opened up for debate. But it is a testament to

---

*Today this is no longer theoretical. In one 2007 demographic projection, if China's sex ratio at birth remains at 2000 levels through 2030, the population will be nearly 16 percent smaller than it would have been with a normal sex ratio at birth.

how unquestionably accepted sex selection was by 1969 that the minutes from the meeting show absolutely no dissent. If anyone present at the workshop worried about the ethical precedent set by such a technology, its implications for societal balance, or what it might mean for the status of women, he—for this group was overwhelming male—kept silent. Instead, in the discussion that followed, the participants decided sex determination was one of the methods they deemed "particularly desirable."[47]

"I can't go along with sex-selective abortion," Segal wrote in his memoir years later. And yet, after planting the technology that led to one of the most sinister chapters in India's sinister history of population control, he returned to the United States to push for that technology's introduction to other lands. Following his 1969 presentation a rough consensus was reached: if a reliable sex determination technology could be made available to a mass market, it would be an effective, uncontroversial, and ethical way of reducing the global population.

Not everyone in the population control movement agreed. There were a few dissenters who objected to the movement's emphasis on sex selection as discriminatory and potentially harmful to society. But they were outnumbered by activists who favored even more extreme tactics. The members of this last camp felt that sex selective abortion didn't go far enough; they pushed for the development of a drug that women could take before sex to guarantee any children that resulted would be male. The "manchild pill," as enthusiasts called it, was the perfect solution: simple, straightforward, with no need for a sex determination test or a late term abortion. It would be, as one proponent wrote in the *Washington Star* in 1978, playing with the biblical term for the food God gave the Israelites on their trek through the wilderness, "a man-ah! from Heaven."[48] In the end, however, the extremists' push turned out to be overkill, for sex selective abortion did the trick alone.

————— ᙇᙇᙇ —————

Not long after Ehrlich's string of *Tonight Show* appearances, a series of global events proved his colorful predictions wrong. The innovations in agricultural technology known as the Green Revolution saved millions from starvation.[49] India, especially, benefited from the new farming techniques, and apocalypse, it turned out, was not just around the corner. When Ehrlich's doomsday scenarios failed to materialize, the television invitations dried up, and he slipped back into academic obscurity. He remained a professor at Stanford, where he returned to the study of butterfly habitats. In the years that followed he wrote papers for scholarly journals with titles like "Checkerspot Butterflies: A Historical Perspective."[50] He also authored a few books on bird-watching.[51] He witnessed his daughter grow up—he and his wife took their own advice and stuck to one child—and in time he had a grandchild, and then a great-grandchild.[52] He continued to write about population, but now he did so for a largely academic audience, expanding his focus to include climate change, resource use, and other environmental causes. He pushed for a byline for his wife, and their later works on population appeared under both of their names. He was also careful to underline his commitment to racial and economic justice. After years in the limelight, however, it was difficult to take it all back. The ideas he put forth in his 1968 blockbuster continued to reverberate.

Four decades after the publication of *The Population Bomb*, I travel to California to meet Ehrlich. I take the train from downtown San Francisco to Stanford one Friday, staring out the window as Silicon Valley, with its hopeful start-ups and twenty-four-year-old millionaires, zips by. Disembarking near campus, I hop on a university shuttle, and as the driver winds through campus I look out to see electric green lawns glistening in a noontime sun. I disembark in front of the engineering building, which is surrounded by students sitting at shining metal tables, absorbed in their laptops.

Ehrlich is across the street and four stories up, on a floor devoted to the biology department, where he works from a small office, happily ensconced in clutter. That is the first thing that strikes me: a certain mad scientist vibe permeates the room. Scattered across an L-shaped desk, a large library table, and the bookshelves lining the walls is an odd assortment of objects—a pair of crutches, two empty Dr. Pepper bottles, a jar that reads ASHES OF PROBLEM STUDENTS. Underneath the desk are several pairs of shoes. One is a pair of royal blue high-top Chuck Taylors, a playfully young choice for a man a few weeks shy of seventy-eight. Everywhere are books and papers, some of them stacked, others in haphazard piles.

"Let me just clear some of this away," Ehrlich says, sweeping a bunch of papers off his keyboard and pushing them to one corner of the desk. A long rubber dental pick now sits in the space left by the papers, propped up between a few keys. He doesn't notice.

"Now." He turns to look at me, flashing a toothy smile. Aside from a slight paunch and thinning hair, he hasn't changed much since his *Tonight Show* appearance. He is even wearing the same style of high-water pants he donned for Carson, though this time with a more subdued plaid shirt. "Why am I meeting you again?" he asks.

I start to answer that I am here to interview him for my book. But he is content, it turns out, to talk about anything and everything. As with the office, so with his mind: quirky, chock full of knowledge, and unafraid of messy or incomplete thoughts. Among the topics he covers within the first few minutes of our meeting are the perils of genetic determinism, American ignorance of Rawlsian ethics, and the evolutionary origins of human sexual response. This tour through his consciousness is delivered carefully, warmly, as if each new story is a secret between me and him. At one point he stops midsentence and asks, "Are you recording this crap, by the way?"

Finally Ehrlich pauses, and I steer the discussion back to population, bringing up the topic I have been wondering about ever since I read *The Population Bomb* a few months earlier: his advocacy of a "simple method . . . to guarantee that first-born children are males." "I looked into how sex determination technology was introduced," I begin. "And I saw you mentioned it in *The Population Bomb*." I sit back, anticipating a defensive answer, expecting him to say, perhaps, that he could not have foretold the damage sex determination would do in the developing world. Or maybe he will stand by his earlier position and tell me why sex selection has been such a great thing for the world. I expect, in short, anything except what actually happens, which is that Ehrlich looks at me curiously. "I did?" he asks amiably. "That's interesting. I don't remember."

He pauses. "If I did actually say that," he says later, "[then] it would be a good idea to let people have their choice so that they could have fewer children and could have what they wanted." It's the same reasoning that appeared in *The Population Bomb*, but it's as if the thought just occurred to him. He resumes his usual pace, and now his voice bubbles with wonderment. He continues, "There have been clearly, from anecdotal situations, people who keep trying in order to have a boy. Obviously if you can give them a boy the first time—"

He keeps going, and now he expands on his old arguments. In some cases sex selection may be better than the fate that awaits females upon birth, he says: "You can be aborted as a conceptus, you can be killed at birth, or you can be sold into slavery and die in a slum someplace." By preventing females from being born, sex selective abortion may save them from grueling lives, he explains. "It would be interesting to know how many females you're keeping out of hideous situations—the ones who are not killed or infanticided but nonetheless not valued." He suggests I research the question.

But even if it were acceptable to reduce a group of people for their own good, there remains the fact that for the women who are born onto this earth, a minority in a patriarchal society, life has gotten worse. I point out that sex trafficking and marriage brokering are on the rise in Asia, that giving people the boys they want has increased autonomy for the middle and upper classes and decreased it for everyone else, particularly women at the bottommost social rungs. Ehrlich doesn't disagree. He even adds to my list of problems: "You're going to have a gigantic mass of horny young men in China," he predicts. But then, without skipping a beat, he dismisses those problems as mere side effects. "Basically, what you're looking at is the old unintended consequences problem," he says. "Repeatedly in my career it has turned out things I never would have imagined were huge factors."

Watching Ehrlich jump from one topic to the next and defend an idea he says he has forgotten, I wondered if perhaps he was just a dreamer, the sort of man who falls in love with ideas without worrying too much about their real-world ramifications. But now I see it is more than that. "Unintended consequences" is a fancy way of saying the end justifies the means. He is not only a dreamer. He is also a utilitarian, a big-picture person willing to see individuals sacrificed in service of a larger cause.

Today Ehrlich says his thinking on many subjects has changed. "Listen," he tells me when I bring up his most famous work again. "If I had to write *The Population Bomb* over, it would be a very different book." In a recent essay published on the fortieth anniversary of the book's publication, he regretted the sensational title, along with his use of doomsday scenarios.[53] Lately he has embraced the fact that providing work and education opportunities for women is an effective way of lowering birth rates. Conservatives do not seem to have noticed his change of heart. Ehrlich has recently come under attack from right-wing critics, who have dredged up a book he and Anne wrote with physicist John Holdren, now President Obama's science adviser, in 1977.[54] In the book the three scholars evaluate a solution that had circulated in population control circles over the previous decades: a sterilizing agent added to municipal water supplies that would render people infertile until they apply for permission to reverse it. The scholars dismiss the solution as unfeasible, and Ehrlich says his critics have taken passages from the book out of context. He has received several threatening voice mail messages.

But explaining the brouhaha to me now, Ehrlich defends the basic thinking behind mass reversible sterilization. Its beauty, he explains, is that it yields a world in which couples have to work to get pregnant instead of work at preventing pregnancy. He ventures the approach is controversial because people are reluctant to cede control over their reproductive organs to their governments, but he says if we could somehow get past that reluctance mass sterilization could—were it technically possible—help us remedy some of the world's more intransigent ills. "If I could wave a wand now and say, we're going to have a system where everybody has to do X in order to have a kid, and it will be a fail-safe, we'd solve a lot of the things that disturb people the most," he says. "It would mean every child a wanted child, and no more abortions, basically." And then I realize that my visit has reminded him of sex selection's potential as a population control tool. For it has apparently just occurred to Ehrlich that mass sterilization could be reworked to take advantage of the widespread preference for boys, so that when couples apply to have the sterilants in their bodies chemically overpowered they might also select the sex of their baby. He continues: "If you could do it"—introduce reversible sterilization around the world—"and determine sex at the same time?"

Chapter 8

THE GENETICIST

*When you come right down to it, the reason that we
did this job is because it was an organic necessity. If
you are a scientist you cannot stop such a thing.*

—J. ROBERT OPPENHEIMER[1]

The bulk of research on sex determination did not come from scientists like Paul Ehrlich, who crossed easily into the policy world and looked to science for its potential to ameliorate problems of global importance. Ehrlich mattered as a disseminator of ideas, and in this role he, along with activists at IPPF and the Population Council, helped bring sex determination technology to the developing world. By the time he got on board, however, the technology itself was already well developed, thanks to a small group of medical researchers who had spent the past few decades working quietly in their laboratories, isolated from the population debate and governed by a different set of motivations. These scientists worked on a small scale. They did not aspire to change the world. At most, they hoped to help a few people. Some were driven by the high of discovery—the force that underlies many of mankind's greatest achievements, as well as some of our most cursed tools. But the story of gender imbalance is their story too.

The groundwork for sex determination had been laid by the 1940s. By then scientists knew humans had forty-six chromosomes—twenty-three from the mother and twenty-three from the father—and that two of these chromosomes determined sex. They had named the sex chromosomes, X and Y, and they knew that what made a man was the presence of both X and Y, while a woman possessed two Xs. From there it would be a gradual but steady journey to identify sex in animals, in adults, and finally in the human fetus. At the time, though, the problem was still at the cell level, where the sex chromosomes were proving stubbornly elusive. Existing methods meant scientists could only discern sex chromosomes during cell division, which entailed waiting around at the microscope for a cell to complete its reproductive cycle, a process that could take a whole day. Even then, a researcher might not be able to see the chromosomes; the low-resolution instruments available at the time left finer cell characteristics blurry. Then one day in 1949 a geneticist with the Royal Canadian Air Force peered through his microscope at the cells of a female cat.[2]

What he saw was a tiny, previously undetected cellular body. A quick survey of cells from other cats revealed only females had the body; males lacked it entirely. The geneticist, Murray L. Barr, quickly realized the new substance could be a shortcut around the sex chromosome problem. Like sex chromosomes, the cellular body indicated the sex of an organism. But unlike the chromosomes, it was relatively easy to detect, popping into view even when cells weren't dividing. Barr, who sported a thick mustache and horn-rimmed glasses, was elated. As he wrote excitedly in *Nature,* the new body meant sex "may be detected with no more elaborate equipment than a compound microscope."[3] Four years later, he confirmed that the sex chromatin—or Barr body, as the substance became known—acted the same way in humans as it did in cats.[4] The discovery earned him a nomination for the Nobel Prize.[5]

In the years that followed, the Barr body proved useful in cases where the sex of an adult was uncertain. The microscopic substance made headlines in 1968, for example, after an Olympic competition in which suspiciously masculine Soviet athletes snagged gold medals in women's events. At the 1968 Games, the International Olympic Committee began analyzing athletes' cells for the presence of sex chromatins, ushering in a controversial era of gender testing. (The sex chromatin test was, in any case, better than the method it replaced, which was asking athletes to strip naked.)[6]

The Barr body had another application, however. Scientists saw it could also help people with sex-linked diseases conceive healthy children. Hemophilia, for example, is carried on the X chromosome but manifests itself in males. Mothers pass along the disease to both sons and daughters, but typically only the sons get sick. (For a daughter to fall ill, she must inherit defective chromosomes from both parents rather than just from the mother—a highly unlikely prospect.) If a pregnant woman knew she was a carrier, scientists realized, and her doctor could somehow identify the sex of the fetus growing in her womb, she could abort and thus avoid giving birth to a hemophilic boy.

There was pent-up demand for such a procedure. Advances in genetic testing meant that people living in the mid-twentieth century knew more about the disorders inscribed in their DNA than ever before.* A burgeoning genetic counseling industry had sprung up to advise prospective parents on what to do with this knowledge, but because science had not yet given these parents control over whether they passed on genetic material, the new counselors were hamstrung.[7] For patients carrying non-sex-linked diseases, they might recommend mating with a specific person—advice that was of no help to people who were already married but was, at least, better than nothing.[8] But for women with sex-linked diseases, who risked passing on their conditions no matter what man they had children with, counselors could only soften the blow of the genetic test results. The women thus had knowledge without the power to act on it. Before, at least, they had remained ignorant of the disorders programmed into their DNA and could start families happily, like everyone else, without worrying about what they might be giving their children. Then the breakthroughs in genetics came along and made decisions about marriage and children more difficult.

There was one hope, however. If scientists could find a way to determine whether a fetus was male or female, they could help these women

---

*DNA was a fascinating concept that the public was struggling to understand. The double helix structure was discovered in 1953, the same year Barr identified sex chromatin in humans.

avoid debilitating medical bills, anxious nights, and heartbreak—and give genetic counselors new recourse. Recent findings about DNA thus propelled research on fetal testing: one discovery demanded another. But Murray Barr had only documented the existence of sex chromatins in adults. In order to help disease-carrying women have healthy children, scientists needed to successfully identify the Barr body in fetal cells. After Barr's report appeared in *Nature,* teams of medical researchers scattered across several continents took up the task.

The tools that would allow scientists to identify the sex chromatin in a fetus were already in place, and it was simply a matter of applying them with precision. The first step was to extract fetal cells. For this the teams turned to amniocentesis, which was then used in the third trimester to relieve women with certain pregnancy complications. After using a needle to extract fetal cells from the amniotic sac, the teams put the fetal cells under the microscope to see whether sex chromatins showed up as readily as with adult cells. They did. As with many other important inventions in the history of technology, fetal sex determination was developed separately and yet nearly simultaneously at different points around the globe, with four teams of scientists reaching the finish line within months of each other in 1955. Those teams of researchers—in Minneapolis, Copenhagen, New York, and Haifa, Israel—today share credit for pioneering sex determination in the human fetus.[9]

One of these four teams, the Danish physicians Povl Riis and Fritz Fuchs, conducted a study for which they recruited women carrying sex-linked diseases. After testing the fetal cells they extracted from the women's uteruses, they made the results of their tests available to the test subjects, knowing the women might find the information useful. Riis and Fuchs appear to have been unaware that elsewhere in the world anthropologists were documenting the connection between sex composition and birth rates, and the decision to be open with test subjects probably required little deliberation. What doctor wouldn't want to help a woman at risk of passing on hemophilia to her children avoid doing so? But by deciding that more knowledge was better, the Danish duo made possible, for the very first time, sex selection. The test subjects who found out they were carrying boys chose to abort. The first sex selective abortions discriminated against males.

In an article in the medical journal *The Lancet*, Riis and Fuchs speculated about the possible uses to which their discovery might be put. Unlike most of the scientists who succeeded them, they weighed the ethics of sex selection, cautioning that doctors should not determine fetal sex merely "to satisfy the curiosity of the parents."[10] They did not believe many parents were in fact curious, however. The Danish doctors noted they had received no requests for sex selection from patients in Copenhagen. But because only Scandinavian countries allowed "eugenic therapeutic abortions," as selective abortions were then called, Riis and Fuchs had no way to assess the interest the technology might attract in other parts of world.[11] Then too the early procedures were no cakewalk. Since in the late 1950s doctors could only perform amniocentesis in the third trimester, a woman looking to abort a fetus of a particular sex had to do so at the point of viability or near viability. It made sense that there would be minimal demand for the procedure. But Riis and Fuchs did not foresee how quickly that would change.

———— ∞ ————

If amniocentesis was used to select for girls before it was used to ensure boys, ultrasound's trajectory is even more fantastical. The technology that ultimately became the dominant method of sex selection around the world began as a tool for navigation. Its story dates to 1794, when an Italian biologist curious about how bats find their way in the dark discovered sonar, or the fact that distance can be determined by bouncing sound waves off a faraway object and measuring how long it takes for the waves to ricochet back.[12] Centuries later, when the growing prowess of German submarines during World War I convinced the Allies that to win the war they needed a way to navigate underwater, scientists put sonar to use. The American, British, and French governments jointly funded research into the phenomenon. The effort succeeded, and by 1918 the Allies were using acoustic echoes to correctly pinpoint the location of German U-boats.[13]

After the war, doctors guessed sonar might have medical applications as well. They first used ultrasound in surgery, where it turned out sound waves could heat and destroy tissue, making them helpful for everything from treating ulcers to performing craniotomies. Then in 1949, the same year Murray Barr identified the sex chromatin in cat cells, a chemist stationed at the Naval Medical Research Institute in Bethesda, Maryland, employed ultrasound to locate gallstones in the gall bladders of dogs, and the technology became a diagnostic tool as well.[14] Physicians began navigating the human body as the World War I submarines had navigated dark waters, bouncing sound waves off the internal organs. Ultrasound proved surprisingly versatile. It could clean teeth, treat cysts, and dissolve kidney stones. It may have been with one of these applications in sight that in 1959 Scottish obstetrician Ian Donald used the new technology on a woman who happened to be pregnant and noticed that the fetus returned echoes as well.[15]

Doctors could not perform x-ray exams on pregnant women because of the risk of damaging the fetus, so Donald's discovery raised the prospect of an alternative form of prenatal imaging, giving physicians hope of monitoring high-risk pregnancies. As with amniocentesis, science moved forward in service of a small group of patients.

The first fetal ultrasound scans were used to take crude measurements of the fetal head, which in turn allowed doctors to track a baby's growth in the womb. The machines employed for this purpose were cumbersome gadgets that towered over the pregnant women on whom they were used. One early ultrasound machine, called the articulated arm scanner, resembled a giant version of the toy cranes fairgoers rent for a few quarters to try their hand at winning stuffed animals.[16] The image the articulated arm scanner produced was hazy, making it impossible for doctors to discern fingers and toes, let alone a tiny penis or vagina.

But it didn't matter that the early ultrasound machines yielded fuzzy images, or that they only proved helpful in a small proportion of pregnancies. To the 1960s public the technology looked positively futuristic. Around the time pregnancy became a choice rather than an inevitability in the West and the business of having children became about more than generating labor for the farm, we began seeking ways to bond with our babies before birth. An image on which to pin parental hopes made that task a whole lot easier, and so it was a breakthrough to have a preview, however muddled, of the baby growing inside a mother's womb. Coming as it did at a time of technological optimism when Americans were enamored of outer space and kitchen appliances alike, an era some were calling the Biological Revolution, ultrasound captured the public imagination.[17]

The high-resolution machines capable of identifying fetal sex and other finer characteristics were still years away, but the press seized on the possibility that portraits of babies before birth might help us control the mystical birth process. The flurry of coverage that greeted the new technology forecasted extensive reproductive manipulation—which newspaper editors saw as a great thing. The headlines were bold and optimistic: "Ultrasound Device Takes Guessing Out of Pregnancy." "Knowledge Is Key to Happy Childbirth." "A New Eye into the Womb." One article dubbed ultrasound "The Electronic Doctor."[18] The headline on the cover of the September 10, 1965, issue of *Life*—alongside a hulking machine whose heavy arm nearly eclipsed the mother under examination—read, "Control of Life: Audacious Experiments Promise Decades of Added Life, Superbabies with Improved Minds and Bodies, and Even a Kind of Immortality."[19]

But public fascination also provided a window for criticism, and ultrasound, unlike other technologies that would one day prompt the disappearance of girls in the developing world, elicited substantial ethical deliberation. Some critics feared overly powerful scientists. Feminists pushing for abortion rights fretted, justifiably, that the machine humanized the fetus. Others worried the new reproductive technologies would be exploited by governments intent on manipulating their populations; the Nazis, after all, had screened newlyweds for genetic diseases as part of their eugenics program. What if the power to create "superbabies" fell into the hands of an evil dictator?[20] The problem was that none of these critiques came close to identifying what turned out to be ultrasound's most pernicious threat. In hindsight, 1960s Americans worried about everything except the possibility that average parents, emboldened by the new knowledge technology brought them, might make small, seemingly innocuous choices—and that those choices, taken together, would add up to disaster.

———⊗⊗⊗———

In the midst of enthusiasm over new sex determination technologies, there was a lone voice of restraint. It came from Amitai Etzioni, a sociologist at Columbia University and a Jewish refugee from Nazi Germany. In a 1968 article for *Science,* Etzioni considered the implications of widely available sex control, starting from the premise that it would lead to parents selecting boys over girls and that an imbalanced society would be a bad thing. "We have much experience and some data on societies whose sex ratio was thrown off balance by war or immigration," he wrote. "A significant and cumulative male surplus will . . . produce a society with some of the rougher features of the frontier town," including "the diminution of the number of agents of moral education and [an] increase in the number of criminals." It is not only women who suffer in a lopsided world: more men will mean unhappy men, Etzioni predicted, writing with foresight of the "sorrows of the unmatable mates." He continued, "We must ask . . . are the costs justified? The dangers are not apocalyptical; but are they worth the gains to be made?"[21]

Etzioni, whose interest in the topic grew out of the fact that he had several sons and wanted a daughter, had a larger point.[22] By the 1960s, science was arriving at a newfound appreciation for the rights of what Etzioni called its "human guinea pigs." Scientists were taking care to ensure that they performed experiments on subjects who had given informed consent and that their research did not harm those subjects in any way. But when it came to a technology's effect on society at large, Etzioni wrote, scientists behaved very differently:

> Western civilization, ever since the invention of the steam engine, has proceeded on the assumption that society must adjust to new technologies. This is a central meaning of what we refer to when we speak about an industrial revolution; we think about a society being transformed and not just a new technology being introduced into a society which continues to sustain its prior values and institutions.[23]

As the pace of technological innovation accelerated, moreover, it was time for scientists—and the government bodies and corporations that accounted for most of their funding—to recognize that research is not an end in itself. "The scientific community," Etzioni continued, "cannot be excused from the responsibility of asking what effects its endeavors have on the community." Work on curing cancer, he put forth, is more important than research aimed at proving biological or intellectual differences among the races. And research into sex control is, in the end, not worth the cost to society.

His article arrived at an important moment in the development of sex determination technologies. The early discoveries would have been difficult to halt. Sex selective abortion, after all, had been developed nearly at once by teams of scientists spread out around the world—scientists, moreover, intent on preventing disease, not giving parents the power to freely choose their children's sex. But in 1968 science was at a crossroads. Sex selection techniques were not yet far enough along to be applied widely, and population control activists with ties to the National Institute of Child Health and Human Development were pushing for more funding—for an end that had nothing to do with preventing disease. The work of narrowly focused researchers and social scientists interested in reshaping the developing world to their whims had finally converged. The U.S. government could either choose to fund the research or to discourage it.

But while the article created a minor stir, in the end it was little more than a cry in the dark. Population control activists like Sheldon Segal got their way with sex determination, and the Biological Revolution pressed on. Etzioni ultimately changed his mind, adopting a strikingly libertarian position on sex selection.* In the late 1960s and early 1970s, U.S. spending on health research and development increased by an average of 10 percent a year. A sizable portion of this money went to genetic research, which advanced more quickly than any other field.[24] Scientists continued searching for ways to improve on sex determination, setting their sights on a new goal: to gain information about a fetus in the second, rather than the third, trimester. From 1970 to 1974, funding for amniocentesis research from the National Institute of General Medical Services, a division of the National Institutes of Health, nearly doubled.[25]

A few researchers also got to work on chorionic villus sampling, or CVS, a procedure that involves taking a biopsy of the chorion, the thin membrane that separates a fetus from its mother in the womb. The villi,

---

*Now eighty-two, Etzioni heads up the Institute for Communitarian Policy Studies at George Washington University. When I call him to discuss his objections to sex control research, he says he looked into gender imbalance a bit further and decided, based on the case of Alaska, that it wasn't so bad. "I did not find enough compelling damage that would lead us to stop science," he told me.

the microscopic hairs projecting out from the chorion, are covered with a thin coating of fetal cells. By extracting these cells, scientists could check them for the presence of sex chromatins, applying the technique Murray Barr had developed back in 1953—and they could test earlier than with amniocentesis. As with that technique, much of the pioneering work on CVS was done by researchers in Denmark because of that country's liberal laws on selective abortion.[26] But when Danish scientists found that the unwieldy fiber-optic device they used to visualize the fetus led to high rates of miscarriage, they abandoned their experiments, leaving scientists in China and the Soviet Union to push ahead, this time with more questionable motives.[27]

In 1975, the same year the AIIMS amniocentesis trials began in Delhi, Chinese doctors at Tietung Hospital in Liaoning province reported in the *Chinese Medical Journal* that in one hundred attempts at performing CVS they had successfully identified the sex of ninety-three fetuses. The Chinese researchers used a rudimentary device with no fiber-optics, and at least three of the one hundred women on whom they performed the test miscarried. But the salient fact for their purposes seems to be the incidence of sex selective abortion that resulted. Of the ninety-three women who had their fetus's sex determined, thirty chose to abort. Of those thirty, twenty-nine were carrying girls.[28]

Elsewhere in the world, delegates to a mid-1970s global conference on prenatal diagnosis adopted a statement objecting "to prenatal sex determination with the objective of aborting the fetus if it is not of the desired sex."[29] But still it appears no one bothered openly to condemn the Chinese study. To the contrary, when research into CVS picked up again in the 1980s, Western scientists focused on replicating the Chinese doctors' success.[30] Ignoring the obvious gender discrimination described in the 1975 study, they considered only what it represented for their research.

———— ∞ ————

In 1976, after years of trials, the U.S. government deemed amniocentesis safe for routine use in second trimester pregnancies.[31] The announcement came from the U.S. National Institute of Child Health and Human Development, which by that point had sponsored two conferences at which sex determination was proposed as a population control method.

The reception of amniocentesis in the developing world would have been predictable, since social scientists and family planning workers had been documenting interest in sex selection for years. Enthusiasm for the new technique in the United States, however, was presumably more surprising. No sooner was amniocentesis approved than doctors started receiving requests from pregnant women hoping to use it. Women gave a whole range of reasons for wanting to know the sex of the fetuses they carried, but a common one was what Danish doctors Riis and Fuchs, back in 1959, had termed curiosity: was it a boy or a girl?

Sex determination, Americans realized, was no longer about helping women avoid giving birth to children with debilitating diseases, and suddenly—for although it was twenty-seven years after Murray Barr began his sex chromatin research and nearly a decade after population control activists first proposed sex determination as a tool for reducing the global birth rate—the country had an ethical debate about the new technologies. The legal scholar Jane M. Friedman weighed the ethics of amniocentesis in an article for the *University of Pennsylvania Law Review*, identifying risks that included "Tampering with the Gene Pool" and "The Risk of Gender Imbalance."[32] Elsewhere Darwin resurfaced. In a story that went out over the wire to newspapers around the country, journalist Patricia McCormack fretted about "the era of electing survival of the fittest fetus and destruction of unfit ones." Amniocentesis raised questions, she wrote, like: "If the fetus is female and you wish a boy, do you abort? If you want only boys, do you abort every time a pregnancy results in a female?"[33] The May 1977 issue of *Mademoiselle*, meanwhile, screamed "Women: The Next Endangered Species?"[34]

At the same time, changes were afoot in the population control movement. Feminists and others on the left had organized and were pushing for a voice in decision making. The shift started with a group of U.S. graduate students, who in 1969 launched the journal *Concerned Demography* to counteract the machismo within the population field. Judith Blake, a demographer at the University of California-Berkeley, outlined what an alternative, more humane approach to population control might look like, listing initiatives like liberalizing sex education, eliminating tax breaks and other incentives for having children, and reversing legal and social sanctions against homosexuality.[35]

Over the next few years, women took over positions that had long been held by men at the Ford Foundation, IPPF, and elsewhere. As the prevailing mood swung to the left, even John D. Rockefeller III—the man who had bankrolled the movement at its chauvinistic height—changed his tune. At the 1974 United Nations World Population Conference in Bucharest, Romania, Rockefeller surprised delegates by saying, "If we are to make progress in achieving population goals, women increasingly must have greater freedom of choice in determining their roles in society."[36] His speech marked the beginning of the end for sexist population politics, and over the following decade the population organizations saw a dramatic shift, culminating in a Pakistani woman, Nafis Sadik, taking over as executive director of UNFPA in 1987.[37] By the 1990s the organizations's work centered on reproductive rights, not population control.

These changes were great for the development of woman-friendly contraceptives and education programs. But for sex selection, which was spreading across Asia with alarming rapidity, the timing could not have been worse. By 1979 amniocentesis could identify fetal sex to nearly 100 percent accuracy. A few years later the continent saw the advent of cheap, mass-produced ultrasound machines. The new female activists mostly stayed silent, though, watching as a technology that had been proposed as a solution to one demographic crisis became crucial in the creation of another, this one affecting their own kind. They neglected to stop sex selection for the memory of *Roe v. Wade*: they had cut their political teeth in the 1970s feminist movement, for which reproductive rights were paramount and any restrictions on abortion were a blow to women's freedom. Prenatal sex determination the activists could abhor. But beyond that their politics made it difficult to address the other cause of the growing gender imbalance: thanks to the earlier generation of population activists, abortion had become disturbingly pervasive in Asia.

Chapter 9

THE GENERAL

*The spirit is received from Heaven but the physical is
the endowment of Earth. So it is said that One creates
Two, Two creates Three, and Three creates a myriad
[of] things. All things are* yin *behind and* yang *in front.
With the effusion of* qi *they unite. So it is said that in
the first month a blob of fat is formed, in the second
sinews, in the sixth bone. In the seventh month [the
fetus] is fully formed, in the eighth it is active, in the
ninth it is boisterous, and in the tenth it is born.*

—THE CHINESE *HUAINANZI*, 2ND CENTURY BC[1]

If he had lived in another era, General William Draper might have been
an anti-abortion activist. He might have made Asia the staging ground for
a politics centered on the fuzzy first stirrings of life. He might have de-
cried forced abortions and worked to obtain political asylum for women
targeted under China's one-child policy. But Draper was born in 1894 and
became undersecretary of the U.S. Army in the 1940s, when communism
seemed the greatest threat to global stability, ideology was a question of
Us versus Them, and a politics revolving around knotty ethical questions
was still decades away. And so it was that Draper, supervisor of Allied
efforts in Asia and Europe after World War II, close friend of President

Dwight D. Eisenhower, and a staunch conservative in other regards, came to be an ardent proponent of abortion.[2]

An arrogant man with thick horn-rimmed glasses and a crooked smile, Draper oversaw General Douglas MacArthur in the occupation of Japan that followed the bombing of Hiroshima and Nagasaki.[3] The occupation, he believed, was not just important for preventing Japan from accumulating power again; it was also critical to winning America's struggle against communism. His concern escalated in the late 1940s, as the Chinese Communist Party amassed weapons left behind by the Japanese and won over beleaguered peasants, threatening to seize control of China from the Nationalists. Japan seemed America's only hope in providing a bulwark against the spread of socialism throughout Asia.

Provided, that was, the country remained placid and stable. When Draper arrived in Tokyo in 1947, the United States was firmly in control. "General MacArthur was Emperor No. 1 and the other one was Emperor No. 2," Draper would later joke, as if Emperor Hirohito wielded so little power he wasn't worth naming.[4] But some factors were beyond U.S. control. Like many countries following protracted wars, Japan was experiencing a baby boom as returning soldiers hunkered down with their wives. For the general, who ascribed to 1940s theories directly linking population size and economic growth, this was deeply unsettling. Draper worried the climbing birth rate would threaten the Japanese economy and undermine the stability of America's strategic Asian foothold. "The whole country was being fed and largely fed by us," Draper fretted.[5] Unless the United States did something, poverty—which, he believed, bred communism—would claim Japan.

The notion of population control was just gaining appeal in the West, and many of the methods under discussion had not yet been tried on a grand scale. Japan, Western proponents realized, was just the place to test them.[6] Liberalized birth control appealed to the Japanese elite, meanwhile, for a very different reason. Eugenics had become fashionable among the upper classes, a faction of whom believed Japan might be improved by forcibly preventing pregnancies among the mentally ill and physically disabled.[7] Western and Eastern interests converged in 1948, when American advisers steered the country toward passing the Eugenic

Protection Law, which legalized abortion and sterilization.* The act made Japan the only country in the world to allow abortion for a variety of reasons.[8]

The experiment worked, at least at the level of raw numbers. As abortion became widely available and people deemed unfit to reproduce were sterilized, Japan's birth rate plummeted—even as gentler, temporary methods of contraception remained illegal. (Japan finally granted women the right to take birth control pills in 1999.)[9] By 1955 Japanese doctors were handling 30 to 50 percent more abortions than births.[10] Poverty diminished, meanwhile, and over the next few decades Japan grew into one of the world's largest economies—and a critical American ally. As Draper watched this shift, the efficacy of abortion as a birth control method struck him. His secretary, Phyllis Piotrow, later recalled that the general "observed at first hand how, with legalized abortion and considerable publicity, the Japanese people had sharply reduced birth rates and achieved their 'economic miracle.'"[11] He returned home to the United States enthusiastic about abortion's potential for furthering American interests abroad.

In 1958, when President Dwight D. Eisenhower selected Draper to head a presidential commission to evaluate U.S. foreign aid priorities, the young general put Asia's growing population front and center. Summarizing his commission's work before the Senate Foreign Relations Committee, he said, "The population problem, I'm afraid, is the greatest bar to our whole economic aid program and to the progress of the world."[12] He became an outspoken advocate of legalizing abortion overseas, and his support helped push global abortion rights from a preoccupation at the fringes of the population control movement to a major concern among the American foreign policy elite.[13] (Draper also lobbied for the establishment of the UNFPA, raised money for IPPF, and popularized the notion of making food aid conditional on countries reducing their birth rates.)[14]

Draper, who went on to help Dixie Cup tycoon Hugh Moore found the Population Crisis Committee, could be callous, and he had his detractors.

---

*With the Nazis' forced sterilization of the disabled fresh in the public mind, American advisers did not want to be seen as supporting eugenics. Advisers therefore pushed from behind the scenes, taking care to make the law appear a homegrown initiative.

Others in the population control movement favored condoms and intrauterine devices over abortion. They saw the risk to maternal health posed by repeated abortions, and they saw how it was easier on women emotionally to prevent pregnancy rather than react to it—or they simply saw the political risks, both abroad and at home, of being seen to promote abortion.[15] But selling Asians on contraception took a sustained educational effort, a task for which Draper's camp argued there just wasn't time. Abortion was also, in a crude way, more practical: family planning workers looking for potential recruits had an easier time spotting pregnant women than they did women who were planning to conceive. And so over the coming years abortion came to be accepted as an important instrument in reducing the birth rate in the developing world—but particularly, and most importantly for our purposes, in Asia.

———&⊙∞⊙———

In the late 1960s and early 1970s dozens of poor or developing countries liberalized their abortion laws, many of them in response to pressure from the United States.[16] The politics surrounding the passage of these laws looked nothing like American feminists' efforts to legalize abortion at home. In the developing world, there was no rallying by women's groups, no discussions about the number of women who die from botched illegal abortions, no impassioned arguments about when life begins. In poor countries, the right to abort was envisioned as serving not women but the state—although even the power of the state could be illusory. India's 1971 Medical Termination of Pregnancy Act, to name just one case, was the work of a government that relied on U.S. funds to sustain whole ministries.[17] "The Western countries had put pressure on India and China from the 1960s, saying India and China were breeding like rats," explains Sabu George, the public health activist. "India was under enormous pressure because it was part of the Malthusian world. The government liberalized abortion laws . . . so that abortion could be used as a population control method."

Back in the United States, meanwhile, the global abortion push brought together some odd political bedfellows. Predictably, Paul Ehrlich was a big advocate of abortion as birth control. At other points, however, the list of abortion's early champions reads like a directory of the Republican Party. Draper's support attracted other conservatives, many of whom assumed a brazenly hypocritical stance. Seeing abortion as a tool, not a right, these population activists promoted its utility abroad without bothering to back legalization at home.[18] George H. W. Bush, for example, declared himself a fan of Draper's work. In 1973, just a few years before Republicans rallied around the rights of the fetus, Bush wrote the foreword to *World Population Crisis,* an account of the population control movement by Piotrow, Draper's old secretary. "As chairman of the special Republican Task Force on Population and Earth Resources," wrote Bush, recounting his days in the House of Representatives, "I was impressed by the arguments of William H. Draper, Jr. that economic development overseas would be a miserable failure unless the developing countries had the knowledge and supplies their families needed to control fertility."[19] Another important advocate of abortion overseas was Henry Kissinger, then secretary of state under Richard Nixon. In 1974, on the eve of India's AIIMS trials, Kissinger signed a classified U.S. government memo stating that "abortion is vital to the solution" of world population growth. "No country has reduced its population growth without resorting to abortion," the memo read.[20] The legalization of abortion abroad, then, came about with support from both sides of the American political spectrum.

But ensuring that women in the developing world could terminate unwanted pregnancies was only half the battle. If abortion were to prove an effective population control method—if it were to truly serve Western interests—women also had to be convinced to abort. Today, press reports from Asia tend to paint a picture of a people who are morally pragmatic, entirely unbothered by the termination of a pregnancy and free from the ethical hand-wringing that surrounds the beginning of life in Judeo-Christian countries. (In the 1970s, too, this interpretation was common. Recall that describing their sex selection experiments, the AIIMS doctors explained women chose to abort female fetuses "without any undue anxiety.") The reality that population workers found when they landed in the 1950s, however, was vastly different.

Throughout Asia, abortion was frowned on. Where it was performed, it was a hushed, shameful affair. Asian religions and philosophical traditions, to varying degrees, opposed abortion. Confucianism held that life begins a few months before birth.[21] Hindu texts, as Jonathan Duncan had pointed out in his efforts to quash female infanticide in colonial India, warned against killing fetuses.[22] The Buddhist monastic code, meanwhile, stated that life begins at conception, and monks could be expelled for helping a woman abort.[23]

These prohibitions had seeped into local cultures and medical codes. Take the case of China. In the thirteenth century one of the country's preeminent medical ethicists penned an ominous parable warning doctors and midwives against performing abortions:

> In the capital city lived a woman whose family name was Bai . . . She made a living by selling abortifacient drugs. One day, she started getting violent headaches: her head swelled up and increased in size day by day. All the prominent physicians treated her, but no one was able to cure her. After many days, an ulceration developed and the smell became unbearable. She cried every night and her crying could be heard near and far. Eventually she gathered her family around her and begged them: "Burn all the prescriptions that I've kept." She also made her children swear not to pass on her trade. Bewildered, her son asked: "You have built yourself up through this work. Why do you want to give it all up?" His mother answered, "Every night I dream that hundreds of little children are sucking on my head. This is why I cry out in pain. All this is my retribution for selling drugs to damage fetuses." Right after saying this, she died.[24]

While other Chinese ethicists condoned abortion, terminating a pregnancy remained, at the very least, highly controversial throughout imperial times. By the 1950s anxiety about the practice had crept into the language: the Mandarin used at the time imbued the fetus with life and the act of terminating a pregnancy with violence. Terms used to describe abortion included *duoshengtai*, "dropping the living fetus," and *datai*, "beating the fetus." Even the Chinese word for miscarriage implied a sort of birth: *xiaochan* means "small labor."[25]

But resistance to abortion wasn't merely the outgrowth of religious baggage. It also stemmed from popular notions about femininity. Across Asia in the mid-twentieth century, cultures rewarded women for becoming mothers. A woman with many children was an attractive woman. Her neighbors looked up to her, and her family held her in high regard. A woman with no children, on the other hand, was to be pitied. Before the introduction of South Korea's family planning program, writes sociologist Seungsook Moon, "The idea of contraception was foreign to most Koreans, who tended to believe that having many children meant good luck."[26] To convince Asian women that abortion was not only ethically permissible but also sometimes preferable to childbirth, then, was a mammoth task. If family planning workers were lucky, it would entail a feat of subtle social engineering. If they weren't, it would mean the use of force.

If Japan was the laboratory that showed abortion could be a useful population control tool, South Korea was where that tool was refined. Emerging from the Korean War in the mid-1950s, it became the next major crisis zone for population workers, under circumstances remarkably similar to those that had made Japan a priority a decade earlier. In South Korea too the end of conflict brought both a baby boom and effective U.S. control. President Syngman Rhee, the unpopular ruler installed on the heels of the war, was essentially a puppet who gave American advisers wide-ranging influence over his country's economic and social policy. After Rhee was deposed in a coup, the United States quickly won over his successor, General Park Chung-hee, a career military man who had received training at Fort Sill, Oklahoma.[27] Yet the stakes were higher than they had been in Japan, for the cold war was in full swing, and McCarthyism was gripping America. "It became evident," recalled Draper, who by that point was the U.S. representative to the newly formed North Atlantic Treaty Organization, "that it would be necessary, with the Korean War on and the threat to Western Europe from Russia, to build up the Western world's mutual defenses."[28]

Fortunately from Draper's perspective, political access meant population control workers had virtual free rein in South Korea. IPPF entered first, forming the Planned Parenthood Federation of Korea on April 1, 1961.[29] The Population Council officially began working with the Korean government in 1962.[30] As funding flowed into Seoul over the coming years, employees of both organizations became fixtures in the city. But family planning was not an entirely Western operation. The foreign experts were joined by an extensive network of local workers and volunteers. By 1964, the Western advisers had at their disposal 1,500 Korean family planning fieldworkers.[31]

Although America's population control emissaries boasted abundant money and political will, they stepped into a world filled with other obstacles. In the 1960s, 20 percent of Koreans lived in townships with no doctor, and in rural areas public transportation was basically nonexistent. In some cases fieldworkers had to walk miles to reach potential recruits.[32] Once they finally reached them, actually convincing couples to change their behavior was another challenge. The fieldworkers were trained to use creative analogies—a man with a vasectomy, they informed skeptical farmers, was like a "sweet seedless watermelon"—and to focus on mild contraceptive methods.[33] But Korean villagers were not so easily convinced. "The habit" of giving birth, one Western adviser noted dryly, "is hard to break."[34] Others observed that many women rejected contraception because they were intent on having a son.[35]

Rather than hindering their work, however, this intransigence merely heightened the family planning advisers' sense of urgency. Before long, Western groups were calling, as they would later do in India and elsewhere, for a "crash" phase of family planning in Korea.[36] "The only meaningful pay-off in this campaign," asserted a report in the Population Council journal *Studies in Family Planning*, "is a reduction in the annual rate of increase."[37] Funders back in New York, it was assumed, knew precisely to what "rate of increase" referred: population growth. There was no other metric that mattered as much.

Park Chung-hee's government was happy to oblige. As an experienced general, he approached birth control "much like a military campaign," at one point assigning actual soldiers to assist.[38] As the crash phase kicked off, the share of Korea's health budget devoted to family planning swelled to 25 percent. (The health minister objected to this lopsided distribution of funds, suggesting some of the money be used to fight tuberculosis, but Western advisers appear to have overruled him.)[39] The issue of transportation, meanwhile, was solved by the U.S. Agency for International Development's donation of eleven reconditioned U.S. Army ambulances. These were rugged Jeeps that had probably been used in the Korean War.

(In photos from the campaign they look like something straight out of the television show *M.A.S.H.*)[40] The agency had the Jeeps painted white in an apparent effort to make them appear civilian friendly and in December 1965 delivered eight of the vehicles to rural family planning posts, where the ambulances were transformed into mobile clinics. USAID later added another fifty Jeeps, along with fifty buses and half-ton trucks. The Swedish International Development Authority, for its part, contributed thirty Land Rovers. [41]

Throughout the late 1960s, the Korean population control fleet roamed the countryside. Each mobile clinic was staffed by a doctor, a nurse, a midwife, educator, and a few volunteers.[42] These teams performed IUD insertions and sterilizations in the backs of the vehicles, in small "operating theaters" measuring six feet by seven and a half feet.[43] Many of the staff had no gynecological experience, and doctors were given a maximum of two days training before being put to work.[44] Still, they were expected to work quickly, with compensation doled out based on the number of procedures they managed to perform in a day. A vasectomy, for example, brought a fieldworker thirty-six cents, while an IUD insertion yielded half that.[45]

Sang-yong Song, former vice president of the Asian Bioethics Association and now a tall, grandfatherly man with a deep, soothing voice, remembers the mobile clinics in the 1960s. Back then he was a chemistry undergraduate student at Seoul National University, which was deeply involved in the population control campaign. The Population Council had backed the creation of a dedicated population research center at the university, and SNU scientists were using council money to monitor fertility trends and conduct sterilization experiments on animals.[46] Song, who had founded a student humanist organization, did his part by traveling through the countryside and giving lectures on the importance of birth control. He says he was not involved with the mobile clinics, but he remembers the impact they left. "It was terrible," he tells me decades later over dinner at a Seoul seafood restaurant, later adding, "Korea was under military rule, and the annual income per capita was $60. All kinds of unbelievable things . . . happened. There was no concept of human rights." Then he downs most of a bottle of *makali,* a potent Korean rice wine.

The foreign population organizations' records do not mention a payment for abortion, which was technically illegal under Korean law. But mobile clinic staff allegedly did that as well. Cho Young-Youl, the suburban gynecologist who would later perform sex selective abortions, was a medical student at the time. When I ask how sex selection became common in South Korea, he begins by describing the population control drive. By the 1970s, he says, "there were agents going around the countryside to small towns and bringing women into the [mobile] clinics. That counted toward their pay. They brought the women regardless of whether they were pregnant." Many of the women were forced: "If a woman wasn't pregnant, the agent would make her undergo surgery—tubal ligation—to make sure she didn't have any more babies. And if she was pregnant, the agent would have her abort and then undergo tubal ligation. There were units that only did [abortion and sterilization]."

The financial reward system described in Population Council documents—eighteen cents for an IUD insertion—confirms that fieldworkers had an incentive to round up as many women as possible. The same reports obliquely suggest Korean women did not seek out the trucks at their own volition: "The women apparently do not mind visiting the units," one account states weakly.[47] Photos taken in villages along the family planning route show women lining up behind the vehicles in the rain, or standing off to one side staring defiantly, their arms crossed over their chests.[48]

Whether directly or indirectly, by working through Korean organizations, IPPF and the Population Council administered mobile clinics, oversaw fieldworkers, and issued targets for vasectomies and IUD insertions in South Korea for over a decade. Foreign funding for family planning peaked in 1974, when UNFPA pledged $6 million for a five-year grant that, among other things, allowed for an increase in the number of Korean fieldworkers to 2,780.[49] Throughout the period of Western involvement, South Korea's birth rate plunged, from forty-seven births for every one thousand people in 1960 to twenty-four per thousand in 1975.[50] While the population control advisers' explanations of Korea's rapid drop in fertility from the time make no mention of forced abortions performed in converted U.S. Army trucks, they do suggest that Korean women who had just undergone abortions were good candidates for IUD insertions and sterilizations—a detail that corroborates Cho's account of forced abortions followed by tubal ligations.[51] "Induced abortion happened so casually," says Heeran Chun, a sociologist at Ewha Womans University in

Seoul who has studied the history of family planning in Korea. It was "a kind of contraceptive method among married women, whether it was chosen—informed or un-informed—or by force."[52]

Western reports also freely admitted that targets for condom and birth control pill acceptance fell short in South Korea and abortion was responsible for the drop in the country's birth rate.[53] Christopher Tietze, the former U.S. State Department researcher and colleague of Sheldon Segal, who in 1969 had promoted sex selection as a method of population control, wrote in *Studies in Family Planning*: "It is . . . clear that induced abortion, regardless of its legal status, has contributed substantially to the success of Korea's national family planning program in reducing fertility."[54] Then again, it would have been hard to deny the role played by abortion in South Korea. By 1977 doctors in Seoul were performing 2.75 abortions for every birth—the highest documented rate of abortion in human history.[55]

Korean teenagers soon outnumbered young children, and in 1983 the country attained a replacement-level fertility rate.[56] But population theories died hard. South Korea's plummeting birth rate had paralleled its economic rise, and President Chun Doo-hwan, the military ruler who succeeded Park Chung-hee, was keen on further stimulating economic growth. Population control had also proven a reliable source of foreign aid. In 1980 the World Bank furnished Korea with $30 million in loans earmarked for family planning, and soon after it funneled millions more into the country through its International Bank for Reconstruction and Development.[57] Instead of declaring victory and relaxing population targets, Chun redoubled his efforts, decreasing the recommended number of children from two to one and denying social benefits to women who violated the restriction.

As Chun launched a second crash phase in 1983, slogans appeared throughout the country informing Koreans that "Even Two Is A Lot."[58] Mobile clinics again spread throughout the country, this time to enforce targets approaching China's one-child policy in severity. "The new, more stringent, policy is designed to counter several trends which imperil the attainment of stated population goals," read a classified U.S. National Security Council brief filed a few months after the campaign's inception. "The most serious is the persistently high cultural value placed on sons . . . Koreans resist birth control until they have a son."[59] The brief explained the government was unveiling policies designed to make daughters more desirable. But certainly Chun and his backers at the World Bank knew that the shortcut around persistent son preference was not improving the status of girls and women but—much as Paul Ehrlich and Sheldon Segal had envisioned years earlier—relying on newly available sex determination technology. The additional pressure the campaign placed on women to restrict their fertility no doubt played a role in South Korea's 1980s binge of sex selective abortions.

Following the months he spent as a student volunteer lecturing villagers on birth control, Sang-yong Song earned a PhD from the University of Indiana–Bloomington, where he says he became a "critic of science." Later, as a bioethicist, he turned his attention to controversies like the 2005 Hwang Woo-suk stem cell debacle, in which a Korean scientist who claimed to have cloned stem cells from a human embryo was found to have fabricated research. Well into his sixties, though, Song has continued to think about what he witnessed back in the 1960s.

Even the Hwang fiasco, he believes, has its roots in the population control movement. As news of the scientist's discovery broke, Korean women lined up to donate their eggs, allowing Hwang to amass a supply of over two thousand human eggs. A casual attitude toward eggs, the embryo, or the fetus clearly violates Confucianism, Song says, tracing this lapse in ethics to the coercion that characterized Korea's decades-long population control campaign.[60] That Koreans think so lightly about their own genetic material today, he tells me over dinner, has to do with the fact that back then the country became a "paradise for abortion." Before he gets drunk on *makali*, he says ruefully that in today's Korea, "there are almost no ladies who haven't had an abortion. The abortion debate—I don't care so much about that. I am pro-abortion, pro-euthanasia, and so on. I am *that* liberal. But I am against utilitarianism. Life is very important, and we shouldn't take it lightly."

Back in the United States, South Korea's family planning program was lauded for its success. A report in the journal *Demography* contrasting Korean birth control practices before and after Western intervention was typical: "Few birth control techniques were known or used: only seven percent of childbearing-age women had tried abortion, and commercial contraceptives were sold only at the county seat at best. Into this setting came mass media information, the fieldworker, and the service, all firmly administered, and the response was of historic proportions."[61] Firmly administered, of course, was a euphemism for forced, but few interrogated this point. As the late 1960s was still the era of General William Draper, and as it had not yet become politically untenable for conservatives to back abortion abroad, Korea's family planning program became a model for other countries in Asia.[62] In Taiwan the proportion of women who had had one or more abortions doubled in just eight years, from 10 percent of women in 1965 to 20 percent in 1973.[63] Take-up was also rapid in India; in 1973, just two years after the country legalized abortion, its hospitals and clinics performed an estimated 23,000 abortions.[64] Decades later, demographer Geoffrey McNicoll bluntly summarized the changes that swept Asia: "The broad sequence entailed, initially, establishment of an effective, typically authoritarian, system of local administration, providing (sometimes incidentally) a framework for promotion and service delivery in health, education, and family planning."[65]

As family planning organizations made inroads in new nations, Western advisers became bolder. Some even extolled abortion as preferable to birth control. "Early abortion is safe, effective, cheap and potentially the easiest method to administer," wrote IPPF medical director Malcom Potts in the *Proceedings of the Royal Society of London* in 1976. "To call it 'a second best' or 'a back-up method,' as is so often done, is to believe a mythology . . . which runs directly counter to the needs of women, the welfare of existing children and the future prosperity—or maybe survival—of mankind."[66] Others turned their attention to China, which was tightening birth quotas in the lead-up to the one-child policy. Beginning in the early 1970s, roving teams of medics and midwives carried out "shock attacks," performing IUD insertions, sterilizations, and abortions on women and sterilizing men.[67] Nearly from the start, many of these campaigns were coercive. In 1973 Western journalists based in Hong Kong reported that pregnant women on the mainland who had more than two children were required to abort or bring up any additional children without rations.[68]

China was in the throes of the Cultural Revolution and isolated from the rest of the world. On family planning, however, it was following an approach that had been dreamed up in the West and already pursued in South Korea, a fact that greatly pleased population control advocates—particularly William Draper, who never lost sight of Asia. He fantasized about getting the Population Crisis Committee involved in shaping Beijing's population policy.

On March 24, 1971, as the U.S. table tennis team prepared to make a historic visit to China, Draper wrote premier Zhou Enlai asking for an exchange of information, explaining, he later recalled, that family planning, like table tennis, is "without particular ideology and without political implications."[69] When he did not receive a reply, Draper commissioned Edgar Snow, one of the first American journalists to report extensively on the People's Republic of China, to look into China's family planning program.

Snow, who tended to be sympathetic to the Chinese government and who enjoyed good access as a result, soon filed a lengthy report peppered with telling anecdotes. Mao Zedong himself told the journalist that son preference was a major obstacle to getting Chinese women to accept family planning. "In the countryside a woman still wanted to have boy children," Snow recalled Mao saying. "If the first and second were girls, she would make another try. If the third one came and was still a girl, the mother would try again. Pretty soon there would be nine of them."[70] Elsewhere, however, Snow found what he interpreted as signs of great progress. In the article he filed for Draper, which appeared in a special China issue of the Population Crisis Committee's magazine, he described a new abortion technique he had witnessed being tried out, using only acupuncture as anesthesia, on a woman who had exceeded her birth quota. "An abortion is being performed on a smiling patient," Snow wrote credulously. "The young woman, a factory worker, is under no anesthesia except two needles painlessly inserted into her earlobes. . . . 'Do you feel any pain?' I ask in Chinese. She smiles and shakes her head. She uses Mao Tsetung Thought, she says. 'Fear neither hardship nor death,' perhaps. In less than ten minutes she is released from the table."[71]

For Draper, such tales apparently only made the country more appealing as a partner in population work. In the introduction to the China issue, he appealed to Chinese leaders a second time, once again comparing population control to table tennis. "Now that the first round of table tennis diplomacy has been so well played out before its world audience, we again suggest to Premier Chou En-lai that some channels of communication might be usefully set up on subjects of common and basic interest, such as family planning programs and their effect on the future of the human race as a whole."[72]

But Draper was hardly the only U.S. population activist who fantasized about securing a foothold in the world's most populous country. In 1976, shortly after Chinese researchers at Tietung Hospital announced their success at identifying and aborting female fetuses, the New York–based family planning organization the Guttmacher Institute ran an approving article in its magazine entitled "China's 'Birth Planning' Approach Transferable to Other Nations."[73] And the next year, as Song Jian got to work using the equations of Dutch mathematicians, IPPF sent a delegation of twenty people to China on a seventeen-day tour of six cities and two agricultural communes.

Despite close government supervision, the group noted incidences of coercion along the way. One member of the delegation told a reporter, "If persuasion fails to work, draconian measures may be used. A woman pregnant for the third time may be pressured to undergo an abortion."[74] But a lengthy summary that IPPF regional director Benjamin Viel drew up upon returning from Beijing did not mention draconian measures, at least when it came to birth control. While he conceded that abortions were performed on Chinese women who had violated the requirement that they wait three years between births, he implied that these were voluntary. "As proof that compulsion plays no part in the program," Viel wrote in a comment that may have been directed at the Chinese authorities as well as Western donors, "we were told that if, in the majority of places, ninety per cent of the children have been planned, there are other parts of the country in which planned children constitute no more than fifty percent of the total."[75] Central government directives, he added, seemed to "reach the periphery in an ideal process of decentralization."

Whether such praise had any effect on cadres in Beijing is unclear. But within two years population control organizations would back up their compliments with hard cash—and China would finally relent and let the Western advisers in.

Chapter 10

THE FEMINIST

Action is indeed better than inaction.
—BHAGAVAD GITA

In December 1979, as preparations for the one-child policy were under way in Beijing, the Chinese government signed an agreement with UNFPA for the organization's first population project in China.[1] The $50 million the agency pledged over four years was the largest chunk of foreign aid China had received since the country severed relations with the Soviet Union in 1961, and it came as a boon to a cash-strapped government in Beijing.[2] The agreement stipulated the money would be used to buy computers, train 70,000 family planning workers, and fund extensive information campaigns to promote smaller families—measures about which China's leaders could have only fantasized before.[3] It also paved the way for cooperation with other Western population organizations, including the IPPF, the Ford Foundation, and the Population Council.

Perhaps because reports of forced abortions and other forms of coercive birth control had been trickling out of China for six years, in announcing the agreement UNFPA director Rafael M. Salas took care to note that China's birth planning network functioned by taking advantage of a cultural knack for collective mobilization. "It is not only an efficiently run program," he told reporters, "a bureaucracy that administers well, but a social consciousness and communal pressure at all levels to promote family planning."[4]

Such comments were grounded in the same strain of misplaced cultural relativism that made it possible to believe an unanesthetized woman lying on an abortion table could steel herself for the procedure by reciting Mao Zedong thought: while Westerners act out of self-interest, in China people sacrifice their own needs for the needs of the group. By the late 1970s Westerner observers knew that collectivism had failed China when it came to industrial and agricultural production. But in the realm of human reproduction the notion the People's Republic was a socialist paradise where individuals put their communities before themselves stubbornly lingered. "Persuasion and motivation," wrote the IPPF's Benjamin Viel in his 1977 report, are "very effective in a society in which social sanctions can be applied against those who fail to cooperate in the construction of the socialist state." A few years later, a review of birth control around the world by the U.S. Office of Technology Assessment explained:

> The underlying philosophy of the birth planning policy is to combine state guidance (education and persuasion as opposed to administrative orders) with the "voluntarism" of the people. . . . Because every unplanned birth in defiance of the community decision means that an eligible couple must give up a birth permission they deserve and have earned, there is a collective interest in seeing that the community plan of births is carried out. Chinese birth planning programs thus involve local communities in the planning and implementation of a policy of vital national importance.[5]

Mere months after the UNFPA agreement was signed, however, press reports clarified the true nature of "voluntarism" in China. As cadres started cracking down on out-of-quota births, tales of forced abortions filtered out of the country. In May 1980, the Associated Press related tales from travelers to Guangdong province who reported seeing "buckets of fetuses" outside Chinese hospitals.[6] In August the wire service carried interviews with village cadres in Sichuan province who alluded to the practice of coercive abortion there. "If women get pregnant outside of our plan, they must have an abortion," brigade leader Fu Shaorong told reporter Victoria Graham. Chen Fenglian, chair of the local women's federation, elaborated: "Most [women] objected to abortions, but cadres go to their homes and explain how poor China is and then they are willing," adding that some of the women who needed convincing were seven months pregnant.[7]

Reports of forced abortions also circulated among family planning organizations. In a January 1980 memo to IPPF director Carl Wahren, information officer Penny Kane warned that Planned Parenthood staff members who had recently visited China reported "very strong measures being taken to reduce population growth—including abortion up to eight months." Kane noted, presciently, that being associated with such incidents could be bad for IPPF: "I think that in the not-too-distant future this will blow up into a major Press story, as it contains all the ingredients for sensationalism—Communism, forced family planning, murder of viable fetuses, parallels with India, etc. When it does blow up, it is going to be very difficult to defend."[8]* But publicly, officials at IPPF and other organizations continued to spout the line that China's communal spirit allowed for smooth and effortless family planning.

Western organizations had been trying to make headway in the world's most populous country for nearly a decade, after all, and now they were being welcomed with open arms. As part of UNFPA's deal with the Chinese government, the agency gained critical access to officials in Beijing, including the right to post around six foreign specialists to China for two-year stints and cycle through twenty others.[9] Western demographers kept quiet for similar reasons. The UNFPA arrangement provided for technical assistance for China's 1982 census, along with the training of local population scholars, and after decades in which the country had been a statistical black hole the advent of professional scholarship meant sudden access to reliable statistics.[10] Then too, many demographers still believed in combating population growth at all costs. In a 1978 survey of Population Association of America members, 34 percent of respondents agreed with the statement "coercive birth control programs should be initiated in at least some countries immediately."[11] Coercion had, after all, already been tried

---

*Later that year, Kane warned Chinese leaders were keenly interested in eugenics, with the aim of weeding out physically and mentally handicapped children.

in India and South Korea, with Western advisers and demographers emerging from their involvement in those countries relatively unscathed. Perhaps they thought they would get off easy in China too.

—⟨∞⟩—

As China's National Population and Family Planning Commission began implementing the one-child policy in late 1980, officials quickly put the foreign funding to use. With the money UNFPA had earmarked for such purposes, the commission trained family planning agents and launched an ambitious propaganda blitz to spread the word that it was serious about birth control.[12] UNFPA probably intended funding for education to go toward posters proclaiming the value of daughters and the benefits of small families. But local officials had other ideas about what they considered effective communication. Village walls soon read

BETTER TO LET BLOOD FLOW LIKE A RIVER
THAN TO HAVE ONE MORE THAN ALLOWED.

and

YOU CAN BEAT IT OUT! YOU CAN MAKE IT FALL OUT!
YOU CAN ABORT IT! BUT YOU CANNOT GIVE BIRTH TO IT.[13]

The newly trained family planning agents got to work, dispersing across the country to implement the birth targets. Arriving in China's villages and cities, they tried several different approaches to birth control, inserting IUDs in women and sterilizing both women and men. But government figures reveal that abortion quickly emerged as one of China's primary birth control methods.[14]

As in South Korea, many abortions carried out in the name of family planning were voluntary. But others were not. Some were difficult to classify, there being a thin line between free will and coercion in 1980s China.

The methods agents used to compel pregnant women to abort were far-ranging. In July 1981, a Hong Kong reporter found that in addition to fines and other penalties, women in Guangdong province who refused abortions risked having their water or electricity cut off, roof tiles re-moved, and houses sealed.[15] Three months later the *Wall Street Journal* reported that women were being "handcuffed, tied with ropes or placed in pig's baskets" before being shipped off to the hospital for abortions.[16] The *Journal* also ran an article by Steven Mosher, an anthropology student in Stanford University's PhD program who had witnessed forced abortions while conducting fieldwork in an agricultural commune in Guangdong province. Mosher described being present at a meeting held at the com-mune's headquarters:

> There were eighteen women, all from five to nine months pregnant, and many red-eyed from lack of sleep and crying. They sat listlessly on short plank benches arranged in a semicircle about the front of the room, where He Kaifeng, a commune cadre and Communist Party member of many years' standing, explained the purpose of the meeting in no uncer-tain terms. "You are here because you have to 'think clear' about birth control, and you will remain here until you do."[17]

According to Mosher, the cadre first tried to reason with the women. He told the women that the commune would provide cars to shuttle them to and from the hospital—most had never ridden in one—and mosquito nets to cover them while they were undergoing the procedure. Then he switched tactics:

> "None of you has any choice in this matter. You must realize that your pregnancy affects everyone in the commune, and indeed affects every-one in the country." Then, visually calculating how far along the women in the room were, he went on to add, "The two of you who are eight or nine months pregnant will have a caesarean; the rest of you will have a shot which will cause you to abort." Several of the women were crying by this point.[18]

At the time of his stay in Guangdong, Mosher was pro-choice, with no professed agenda other than observation. At Stanford, he had been heavily influenced by the ideas of Paul Ehrlich, and he estimates he read *The Population Bomb* four times. He had gone to China believing "China had an overpopulation problem and the Chinese government should take serious measures to deal with it."[19] But the bullying he witnessed angered him, and when he left China he smuggled out photos of heavily pregnant women undergoing abortions. One image showed a woman at seven and a half months lying on the operating table as a doctor came at her belly with a scalpel. The physician had not bothered to give the woman a gown, and her coarse peasant's pants were bunched around her ankles.[20]

Other observers had begun to note that resistance to the one-child policy was strongest among Chinese couples seeking sons. "The desire for a son," wrote New York Times reporter Christopher S. Wren in 1982, "appears to be the main reason why more couples do not take out a 'single child certificate,' in which they pledge to have no more children in return for preferential medical and schooling benefits."[21] Wren related how the Chinese journal Health News had reported that women were aborting female fetuses.[22] A few months later Victoria Graham, the same reporter who had called attention to coercive abortions on the eve of the one-child policy's implementation, warned in a wire story published in papers across America: "Many Chinese women, convinced that boys are better, are seeking unethical sex tests of their unborn babies and rushing to abort healthy female fetuses. . . . These are not isolated cases. . . . Demographers are warning that if the balance between the sexes is altered by abortion and infanticide, it could have dire consequences."[23] But Western organizations that now had emissaries in Beijing made no move to intervene, and the next year the Chinese government tightened its birth control push as part of a wave of general repression.[24]* Fourteen million women— accounting for two-fifths of all pregnancies—underwent abortions that year.[25] Sex selection increased as well.

Again, rather than pull out of China, the organizations redoubled their support. In 1983, IPPF chair Carl Wahren requested increased funding for China.[26] Around the same time, Stanford University expelled Steven Mosher, the PhD student whose reports had helped call attention to forced abortions. Ostensibly, Mosher's offenses were twofold: he had vio-

---

*The government also cracked down on blue jeans and other forms of "spiritual pollution."

lated anthropological ethics by publishing photos of his subjects, and he had traveled without obtaining the proper permits from the Chinese authorities.[27] But a Chinese Academy of Social Sciences official also pressured Stanford at several points throughout the review process, implicitly threatening to bar other researchers from China if the university allowed Mosher to continue his degree.[28]

The Chinese government's zeal for population control especially pleased UNFPA leaders. In September 1983 the organization jointly awarded Qian Xinzhong, the former People's Liberation Army general charged with administering the one-child policy, and Indira Gandhi, who had overseen both India's mass sterilizations and the AIIMS sex selection experiments in the 1970s, with the first United Nations Population Award. At the award ceremony for the $12,500 prize in New York, secretary-general Javier Pérez de Cuéllar was effusive. "Considering the fact that China and India contain over forty percent of humanity," he said, "we must all record our deep appreciation of the way in which their governments have marshaled the resources necessary to implement population policies on a massive scale."[29]

But for those who worried about human rights as well as reducing population growth, the prize announcement was the final straw. An adviser to the prize selection committee, Nobel-winning economist Theodore W. Shultz, quickly went public with his disapproval, calling the decision damaging to the cause of family planning and asking UNFPA to remove his name from all committee materials.[30] From then on, population control—and, by unfortunate association, reproductive health work—became a lot trickier.

Soon after the prize was announced, America's nascent anti-abortion movement seized on coercive birth control in China to push for eliminating UNFPA funding altogether. The story of reproductive rights organizations bankrolling forced abortions was, as IPPF information officer Penny Kane had predicted back in 1980, too juicy to pass up. At the 1984 UN World Population Conference in Mexico City, anti-abortion protestors showed up wielding evidence of forced abortions, female infanticide, and sex selective abortions in China—and reserving special vitriol for IPPF and UNFPA.[31] The next year, Congress passed the Kemp-Kasten Amendment, which barred the U.S. government from funding any organization that contributes to forced abortions or sterilizations, and President Ronald Reagan cut off $46 million in USAID funds to UNFPA, drying up the agency's largest source of government funding.[32] (Today Reagan's executive order, which also withheld U.S. funding from NGOs that lobby for, perform, or provide referrals for noncoercive abortions abroad, is sometimes referred to as the "global gag rule.")

By that point the makeup of organizations like UNFPA had begun to shift, with more women assuming positions of power. But the new leaders had fought hard for a woman's right to terminate a pregnancy in the United States, and in some corners of the globe the battle for reproductive rights was not yet won; at least a quarter of the world's women lived in countries where abortion was mostly prohibited. (This is still true today.)[33] That was certainly not the case in China, however, and throughout the 1980s UNFPA leaders reacted to allegations of complicity by alternately denying that the one-child policy was coercive and arguing the Chinese government only used the organization's money to carry out education and improve the state of Chinese demography.* In 1989, when the agency agreed to fund a five-year, $57 million program in China, UNFPA secretary-general Nafis Sadik told the *New York Times* that Chinese officials had admitted to isolated incidences of forced abortion but had pledged to eradicate them—and that they had assured her their policies only allowed for voluntary abortions.[34] The United States continued to withhold funds.

The struggle over UNFPA funding has continued up to the present, with each U.S. president since Reagan withdrawing or reinstating the gag rule, soon after taking office, along partisan lines.[35] Despite claims by anti-abortion groups to the contrary, today UNFPA plays a very different role in China—as does the Chinese family planning commission, which is no longer solely obsessed with birth rates. But the wrangle over coercion in China has had the unfortunate side effect of obscuring an important trend—one very much connected to China's sex ratio imbalance. To activists concerned about women's health, the sheer number of abortions performed under the one-child policy, and the frequency

---

*This was a difficult case to make. The computers bought with UNFPA funding, for example, were ostensibly for tabulating census results, but as China had very few other computers at the time they were almost certainly also used to track compliance with birth targets.

with which they occurred in the second and third trimesters, should have been alarming. Between January 1981, shortly after the policy was introduced, and December 1986, Chinese women underwent 67 million abortions.[36]

The best indication that something went seriously wrong with abortion in Asia is to compare the continent with the West. In North America and Western Europe, the legalization of abortion has typically been followed by a *decrease* in the number of terminations performed. That is not as paradoxical as it seems; when societies liberalize abortion laws, they tend to improve access to contraception as well, so that with the right not to give birth comes the right not to get pregnant in the first place.[37] But in Asia and much of Eastern Europe, where family planning polices were developed without concern for the needs of women and abortion was introduced as a crash population control method rather than as backup to contraception, legal abortion has instead meant more abortion. "Family planning policy has been deprived of the gender perspective," explains Whasoon Byun, the Korean Women's Development Institute researcher. In South Korea, she says, "The woman's body is the instrument. So instead of the pill we use abortion."[38]

In the United States, the average woman seeking an abortion is in her first pregnancy. Usually she is unmarried. Very often she is young and getting rid of what is sometimes called a mistake. In Eastern Europe and Asia, the typical woman going in for an abortion is married and has children. Odds are she has already had two or three abortions. (The average Azerbaijani woman has 3.2 abortions over the course of her lifetime. Her Georgian counterpart has 3.7.)[39] And after years of having population targets pummeled into her consciousness, she is likely using abortion to control the number of children in her family.

I once began explaining my research to a Korean friend who grew up in the 1980s, and before I had said much she became solemn. "My mother had three abortions when I was a child," she said. My face probably betrayed concern, for she shrugged. "It was common then."

Even with coercion looming over their heads, women had a hard time letting go of old ideas. Asked to ignore their religions and reconfigure their conceptions of femininity, they demurred. When in the late 1990s the bioethicist Nie Jing-Bao surveyed Chinese women who had aborted fetuses, several used the phrases *tongbu yusheng*—"so painful as to not want to live"—and *kubu kangyang*—"so bitter that no words can describe it."[40] One woman told Nie: "I remember it as though it happened this morning. I will remember it for good. While I was waiting for the abortion, my mind was in a state of great turmoil. I worried I would become infertile. I worried my health would be damaged. During the operation, I realized that it was really not easy to be a woman. It is painful, very painful."[41] Elsewhere, women continued to assign each pregnancy importance, even as they adapted to their countries' population control programs. In Vietnam, many women name the daughters growing inside them before aborting.[42] A recent report by the Indian NGO Centre for Youth Development and Activities concluded that even after decades of state-condoned abortion many Indians "see abortion as clearly the killing of life (a life that has to be given the same status as a human being) and therefore as ethically wrong."[43]

To a large degree, though, thinking in Asia *has* changed. It is rare to go far in a Chinese village today without encountering a sign advertising cheap and easy abortion. These ads are printed in bold black characters, photocopied, and then pasted to the walls of houses, stores, and communal toilets. Once while urinating in a Suining outhouse, I counted five such flyers on the earthen wall facing me. Chinese abortion clinics run television commercials during prime time, and promotional ploys abound; some even offer discounts to students.[44] As a Western woman living in the country, I sometimes find this openness reassuring—a refreshing contrast to the United States, where a woman seeking an abortion may have to brave picket lines. But for the most part the nonchalance surrounding abortion is disconcerting. Take the language: the evocative words hinting at the magic of pregnancy and the sadness of terminating it are gone. The Chinese term Liu Li used to tell me about her sex selective abortions was *dadiao:* to wipe out.

In Nie's research, women who admitted to being affected by their abortions were equaled in number by those who thought abortion utterly commonplace. In a questionnaire he distributed to over six hundred men and women in 1997, 29 percent believed abortion acceptable when a pregnancy affects the mother's looks; 34 percent thought severe morning sickness was grounds to abort.*[45] "Abortion is "a very natural thing, like eating and drinking," one told him. "It's a rather common occurrence, [like eating] an ordinary kind of food," echoed another.[46]

That attitude is also common among Delhi's elite. Even the analogies are the same. For some of his patients, Puneet Bedi tells me, abortion is "like having a cup of coffee. I have patients who come and say, 'I want to abort because if this baby is born it will be a Gemini, but I want a Libra,' believe it or not." Elsewhere in India popular objections to abortion are more entrenched, but they are overshadowed by a lingering government fixation on abortion as a population control tool. A recent assessment of reproductive health pamphlets in the state of Rajasthan found flipcharts implying that "a woman should seek abortion if she was poor or already had three children"—regardless of whether she wanted one.[47] As a result, many Indian women accept the practice with a sort of fatalism, divorcing it from ethics even as they see it as morally wrong. Women in India, the Centre for Youth Development and Activities report states, "do not see [abortion] as a matter of legal or human rights."[48]

Years of casual abortion carried out in the name of population control, scholars in Asia say, have made it a lot easier for women to abort for a reason as frivolous as a fetus's gender. "What would have happened if the [Korean] government hadn't allowed for such easy abortion in the era of high fertility?" posits Heeran Chun, the sociologist in Seoul. "What if the government hadn't permitted abortion?" She tilts her head to one side and considers what an alternate scenario might have looked like. "I don't think sex selective abortion would have become so popular."

———— ∞ ————

Years after UNFPA's indirect involvement with forced abortions in China led President Reagan to withdraw its funding, the issue continues to haunt the organization. If feminists and reproductive rights activists

---

*Disturbingly, 75 percent—and equal numbers of men and women—also agreed with the statement, "Under some situations, it is necessary to force a woman to have an abortion."

bring up abortion in the developing world today, it is ordinarily to point out how many women die of botched operations in countries where abortion is illegal. They don't talk about abortion being used for dark purposes. They don't talk about how the culture surrounding abortion has changed in Asia, about how the pervasiveness of the procedure alarms even the doctors who perform it. And they certainly don't reveal that the number of sex selective abortions far outnumbers the toll taken by back alley operations.[49]

Most reproductive rights organizations, in fact, deal with sex selection by attempting to dodge abortion entirely. The pamphlet that the UNFPA India country office distributes to artists and performers interested in campaigning against sex selection, for example, cautions against using the word "abortion," offering instead the official term preferred by UNFPA: "prenatal sex selection."[50] "One of the fundamental ways to address the problem," India representative Dhanashri Brahme explains, "is to focus on selection and discrimination" rather than abortion.[51]

That reasoning confounds those who are familiar with the issue. As one of the foremost experts on sex selection, Christophe Guilmoto has done research for UNFPA on several occasions, compiling detailed analysis and demographic projections into documents intended for journalists and scholars. Several of his reports have been rewritten because of political concerns. UNFPA "doesn't like the 'abortion' word too visible," he tells me. "They don't want to project abortion as the ultimate reason for sex selection. And I understand their point. But I was surprised, because when you call it prenatal sex selection it's not exactly clear what it is. And mostly it *is* abortion—in 95 percent or 99 percent of cases."

After decades of fighting for a woman's right to choose the outcome of her own pregnancy, it is difficult to turn around and point out that women are abusing that right—that in union with population pressures and technology, choice has been perverted. Privately, UNFPA officers say they are in a bind. "We have had a challenge making sure that when we communicate we are able to preserve women's right to abortion but at the same time say that sex selection on the basis of the gender of the future child is incorrect because it amounts to discrimination," one UNFPA employee tells me. "How do you hold on to this discrimination tag and at the same time talk about safe abortion and access to it? It has been a *huge* challenge for us. . . . We are walking a tightrope."

But rather than start to reframe the abortion debate, officers divorce sex selection not just from abortion but also from the very notion of choice, maintaining Asian women typically don't have a say in whether to carry their pregnancies to term—and that sex selection therefore can't be a decision arrived at through free will. Newspaper and magazine articles sourced from UNFPA reports are cast with women whose husbands beat them or threaten divorce if they don't produce an heir. Internal directives, meanwhile, explicitly instruct employees to emphasize the powerlessness of women requesting sex selection. The pamphlet for artists and performers in India, for example, reads: "Avoid language that holds the mother responsible for sex selection. She has very little control over the decision. . . . Choice in the absence of autonomy is no choice."[52]

Guilmoto encountered resistance from the organization here as well. "From time to time," he recalls, "I got in trouble with UNFPA because when I said 'women who did this' they would correct it to say 'couples who did this' or 'parents who did it.' It's all very nice to bring the male or husband into the picture, but it's a bit confusing. Because we know that women have some independent agency in the process as well, and there is no reason to forget about it."

For the most part, though, even thinly sketched explanations downplaying the role of abortion and female autonomy are poorly disseminated. UNFPA officers have known about the global sex ratio imbalance nearly since its inception—since well before Amartya Sen shook up the social science world with his 1990 *New York Review of Books* essay. Demographer Joseph Chamie spent decades at the UN Population Division, serving as its director for twelve of those years. The division is charged with collecting statistics and, unlike UNFPA, does not get involved in population advocacy work. He says the disparity in male and female births in Asia was common knowledge within the UN early on. "We knew about it in the eighties," he says. "We knew about it in the nineties. In every demographic publication there are two factors you always report. One is sex distribution and one is age. Sex and age. A lawyer may look at legal aspects. An MD may look at health aspects. For demographers our eyes are on sex and age—first thing." But it wasn't just the numbers that circulated within the UN. Officers also knew "that the technology kept improving." They knew about the development of handheld ultrasound devices. It was just that their existence clashed with other UNFPA goals.

(Chamie says UNFPA's leaders also balked when he published figures, like evidence of population aging around the world, that they believed contradicted their work.)

Several decades after unequal male and female birth totals first appeared in Asia, UNFPA still has not formulated an official stance on sex selection. The global office in New York relegates sex selection to the nether regions of its website, prioritizing honor killings and domestic violence as more pertinent population issues. The China office has remained virtually silent on sex selective abortion, and the Albanian office continues to actually thwart progress on the issue. While the country offices in India and Vietnam are more active, India's work came belatedly, after years of denial. Activist Sabu George remembers begging the director of the India office to do something about the problem back in the mid-1990s. At that point George had been working on the issue for over a decade. The Indian press had been reporting on sex selection for even longer; Indian feminists, recall, had begun organizing in the late 1970s. But George says the UNFPA officer turned him down. "For them these are not problems," he says. "They didn't see [sex selection] as an issue."*

The India office finally turned its attention to gender imbalance several years later, and its headquarters in Delhi is now plastered with posters from a campaign called Delighting in Daughters. But Guilmoto says the right to abort remains UNFPA's "priority issue," while George alleges the fear of impinging on that right renders most of the India office's work irrelevant. "Look at what they're doing!" he says. "Most of the money they're spending they're wasting. They don't want any strong action. People pretend they are working on the issue, but basically very little is done."

—⟨∞⟩—

UNFPA's leaders do not have to let the memory of its troubling involvement in China silence them. They could separate the past from the

---

*The Ford Foundation, to its credit, has taken a more active role in fighting sex selection, bankrolling a Chinese program designed to incentivize daughters and ensure compliance with the country's ban on prenatal sex determination.

present. They could call attention to the abuses of William Draper, reminding conservatives that the use of abortion as birth control in Asia is mostly their legacy—and then point out how dramatically the reproductive rights movement has changed. At the very least, they could uphold the precedent set by another arm of the United Nations.

In 1995, the UN Commission on the Status of Women sponsored the Fourth World Conference on Women in Beijing—an appropriate backdrop against which to address the world's sex ratio imbalance. The resolution delegates adopted at the end of the conference called attention to growing violence against women, which they defined as "violation of the human rights of women in situations of armed conflict, in particular murder, systematic rape, sexual slavery, and forced pregnancy . . . forced sterilization and forced abortion, coercive/forced use of contraceptives, prenatal sex selection and female infanticide."[53]

But rather than point to the Beijing Conference declaration as evidence of early UN action on a mounting problem, UNFPA leaders today refuse to acknowledge it. Reviewing the document years later, someone within the organization apparently worried the declaration could be construed as bestowing personhood on the fetus, for a 2010 internal staff memo warns country officers that they should stay away from the Beijing Conference definition at all times. If country offices choose to take up the issue, the memo advises, "refer to the human rights concerns which are related to sex selection (e.g., gender inequalities in general, or specific cases such as women who are forced to abort), or the human rights consequences that may result (e.g., trafficking, early marriage)." Officers should be careful, the memo stresses, to "not identify sex selection itself as a human rights abuse."[54]

The effects of the major UN agency tasked with population advocacy distancing itself from the issue of sex selective abortion are immense. Foot-dragging within UNFPA prevents other global funds from being directed toward meaningful work on gender imbalance. One day in Christophe Guilmoto's Paris living room I meet Sharada Srinivasan, a feminist sociologist at York University in Toronto who has flown in to discuss collaborating on a paper. Srinivasan, who has a mop of unruly, jet-black curly hair and a personality just as large, recalls attending a conference on women's issues in the Netherlands in 2009. The woman she sat next to at the conference introduced herself as the World Health Organization's point person on female genital mutilation.* It struck Srinivasan that she had never heard of a similar role at an international organization for sex selection; there are no point people on gender imbalance, despite its occurring across a wider swath of the world and affecting many more females—or potential females—than FGM.** "If you go to the UNICEF website, to the UNFPA and World Health Organization websites, you will see material on FGM right up front," she says. "It could be right on the first page. But you will not see *anything* on missing girls. Why is it left to local officers in Southeast Asia or South Asia to look at it as a local problem? At international forums people talk about [FGM]!*** This is not the case with sex selective abortion—not with missing girls."

Srinivasan believes those concerned about sex selection can learn a thing or two from FGM activists. The most obvious problem with FGM is that it constitutes a human rights abuse. But beginning in the 1990s activists managed to elevate the issue beyond the realm of injustice by arguing that it threatened women's health. "The WHO now has FGM as a health issue," Srinivasan says. "And that's it. Period. They talk about all sorts of health consequences for women, including maternal mortality, fistula—it's linked to all kinds of things. So it's a very compelling way to mobilize governments to do something and put pressure on the different African states that are doing this." She points out that multiple late-term abortions done in quick succession also carry health consequences—a point echoed again and again by doctors I interview. In India, 13 percent of all maternal deaths occur because of unsafe abortions, some of them performed on mothers who are determined not to have daughters.[55] But Srinivasan recognizes that her strategy is just wishful thinking. Drawing

---

*Female genital mutilation, also known as FGM, is a practice common in some African and Middle Eastern cultures that involves removing a girl's clitoris or other parts of her genitalia once she reaches adolescence.

**The number of women and girls over ten years old who have undergone some form of genital cutting is estimated at 91 million—72 million fewer than the number of females deemed to be missing from Asia's population.

***FGM even has its own UN awareness day. February 6 is International Day of Zero Tolerance to Female Genital Mutilation.

attention to the health effects of late-term abortions, even late-term abortions involving female fetuses, would simply be too much of a political liability for women's groups. "The moment you say, 'Here are these women who are going through so many abortions to get a boy,'" she says, "you know the Vatican will be the first one to say, 'Ban abortion, make abortion illegal!' And that's it. So UNFPA doesn't want to touch the issue because of that A-word."

But it isn't just population organizations like UNFPA that should take on more responsibility for fighting sex selection, Srinivasan adds. At some point, feminists need to go out on a limb and define sex selection as a human rights abuse. "It's very important to establish up front that whether it is sex selective abortion, female genital mutilation, or domestic violence, it is a form of patriarchal oppression," she says. "There is something common that runs through all of this."

Trepidation about the "A-word," however, has also immobilized the very people who should be crying oppression. Longtime gender activist Gita Sen recently told a journalist, "The biggest danger, which is the one we're dealing with right now, is that the anti–sex selection campaigns not turn into anti-abortion campaigns."[56] One might respond that the biggest danger we are facing is a dramatic reduction in the number of women and girls—that sex trafficking, bride buying, and general instability, when they arrive all at once, amount to one whopping danger. In a world in which women are unnaturally scarce, the right to abort will be the least of our worries.

PART THREE

THE WOMANLESS WORLD

Chapter 11

THE BRIDE

It is a truth universally acknowledged, that a single man in possession of a good fortune, must be in want of a wife.

—JANE AUSTEN, *PRIDE AND PREJUDICE*

Please don't treat your brides like goods.
—MALAYSIAN CHINESE ASSOCIATION PUBLIC
SERVICES AND COMPLAINT BUREAU
DIRECTOR DATUK MICHAEL CHONG,
ADDRESSING MEN WITH VIETNAMESE WIVES[1]

Cheng Ching-huang and Nguyen Thi Mai Chau got engaged the same week they met. That was fast for both of them, but it couldn't have happened any other way. Cheng had to catch a flight back to Taiwan, and Nguyen, who had been brought to Cheng's Ho Chi Minh City hotel by an acquaintance who dabbled in matchmaking, was awaited in her village, where it would have been better not to return than to return unattached. There was no time for courtship, and had there been time romance probably would have eluded them.

They didn't speak the same language, and they had little in common. Cheng had grown up in Taiwan during an era of prosperity. A simple man, a fruit farmer, he was nonetheless educated, keenly interested in the world outside his village, and relatively well-off at age thirty-one, a quality outwardly evident in his fleshy, generously nourished physique. Nguyen was Vietnamese, twenty, and petite. The ninth of ten children in a poor family from rural Vinh Long province, she had left school at fourteen to work as a maid. Few qualities bound her and Cheng, and in their case opposites most definitely did not attract. When she first laid eyes on Cheng, Nguyen thought, "He's so fat!" Cheng, meanwhile, fixated on the fact that the woman before him looked like a scared girl. He worried he'd have to teach her everything about life.

He asked for her hand in marriage anyway. A few years earlier, Cheng had resigned himself to the idea that he would never marry. His older brother, who farmed the family plot in the hills outside Taichung with him, had remained a bachelor, as had many men of his age throughout Taiwan who had the bad luck of being born at a time when Taiwanese were aborting female fetuses by the thousands. All told, Cheng's generation had nearly three-quarters of a million more men than women—a substantial gap in a country with only a few million working age adults.[2] To make matters worse, gender roles had changed. Not only were Taiwanese women scarce, but they chased jobs rather than family now, fleeing rural areas after high school for cities like Taipei in search of university degrees and good careers. Cheng knew it had become difficult to convince a modern Taiwanese woman to live on a farm. Then his sister suggested he find a wife in Vietnam.

Vietnamese women willing to wed strange men they had never met and move to strange lands they had never visited tended to come from remote villages in the Mekong Delta reachable only by boat. Their parents expected money in exchange for their daughters, and the negotiation process could prove complicated. But by 1999, when Cheng first looked into it, enough Taiwanese men had already married Vietnamese villagers that networks had sprouted, with the wives who arrived first serving as matchmakers for their husbands' single friends. A few enterprising women had started agencies that simplified the process by offering all-inclusive trips to Vietnam. For a mere $10,000, a man could buy a flight to Ho Chi Minh City, hotel, meals, transportation, and a wife. Cheng decided to give it a try.

Marriage had only recently occurred to Nguyen too, who thought she had a few more years of single life ahead of her. After the maid job didn't last, she spent several years jumping from one profession to the next, working at a shoe factory assembling high heels and later at a coffee shop near Ho Chi Minh City, always sending some of her earnings to her family. She was at the coffee shop when her mother sent word that she was sick, summoning Nguyen back to their village. When the young woman arrived she found her mother in fine health but with a mind fixated on one thing: it was time for her youngest daughter to *really* help the family.

Nguyen knew what that meant. A few women in her village had married Taiwanese men, and the money and gifts those marriages had brought in raised their families' standing and wealth to such a degree that locals had taken to talking about the Taiwanese Dream.[3] Beyond that everything got a little hazy, though. Nguyen had no idea what life in Taiwan was like. She knew the names of only a few of the countries outside Vietnam's borders, and her encounters with Taiwanese men extended to a few barked comments from her boss at the shoe factory. But she was an obedient daughter, and she agreed to her mother's plan. The next thing she knew, she was at a dreary Ho Chi Minh City airport hotel, clutching the bouquet of flowers the matchmaker had instructed her to buy (she wondered why she should be the one to give flowers but was too shy to ask) as she waited with other women for an evening flight from Taipei to land.

Finally the men arrived. The matchmaker introduced the couple, and then Nguyen stood before Cheng silently, her eyes averted, and waited. "So?" the matchmaker asked him after he had had a few minutes to stare. "Will you marry her?"

⸙

They wedded in Nguyen's village, and Cheng brought Nguyen back to his farm near Taiwan's western coast, in the rolling hills outside Taichung. When they reached his driveway, she looked out the car window to see persimmon trees marching up the hills in orderly rows, their trunks held rigid by metal bars. Her parents, like Cheng, farmed fruit, and at first there was that to latch onto: in some ways, raising persimmons in Taiwan was not so different from growing longans in Vietnam. But in Taiwan a farm was a lonely place—mechanized, organized, and mostly devoid of people—and Nguyen struggled until she got word that a Vietnamese wife who had arrived before her had set up a small café in the area. With time more local men bought the brides who had eluded them, the houses

surrounding Cheng's farm filled with Vietnamese women, and life got
better for Nguyen. She had two children, a girl and a boy. She learned to
make chicken in the Taiwanese style, to flavor noodles to Cheng's liking,
and finally to speak Mandarin. In this way the years passed.

Eleven years after they married, I find the couple sitting on overturned
buckets in their storehouse, boxing persimmons. Nguyen has full lips and
small wrinkles at the corners of her eyes. She is wearing a coral mock
turtleneck and dangly silver earrings, and next to Cheng, who is clad in a
black and red leather bomber jacket that accentuates his stocky figure, she
looks slight. Her personality is also smaller, and at first only Cheng talks,
reflecting on their marriage as he slips the fiery orange fruits into protective Styrofoam sheaths. "We fell in love *after* we got married," Cheng de-
clares happily, chuckling. "And we're still falling in love." Nguyen says
nothing. A few minutes later, as if in silent reply, she raises herself from
the bucket, strolls over to her husband, and carefully removes a fleck of
Styrofoam from his right eyebrow.

I spend the day with them, and by the time I leave it is clear to me that
the marriage has improved Cheng's life. Relatives say he was always fun-
loving and personable, but it is easy to believe that his outgoing personality blossomed after finding a wife, with the benefits that brought: two
sweet children, a companion on the farm, a kitchen fragrant with rich
broths and spices. The marriage also expanded Cheng's horizons. He has
returned to Vietnam a few times with his wife to visit Nguyen's family, and
he enjoys drinking rice wine with her father and uncles. He speaks only a
few words of Vietnamese, but he finds his inability to communicate oddly
freeing. "In Vietnam I can give my brain a rest," he says. After lunch he
shows me to his family's den, where he puts on a home movie he filmed
on a recent visit. The television fills with garishly colored houses, men
on Honda Dream motorcycles, and children running alongside muddy,
swollen rivers. Over the top of these images comes Cheng's voice, narrat-
ing in enthusiastic Mandarin.

Vietnam is an adventure for him, and no doubt that means something to his wife, whose eyes light up as she watches her country reel by
on film. But when I ask if she misses Vietnam she dodges the question.
"We go back there to have fun and see my father and mother," she says
unsentimentally. "But after we're finished having fun we come back." She
doesn't know much about the demographics that brought her to Tai-

wan, but she has determined staying is her fate. "I don't want to live there," she says. "Life is better here. That's how it is."

⎯⎯⎯⎯ ❧ ⎯⎯⎯⎯

There are women like Nguyen everywhere there has been sex selective abortion for any extended period of time. Scholars call them marriage migrants; locals simply say foreign wives; you might think of them as bought brides. In wealthier countries like Taiwan, South Korea, and Singapore—the first nations to develop skewed sex ratio imbalances—the trade in women is now an entrenched industry negotiated by established agencies. A Singaporean man seeking a wife can choose from among J & N Viet-Bride Match-Making Agencies, First Overseas International Matchmaker, and Ideal Marriage Centre.[4] In South Korea there is Interwedding, which offers brides from a smattering of poorer Asian countries.[5] In Taiwan, Lotus 2000 specializes in Vietnamese women.

Typically the search starts online, where men browse photos of the various agencies' merchandise—often full-body shots showing thin, demure near-girls balancing in high heels on bare cement floors. Enough men follow through on their searches that the broker business is booming. In 2003, one-third of all marriages in Taiwan were between a local and a foreign spouse, the vast majority of them between local men and foreign women.[6] In South Korea over a thousand international marriage agencies have registered with the government.[7] Marriages to foreigners accounted for nearly 11 percent of all 2008 weddings in that country.[8] The rate was even higher in rural areas, where 40 percent of Korean farmers and fishermen who married that year wed foreigners.[9] Weddings between wealthy Asian men and women from poor neighboring countries are so common that the phenomenon has inspired movies (South Korea's *Wedding Campaign*), popular books (Taiwan's *Don't Call Me a Foreign Bride*), and dating programs (in one Taiwanese show, bachelors try their hand at winning a Vietnamese bride for free).[10]

When the numbers of marriageable males and females diverge significantly in a society, demographers say there is a "marriage squeeze." The dynamics of a marriage squeeze may sound intuitive, and to a degree they are: men have trouble finding wives when women are scarce. But various factors can also cause a squeeze to snowball. For the first generation in which men outnumber women, surplus men often marry younger women, meaning that the shortage of females does not really affect them. A few years down the line, though, as younger men come of age, things get tricky. Since the men in this new cohort have to compete with both older men and men their own age, they feel the shortage of women acutely. The surplus, as Christophe Guilmoto put it to me in Paris, "piles up," and many men in the second generation are left unmarried.

If a country's fertility rate dropped over the same period in which parents selected for boys (as has happened in both Taiwan and South Korea), the squeeze is intensified. Since fewer people in each successive generation translate into fewer young women, later crops of bachelors have an even harder time finding wives.

For men not inclined to be with women in the first place, of course, a marriage squeeze may not be so bad. In much of the developing world, gay and bisexual men come under significant pressure to marry women. As it becomes more common for men to remain unmarried, the marital arm-twisting may decrease, saving some men from living out lies. (For lesbian women, on the other hand, the gender imbalance has the opposite effect. When potential wives are scarce, women are pushed into marrying and having children, whether they want to or not.)[11]

Demographer Zhu Chuzhu, who has been writing about China's sex ratio imbalance since the 1980s, says gay rights groups have lately taken an interest in her work. At a conference on gender issues in Beijing in 2009, she recalls, a male activist approached her to critique a presentation she had just given. "You only focus on heterosexual relationships," the activist said. "But gay people aren't interested in those. So the imbalance may not be as serious as you all say."[12] In South Korea scholars speculated about a link between a surplus of men and an increase in male homosexual activity early on, and today in Mehsana, a high sex ratio district in northwest India, newspaper reports say the dearth of women has sparked demand for male prostitutes.[13] "I get at least eight to ten calls each month from [men in] Mehsana who pick me up from Ahmedabad," the Times of India quoted a male sex worker as saying. "We check into guest houses on the Ahmedabad-Mehsana highway."[14]

But most Asian men do want to marry. As the region develops rural weddings have become extravagant affairs; in China today they often entail hired sedans and white horses. The people I met in Suining were so fascinated by marriage that it sometimes seemed they didn't talk about anything else.[15] "If you don't get married," one bachelor told me, "you're like a child."

Vietnam is one of the most popular sources of women for desperate East Asian men. But wealthy bachelors also buy brides from Thailand, the Philippines, Uzbekistan, Russia, Malaysia, North Korea, and mainland China. Some of the sending countries have—or once had—women to spare. In some cases, war and regional conflicts killed many males. (In the Mekong Delta, the Vietnam War did the trick. "The Americans played a role in this," demographer Wen-shan Yang told me when I met him in Taipei to talk about Taiwanese men buying wives from Vietnam.) In other cases, a large proportion of adult men are working abroad. But the surplus of women is quickly drying up as surplus men from other countries come of age. The Caucasus countries, the Balkans, and, to a lesser degree, India, are all due for a very large marriage squeeze in the next two decades.* And some countries that send women abroad, like China and Vietnam, now have sex ratio imbalances of their own.

By 2013, one in ten Chinese men will lack a female counterpart. By the late 2020s, a projected one in five men will be surplus. According to one estimate, marriageable women will remain scarce until 2045, leaving around 15 percent of men lacking potential wives.[16] In another calculation, the number of Chinese surplus men in their twenties will soon outstrip the entire female population of Taiwan.[17] A similar scenario will play out across Asia. Between 15 and 20 percent of men in northwestern India will be surplus by 2020, a significant change in a society where until now the proportion of men who remain bachelors has hovered around 1 percent.[18] Scholars haven't yet begun to calculate the effect the sex ratio imbalance will have on marriage rates in Armenia, Albania, and Georgia. But high levels of female migration in the region could make the fate of boys there even bleaker.**

---

*Indian men are relatively better off because the country's fertility rate is higher.
**While it was once men who left for Western Europe or the United States in search of wage work, today women go in larger numbers, drawn in part by the demands of aging industrialized countries for more nurses and caretakers.

Some Chinese bachelors are following the example of Korean and Taiwanese bachelors in seeking wives in Vietnam. But most men in China and India can't afford to go abroad to find women. Instead, they seek wives from impoverished regions within their own borders. At a 2003 Congressional-Executive Commission on China forum on women's rights, historian and gender studies professor Christina Gilmartin said the number of domestic marriage migrants in China—largely poor peasants' daughters who marry men in wealthier areas—had reached 4 million. The figure is bound to increase, Gilmartin added, as the sex ratio imbalance worsens.[19]

Where scholars don't monitor the flow of women across regions and borders, it can be tracked by comparing the sex ratio at birth of a particular area with its adult sex ratio twenty or thirty years later—by counting how many girls are born in the area and then plotting that figure against how many remain or are added to the population as a generation grows up. The results are startling. Trouble spots like northwest India and eastern China, where baby girls are in short supply, have much more normal sex ratios among marriage-age adults. That disparity is made possible by a massive trade in girls and adult women.[20]

⊶⊷

To a degree, East Asia's marriage agencies are like American mail-order bride services, playing to the desire of some men for feminine and subservient wives. Vietnamese women, the agencies' marketing materials claim, care about family. They listen to their husbands. They are "traditional." Graeme Hugo, an Australian geographer and migration scholar at the University of Adelaide who has studied the trade, says many of the Asian men who use agencies approach the process with chauvinistic ideas about the kind of woman they want. "They're looking for a very different type of partner, one who is less questioning and more submissive," he says.[21]

But unlike American companies, which tend to exoticize foreign women, the Taiwanese and Korean companies emphasize the Vietnamese brides' sameness. The websites give the sense that they serve men who are simply longing for a woman—any woman, but particularly the girl next door. "As I run an agency for Vietnamese brides," writes a Taiwanese broker on the site www.vietnambride.tw, "people often ask me: Vietnamese

brides, mainland Chinese brides, Russian brides, Ukrainian brides—
which are best? If you ask me this question, I'll answer you this way: I
think Vietnamese brides, mainland Chinese brides, Russian brides, Ukrainian brides, and other foreign brides are all bad! Taiwanese brides are the
best!"[22] But, the broker continues, if you can't find a Taiwanese wife, Vietnam is a good option, and to that end she is here to help.

Vietnam is a popular source of women in part because—unlike
Thailand, Cambodia, or the Philippines—it shares some traditions with
its East Asian neighbors. A long history of Chinese influence has left the
Vietnamese with a Confucian hierarchy, a similar approach to ancestor
worship and lineage, and a mostly patriarchal family structure. Cheng
Ching-huang, the Taiwanese farmer, can tick off a list of these similari-
ties: both Taiwanese and Vietnamese worship at Buddhist temples, both
place family altars in their homes, and both celebrate the lunar new year.
Men like him are not seeking exoticism. They just want wives.*

Another difference between West and East when it comes to marrying foreign women is that in Asia the import of brides is encouraged by
governments intent on bringing up sluggish birth rates.[23] One South
Korean province briefly sponsored trips to Vietnam, covering men's expenses as they went in search of women, and the national government
now endorses the trade in other ways, recently setting aside around $23
million for adaptation programs for new brides.[24] Most of these programs focus on assimilating the women to Korean culture: foreign brides
can take courses in which they learn to speak Korean, deal with in-laws,
and make kimchi. Korean roadways, meanwhile, are dotted with advertisements for marriage agencies that declare

A VIETNAMESE DAUGHTER-IN-LAW OBEYS.

and

FAST AND SUCCESSFUL MARRIAGE WITH FILIPINO,
CAMBODIAN, AND VIETNAMESE WOMEN.[25]

---

*Similarly, Korean men often seek ethnically similar wives in Uzbekistan and main-
land China, both of which have Korean minorities.

The Taiwanese government has made a greater effort to safeguard the rights of Vietnamese women. Newly matched couples seeking marriage permits are required to undergo a course in Ho Chi Minh City outlining Taiwanese law on everything from domestic violence to inheritance.[26] But the government focuses on regulating the process, not stopping it, so that brides arriving in Taiwan can obtain the 130-page *Handbook of Living Information for Foreign Spouses in Taiwan*, which is conveniently printed in Vietnamese, Thai, Burmese, Cambodian, and Indonesian.[27]

And this is just the beginning. Taiwan and South Korea are small countries, and the impact they can have on the balance of sexes in a country like Vietnam is limited. As the Chinese and Indian economies take off and men in those countries make enough money to look abroad for wives, the repercussions will be grave. Already interest in marriage agencies has been piqued in China by Internet testimonials from men like Dai Wensheng, who bought a wife from Vietnam in 2009. "Most women I met in Vietnam are traditional, low maintenance, and quietly charming," Dai wrote on a forum a few months after settling with his new bride in the city of Nanjing. "My Vietnamese wife takes care of the laundry, cooking, and cleaning, and even peels the shells off shrimp for me. For the first time, I feel loved and spoiled."[28]

Doo-Sub Kim, a migration scholar in Seoul specialized in Asia's marriage trade, told me the resettlement of poorer Asian women in South Korea, Taiwan, and Singapore could augur a massive scramble for females elsewhere on the continent. This is just the tip of the iceberg, he says: "In the next twenty-five years, if the situation we have here [in Korea] continues in China, there's going to be a huge migration from Southeast Asian countries to the mainland. It's going to be total chaos."

Despite the rising number of bought brides and other evidence to the contrary, some scholars stubbornly maintain the laws of supply and demand apply to gender—that the value of women rises as their ranks thin. "As children become adults in cohorts with a high ratio of boys [to girls]," wrote economist Gary Becker and theorist Richard Posner in 2009, "the advantage of girls and women increases since they are scarcer." (Economists are particularly prone to this mode of thinking.) In a society with a sex ratio imbalance, the scholars continue, it is men, and not women, who find themselves at a disadvantage: as "the value of girls as wives and girlfriends, and in other ways, rises because they are scarcer . . . the value of boys as husbands and boyfriends tends to fall."[29]

This assessment is true only in the crudest sense. For women born into high sex ratio areas, scarcity can give them more bargaining power when it comes time to marry. In wealthy cities in eastern China, men now complain that women won't marry a suitor unless he has a house, a car, and a good job.[30] But attracting a high bride-price is not the same as gaining more autonomy, and the increased value experienced by the eastern Chinese woman occurs only on the most basic level, since the real test of equality is not what material goods a woman can ask a man to deliver but how she can expect him to treat her after marriage. A groom in a high sex ratio area may be kind and appreciative of his new wife, or he may fixate on the amount of capital he amassed in order to attract her and watch her like a hawk out of fear she will leave him. No majority group has ever aspired to become a minority under the illusion that a decrease in numbers will somehow lead to the group's members to be more valued by the rest of society, and so it is with women. And in the case of women born into poor areas where they are likely to be bought, an imbalance often makes life considerably worse.

Asia's imported brides typically arrive in their new countries unable to speak their husband's language and dependent on the men for money and immigration status. Almost always they are younger, with the age gap frequently extending to fifteen to twenty years.[31] Youth is important because the women are expected to produce babies, but they are also chosen on looks, and sometimes on more archaic qualities. The Singaporean agency Life Partner Matchmaker medically examines its Vietnamese brides to ensure they are virgins. (Other agencies, warns founder Janson Ong in a video posted on the agency's website, simply teach women how to fake it.)[32] Since these are not what most marriage counselors would describe as the ingredients of a lasting relationship, the women have their work cut out for them.

Of the bought brides I met in Taiwan, South Korea, and China, only Nguyen Thi Mai Chau seemed to have achieved anything approaching contentment, and even hers was fleeting: two weeks after my visit Cheng Ching-huang suffered a heart attack while out tending his persimmon trees. He died soon after. In the months that followed, his family chipped in to help Nguyen make ends meet. Still, money became so tight that she had to relinquish the farmland Cheng had rented and apply for assistance from the Taiwanese government, which sets aside funds for foreign women whose husbands pass away as part of its support program for bought brides. There was no question, it seemed, of Nguyen returning with her children to Vietnam.

❧

Most foreign brides live a life closer to that of Do Thi Nguyet, a thirty-four-year-old woman with a heart-shaped face, neatly permed hair, and a deep scar slicing across her nose. I meet Nguyet in the small eatery she runs outside Taipei, in an area that is rapidly becoming the city's Little Vietnam. She sets down the knife with which she has been chopping vegetables to talk to me, wiping her hands on a red apron and taking a seat at a greasy folding table. Around us, customers are slurping noodles, chatting away in Vietnamese, and silently tending babies. All but one are women.

I ask Nguyet how she came to live in Taiwan, thinking it a good warm-up question.

She bursts into tears.

Over a decade ago, Nguyet left her village in the Mekong Delta to marry a Taiwanese man fourteen years her senior. When she arrived in Taiwan her dreams of sending money home to her parents were quickly shattered. She discovered her new husband was an abusive philanderer with no job, an alcohol problem, and domineering live-in parents who treated her like a servant. But there were few other options available to her, and so she stayed. As the years rolled by, she gave her husband two children, raised them to adolescence, and even arranged for her older sister to journey from Vietnam to marry her husband's brother.

After her sister arrived, she finally worked up the courage to leave. The two women divorced their husbands on the same day, moved into a rented house, and opened a café with their meager savings. In the legal battle that followed, Nguyet's husband won custody of their children. But the children continued to run to her to be fed and clothed, and now here she is, a single immigrant mother of two, serving up bowls of noodles to make ends meet. I ask Nguyet what she would say to Vietnamese women from her village who are contemplating marrying Taiwanese men, and she replies without hesitation. "I would tell them not to do it," she says. "Taiwan is good. But the men who want to marry Vietnamese women are not."

Later I learn of more extreme cases and realize that Nguyet is fortunate, in a twisted way, in that her ex-husband at least allowed her to get a divorce. In Seoul I stop by the Korean Women Migrants Human Rights Center, an NGO set up by feminists to empower foreign brides. The center operates a shelter for women who are victims of domestic violence. All twelve spots are full, and activist Yeong Sug-heo tells me she has to turn away women in need of help. One-fourth of foreign wives in Korea report feeling physically threatened by their husbands.[33]

Even so, Yeong says only a fraction of abused women ever visit centers like hers. Many have mothers-in-law who won't let them out of the house, she says: "They paid a lot of money to get the women, so they trap them and keep them from going out." Occasionally wife abuse escalates into a headline-grabbing incident. In the summer of 2010, twenty-year-old Vietnamese Thach Thi Hoang Ngoc was stabbed to death by her forty-seven-year-old husband just eight days after she arrived in South Korea.[34]

In Taiwan, meanwhile, Vietnamese Catholic priest Peter Hung ministers to suffering brides in the industrial city of Taoyuan, arranging legal representation for runaways and sheltering them in the building attached to his church. "There are so many problems," Hung tells me when I meet him at his shelter, which he calls the Vietnamese Migrant Workers and Brides Office, one Sunday afternoon. He talks about a woman whose Taiwanese mother-in-law forced her to watch pornography in the belief it would help her produce a baby, of a woman married to a mentally ill man, of a woman who has herself gone crazy.* We talk in a small office on

---

*Another case reported by the Taiwanese press involved a man who tortured his wife for seven months, binding her hands with duct tape, shooting rubber bands at her eyelids, and cutting her with a small knife.

the second floor of the shelter while in the next room a handful of escaped women gather around a karaoke machine, singing to a backdrop of tinny synchronizer beats. The incongruously joyous music wafts through the thin office door. "So many problems," Hung continues. "But I think the most serious one is that the concept of marriage for these Taiwanese isn't marriage. It is buying and selling." Indeed, in 2004 three Vietnamese women were listed for sale, at the bargain price of $5,400 each, on Taiwan's eBay.[35]

⸺ ⚬⚬⚬ ⸺

Even the harshest critics of the marriage trade are quick to point out that it is reshaping Asia's homogeneous societies in interesting ways. In South Korea and Taiwan, the children born to mixed marriages pose a powerful challenge to a prevailing concept of nationality that is deeply linked to race. Once, biracial children of American servicemen stationed in Korea were ostracized. Now international marriages happen with such frequency—and produce, on average, more children than marriages between two Koreans—that exclusion is not an option. In India, meanwhile, interregional marriage is breaking down the caste hierarchy. "Now because of [female] scarcity you see marrying outside of caste," says Sharada Srinivasan, the feminist sociologist I met in Christophe Guilmoto's living room. "Some of these barriers that go back a long time are beginning to weaken, and in some cases women are being married without dowries. So there might be some good coming out of this."

Women who migrate as brides also manage to send money home. Either at the wedding or in the months following it, Vietnamese families typically receive $1,000 to $2,000 in exchange for their daughters.[36] This is only a fraction of what men pay to agencies, but on later visits home a woman may bring as much as $10,000—nearly ten times Vietnam's per capita income—in gifts.[37] That amount has surprised many of the scholars who study the trade, and efforts to understand exactly what happens after men marry foreign women have yielded unexpected discoveries. In some cases, new brides convince their husbands to periodically fork over cash as a sort of guarantee of a harmonious marriage. In others, women earn money themselves by taking low-paid work upon arrival in Korea or Taiwan. "It's wrong to depict all of these women as victims," says Hugo, the Australian geographer who studies marriage migration. "It's clear that some of them become empowered at the destination."

To an extent, the increased earning potential of Vietnamese women who marry abroad has raised their status within their families. Because they furnish the cash that pays for remodeling projects, new appliances, and their brothers' weddings, overseas daughters are often consulted on important decisions.[38] But at the end of the day a Vietnamese bride is still mostly a medium for transferring money. Her value has risen, but again only crudely, benefiting her husband, her marriage broker, and her parents—everyone but herself.

Before he passed away, Cheng Ching-huang told me he recognized his marriage put his wife in a difficult situation. Vietnamese parents, he said, are typically more concerned about accruing appliances than they are about their daughters' happiness. "When you go back, they just look at how much money you're bringing," he said. "They don't care whether or not you're good to your wife."

To Lena Edlund, the Columbia University economist who uncovered evidence of sex selective abortion among Asian Americans, that makes intuitive sense. She finds economists who apply supply-and-demand logic to women maddening. "Okay, the value of a woman goes up" as the total number of women decreases, she says. "But does that mean that she will enjoy higher status? Not necessarily. Because she might be sold by her parents, or she might be kidnapped. So it's a bit of a paradox, but the more valuable women become, the higher the risk that they might get deprived of that value. Somebody might try to capture it."

Supply-and-demand reasoning also ignores the roles women are expected to play in high sex ratio societies. In Taiwan, South Korea, and other areas where females are scarce, women are coveted as wives, mothers, caregivers, housekeepers, and sex partners; when men list the qualities they hope to find in a Vietnamese wife, they do not mention intellect or a sense of humor or a desire to build an equal partnership. Historically, high sex ratio societies have exceptionally low rates of literacy and female workforce participation, and today's skewed societies maintain an emphasis on traditional gender roles.[39] Women who conform to those roles are valued, while those who buck expectations—by choosing to become

lawyers or scientists, to remain unmarried, or to not have children—are
perceived as threatening.

∽∾∿

Life on Tan Loc is regulated by the monsoon. The rain starts like clock-
work every morning around 11:00 and pounds down long enough to fill
the island's motor paths and swell the river that encircles it to capacity. In
the hours that follow locals wait for the water to recede. Afternoons are
languorous, with the island finally waking up again at dusk. The weather
is a stark reminder that one's fate is tied to the land, that to be born into
a Mekong village is to have your future circumscribed by your origins.
Perhaps that is why so many women leave to marry foreign men—why a
decade or so into the marriage trade, Tan Loc is also known as Taiwan
Island.[40]

I travel to Tan Loc on a motor scooter driven by Ms. Ha, a moonlight-
ing middle-aged tour guide who accosted me in the lobby of my hotel,
handing me a card that read, "Mekong Delta experience: People in the
street pretending to be my brother or sister lie." A contact had inquired
about a trip to Tan Loc on my behalf, but local officials apparently wary
of the coverage the trade in brides was getting had sent back word that
I was not welcome on the island, and that if I came they would know. So
I invented a weak alibi and set out instead as a tourist. (Before departing,
Ms. Ha and I mapped out a route to a stork sanctuary, one of the area's
few tourist attractions, that conveniently passed through Tan Loc.)

Forty percent of people in Can Tho province live in poverty, and I expected to find the ride depressing.[41] Instead Ms. Ha's motor scooter trav-
erses clean villages dotted with brightly colored houses and lush, thriving
gardens. When after an hour on the road we arrive at Tan Loc, it turns
out to be the nicest village of all—its motor path newly paved, its houses
freshly painted and tiled, their courtyards swept clean and guarded by
shiny stainless steel gates. In the surrounding villages, the gardens were
mostly practical plots filled with cucumbers, green beans, and eggplants.
On Tan Loc, they are decorative accents bursting with colorful flowers.

Local women started marrying Taiwanese men in the late 1990s, and
by the turn of the millennium the outward flow of women had begun to

change the island's fabric. As newlywed brides remitted payments to the parents who had sold them, Western Union set up a branch on Tan Loc, and from that point on money flowed in easily. It is customary in this part of Vietnam to carve the year a house is built into the doorframe, and the structures erected after the island's women started marrying foreigners—the houses whose frames read 2001 and 2004 and 2007—are outrageous things painted baby blue or mint green or bubblegum pink and sometimes all three and topped with Spanish tile roofs holding humongous television antennas. (Families in the Tan Loc area who have sent women abroad are more likely to own televisions—along with radios, motor scooters, cell phones, and air conditioners—than families with no women overseas.)[42] A few buildings have overgrown their foundations, yielding a sort of architecture on steroids.

Small one-story houses built earlier, meanwhile, have mushroomed into three-story towers outfitted with fake brick exteriors, tile patios, and appendages galore—porches, decks, balconies. Still others are works in progress, their exteriors crisscrossed with scaffolding and their yards strewn with paint cans. Several front doors are adorned with bright red cardboard cutout "double happiness" characters—signals of recent weddings.

But the story of Tan Loc is not entirely rosy. Before leaving for the island, I met Xoan Nguyen, a sociologist at Vietnam National University, at a coffee shop in Ho Chi Minh City. A thin, bubbly woman clad in a flouncy shirt, jeans, and flip-flops that reveal silver toenails, Nguyen focuses, unlike most scholars who study the marriage trade, on its impact on Vietnam. In her fieldwork, she catalogs overlooked details: the traits shared by women who marry foreigners, how much money they send back after they leave, and how many get divorced. (This last figure is striking, she says, but you wouldn't know it from looking at the demographic makeup of a place like Tan Loc. A large number of women return to Vietnam but only stay long enough to find a new foreign husband.)

Nguyen also looks at the effect the bride exodus has on local men. "A lot of ladies already have boyfriends, but the boyfriends are poor, so they leave them to find some Korean or Taiwanese men," she says. In 2005 she coauthored a study that found in some Mekong districts as many as half of recent weddings were between local women and Taiwanese men.[43]

"The men who are left behind have no chance to find partners," she continues. "It's very sad."

During my day on Tan Loc I meet no women over thirty. The island is, however, filled with young men and boys. Before we leave, Ms. Ha and I stop at an open-air café near the ferry for some noodles. The café's customer base is exclusively male, and as we wait for our food I count over a dozen young men in various iterations of boredom: men drinking tea, men napping in the hammock, men playing billiards at a table whose green felt has worn down to a colorless nub.

After a while the loungers come together from their corners of the café and gather around a folding table, where the younger ones watch as the older ones begin a game of poker. They play for cigarettes, the action punctuated by dramatic gasps and fists pounding on the table and exclamations Ms. Ha translates as "Oh my god!" One of the bystanders wears a white T-shirt adorned with a sketch of a naked woman in profile. The caption reads, "What Men Want."

In Vietnam, as in China, even marriage between two locals typically involves a bride-price to the bride's family. But such payments never rivaled the amount of money that changes hands in marriages to foreigners—until recently, when competition started driving bride-price up. Should the men in the café succeed in finding women to marry, saving up enough money to secure the deal will be a challenge: parents of local young women now require suitors to furnish as much as twice the amount of goods they once did.[44] In 2007 Tran Giang Linh, a researcher at the Institute for Social Development Studies in Hanoi, surveyed hundreds of households in the Tan Loc area. "Almost all young pretty local women [have] already married abroad," one single man told her. "We—poor men—really have difficulty in getting married. Many of my friends had to find wives in . . . other proximate communes. I am also thinking about [doing] that."[45]

To make matters worse, Vietnam's own sex ratio imbalance means that by 2040 an additional 4.3 million men, mainly in the northern part of the country, will be unable to find wives.[46] Since most Vietnamese men can't afford to buy women from overseas, the imbalance will further increase pressure on the Mekong region to supply women.

———∽∾∾∾∽———

The struggles of men in Tan Loc suggest one of the ugliest features of the trade in brides: the people who select for boys are not the same ones who have to watch their sons grow old alone. Just as globalization allows consumers to buy cheap goods without considering the toll those goods take on the workers who produce them, so too does it allow parents to ignore the impact of their actions by hiding away the unsavory aftermath of sex selective abortion in places like Tan Loc. Wealthy parents in Taiwan and South Korea make decisions, while poor families in Vietnam feel their effects.

The Vietnamese government has not been entirely passive in the face of its women leaving, and officials have tried to staunch the flow of women to neighboring countries. After 2000, when more than 220 women were found crammed into seven rooms at a business hotel in downtown Ho Chi Minh City, where they were being held by brokers as they awaited selection by foreign men, the Hanoi government cracked down on the marriage trade.[47] State-run newspapers ran features debunking the Taiwan Dream. "Taiwan Disillusionment," the headlines called it.[48] In 2002 the government outlawed matchmaking agencies.[49]

But sociologist Nguyen says the crackdown simply had the effect of pushing the trade underground. After leaving their villages, women now gather in Cholon, Ho Chi Minh's Chinatown, where they are held in grimy back alley motels, packed six or more to a room, to await inspection by Taiwanese and Korean men. Waiting is not merely unpleasant. It is also a liability, for in some agency deals men have to cover the lodging fees of their new wives, making a woman who has sat on the shelf for weeks costly. A second consequence of the crackdown has been to propel the trade in women to the poorest corners of the earth. According to a 2008 International Organization for Migration report, the Asian marriage trade is now expanding into Cambodia.[50] The sex ratio imbalance has spawned a matrimonial race to the bottom.

When sex selective abortion arrives in the Mekong region, meanwhile, some scholars believe it will carry a twist: locals will select for girls. "Daughters nowadays are more preferable than sons because daughters can marry abroad and help families economically," a villager told Tran Giang Linh, the researcher who surveyed locals on the trade in women.[51] "Many people . . . feel unfortunate that they do not have daughters at marriageable ages," a middle-aged resident informed Nguyen in a focus group she conducted in An Giang province.*[52]

If the surveyed parents make good on these desires, Vietnam's sex ratio at birth will become more balanced—but the child populations of other, still poorer countries could start to skew female. As sex selection technology becomes cheaper, more sophisticated, and more widely available, and as the number of boys born to the world's upper and middle classes increases, predicts Lena Edlund in one paper, the poor will sense an opportunity: to select for daughters who can then be sold to wealthier families. "[T]he greatest danger associated with prenatal sex determination," she writes, "is the propagation of a female underclass."[53] In this scenario, we are left with a reality in which gender divides along income and class lines, and women go from not being born to being born into poverty.

---

*Similarly, in parts of Asia where large numbers of women go into sex work, parents tell researchers they celebrate the births of girls. In the 2001 book *Sex Slaves*, Louise Brown writes of rural Nepal: "[T]he birth of a daughter here is no longer a cause for lament. Sex work has given them a market value."

Chapter 12

THE PROSTITUTE

Our national ability to pick up chicks will reach heights unparalleled in human history.

—2007 FORUM THREAD ON THE SKEWED SEX RATIO
AT BIRTH ON THE CHINESE PORTAL TIANYA.CN[1]

The girls said good-bye to the madam and left the brothel, making their way down the unfamiliar Chinese street in the murky early evening light. One was sixteen and the other only fifteen. They were out for the first time in a foreign country, and yet they were calm; so far everything was going as planned. They walked toward the appointed hotel slowly and deliberately, thinking their pimp wouldn't bother to follow them. His policy of allowing girls to leave the brothel and visit customers in pairs, they figured, was based on a sort of perverse confidence, on the belief that everything he had put his prostitutes through—the kidnapping and the furtive border crossing, the crass sale of their virginity to the highest bidder, and the months of having sex with seventeen customers a day without pay—had left them meek and untrusting. One girl might flee, but never two. They thought they were not being watched, and so halfway to the hotel, when they spotted the taxi waiting in the appointed place alongside the road, they scrambled inside without bothering to glance behind them.

When their eyes fixed on the other passengers, the two men who spoke their language and knew their trauma and had come to rescue them from it, the girls relaxed, and for the first time in seven months they experienced a feeling close to security. Lam Huong Duong, the fifteen-year-old, had reason to feel especially relieved, as the soft round face of one of the men was familiar, a reminder of the classes and after-school activities and other adolescent doings she had left behind in Hanoi.* Settling into the seat, perhaps edging close to the other girl, she waited.

The familiar-looking man, whose name was Tran Tuan Dung, signaled to the driver to pull away, and the taxi sped off toward the Vietnam border, toward the country they called home. And then the plan unraveled. The girls had been riding in the speeding taxi for just a few minutes when they looked out the rear window to see two men racing toward the car on a motorcycle. They didn't recognize the men, but in a flash they realized they must have been sent by the brothel to hunt them down. Perhaps it was the fact that the man on the back of the motorcycle wielded a long metal rod, which he was shaking menacingly at the taxi.

The next thing they knew, the motorcycle was racing alongside the car, and the girls watched in horror as the man on the back of the vehicle swung the metal bar toward the taxi's side windows. "Go! Go!" they heard Tran yell to the taxi driver. He shouted in Vietnamese, a language the driver didn't speak, but the message was obvious. The driver motioned that he wanted more money, and Tran shoved a few sweaty red hundred yuan notes into his hand. Finally the driver stepped on the gas and the car lurched forward. Just kilometers ahead beckoned the border and the prospect of freedom. But speeding right behind them was the motorcycle. The girls watched silently as the vehicle's driver accelerated and the gap between the motorcycle and their car closed once again. They said nothing, but inwardly they must have wondered whether they'd reach the border before the thugs bashed in their windshield.

Tran eyed the road ahead as he struggled to get control of the situation. A lawyer by training, he had never dreamed his work would one day entail cross-border rescue operations. After graduating from law school,

---

*The name of the trafficked girl, along with the name of the NGO worker who rescued her, has been changed.

he decided corporate law wasn't for him and took a job as legal representative for a Hanoi NGO that works with poor children. Then one day Lam, the daughter of scrap metal collectors from poor central Vietnam and a good student, disappeared. Tran knew trafficking networks targeted disadvantaged girls, kidnapping them off the streets of Hanoi and shuttling them across the border to China, where they were often sold into prostitution. The trade had picked up over the past few years, as China's first cohort of surplus men came of age and demand for prostitutes spiked. An increasing number of Vietnamese girls were now forced into marriage as well. Tran's worst fears were confirmed when a coworker finally received a frantic phone call from Lam, who said she had been kidnapped and was being held in a brothel somewhere in China. She was scared, she said, and she wanted someone to come get her. She had pieced together the name of the town where she was: Hochai. And that was all she knew.[2]

As the NGO's lawyer, Tran took the case to the Vietnamese authorities. But the Hanoi police came back with discouraging news. Because this was an international case, they told him, investigating would require a special permit allowing the officers to cross into China. Obtaining that would take time, which was precisely what Tran didn't have. He decided to take justice into his own hands.

Friends at the International Organization for Migration told him Hochai was a small satellite of Pingxiang, a major crossing point along the Vietnamese-Chinese border that had lately become a hot spot for trafficking. Tran recruited a colleague to accompany him, got a three-day visa to China, and set off for the border.

Hochai's downtown covered only a few blocks, and the red-light district—sizable for such a small town—was not hard to find. It consisted of a collection of dingy buildings (some lit by actual red lights), flanked by women in tiny shorts, high heels, and caked-on makeup. Tran had no idea which brothel held a frightened Lam, so he started at one end of the street and worked his way down to the other, entering each institution and asking to see the girls line up. When they stood at attention, he greeted the girls one by one, surveying them up and down as if they were goods for sale in a store. "*Nihao, xiaojie,*" he said to each girl, trying to hide the fact he was Vietnamese. "Hello, miss." Then he left, feigning disappointment.

The girls were too ugly, or too thin, or too timid, he explained as the madams showed him to the door. Finally in the eighth brothel he entered, he stayed. It was there that he spotted Lam.

Tran and Lam hatched the escape plan in a tiny room reeking of semen and furnished only with a thin, heavily soiled mattress shoved into one corner. Tran couldn't help thinking that if he were the sort of man who paid for sex, he would never want to do it in that room. But on that day the room that embodied Lam's imprisonment became the site that gave rise to her freedom. She was intent on escaping, and she had been watching her pimps and madam carefully, searching for gaps in their vigilance. She told Tran of the one that appeared most promising: a call from a hotel, a request for two girls at once, and a taxi surreptitiously waiting along the road.

That day, in that dirty room, the plan had seemed solid. But Lam hadn't considered that the pimp would be one step ahead of her—that she was not the first to attempt to escape from a daily regime of sleeping with surplus men. As the taxi raced along, she and the other runaway slunk down into their seats. The men who had traveled so far to rescue them trembled. All four of them thought about the border, about the homes that awaited them beyond that line, and hoped.

The story of Lam's rescue is unusual for its thrilling cross-border drama: for the crusader who sets out single-handedly to recover a girl from her abductors, and for the lucky coincidences and harrowing misadventures that ensue. But what happened to the girl up until that point—the kidnapping, the journey to a distant and unfamiliar land, and the loss of her virginity to a man who purchased it—is disturbingly common. In recent years an estimated thousands of Vietnamese women and girls have been trafficked to China.[3] Some of those women end up, like Lam, in Chinese brothels. Many others—by some accounts the largest share of Vietnamese female trafficking victims—are sold into marriage with Chinese men in high sex ratio provinces.[4] Such unions have none of the niceties of those arranged by Asia's marriage agencies. Gone are the photo exchanges, the gifts to the bride's family, the professions of love. The vast majority of trafficked Vietnamese females are never rescued.

The illicit trade in women from Vietnam to China goes back to at least the nineteenth century, when Southeast Asia was under French rule. Back then colonial officers in Tonkin, or what is now Hanoi, catalogued case after case of young girls being kidnapped by crooks and sold to gangs of traffickers. The traffickers dressed the girls in Chinese clothing and posed as their parents in order to smuggle them across the border. Even as colonial administrators attempted to crack down on the practice, French soldiers allegedly aided the traffickers.[5] After the French lost control of Indochina, the shady networks endured, expanding and contracting as demand for women ebbed and flowed. But today the gangs are more active than ever.

This is attributable in part to a cooling of international tensions. In 1992, after decades of fraught relations, the Chinese and Vietnamese governments agreed to reopen the border between their two countries, greatly simplifying the work of traffickers.[6] But the spike in kidnapping and sex trafficking has a larger and more direct cause, which is that as more and more surplus males have come of age in China, demand for females has skyrocketed. From 2004 to 2010, nearly two-thirds of trafficking busts by Vietnamese authorities involved women and children destined for China.[7]

Some women depart Vietnam with a rough idea of where they will end up. They reach their early thirties, an unmarriageable age in rural Vietnam, or find themselves divorced, a difficult status in gossipy villages, and leave with the vague expectation of finding work or a husband in China. Others are kept completely in the dark from the beginning. They are approached in the market, or on the street, with an enticing pitch—*I know where there's work; I'll find you a job that's better than this one; carry this bag across the border and you'll get a wad of cash in return.* Often the person who makes the pitch is another woman.[8]

Lam was captured through a strategy attuned to the interests of urban teens. She first encountered her traffickers online, in a chat room where she met what she thought was a nice teenage boy. After a few conversations she and the boy set a date to meet in person. When she showed up at the appointed place, she was kidnapped.

I learn of Lam's story from Doan Thuy Dung and Nguyen Quoc Nam, anti-trafficking activists with the International Organization for Migration whom I meet in a conference room in a Hanoi skyscraper. Doan and

Nguyen work on reducing the flow of women away from villages in northern Vietnam. It is an uphill battle, they say, because trafficking has become so pervasive. The number of women trafficked as sex workers, in particular, has grown over the past decade. Trafficking "happens everywhere," says Nguyen, a man with a voice so soft it competes with the motor scooter and car honks from the Hanoi streets seven floors down. "If you go to any province or any commune, you hear about it from the people there." The trade is especially difficult to thwart in cases where traffickers target their own communities, he adds.[9] In interviews IOM researchers did with hundreds of returned victims in Quang Ninh, a Vietnamese province bordering China, 70 percent of trafficked women and girls said they had followed someone they knew.[10] Youth, and the innocence that comes with it, is another obstacle. Twenty percent of the women surveyed in Quang Ninh were eighteen or under at the time they were trafficked.[11] Nguyen believes that percentage is now larger. "If you look at the victims," he says, "their ages are becoming younger and younger."

Doan nods vigorously, her face framed by rectangular red glasses. "Some are just eleven or twelve," she pipes in. "Even ten."

The number of prostitutes in China has exploded since 1980s economic reforms began allowing for freer internal migration, with an estimated ten million sex workers flooding the country's booming cities.[12] But with demand for prostitutes rising and fewer Chinese females to go around, foreign women are now highly coveted, and to be a poor woman living on the outskirts of the rooster-shaped Middle Kingdom is to be at risk. Because of its history of trafficking, Vietnam has been particularly hard hit, but in other countries bordering China the outlook for young girls is similarly bleak. Along China's western border, Burmese women enter China through the town of Ruili, which is thronged with matchmakers and brothels. In northeastern China, meanwhile, a major source of females is North Korea, where, as in Myanmar, the cruel mixture of authoritarianism and poverty makes women eager to leave. They do so in such numbers that in 2010 the director of the Durihana Association, an organization that aids North Korean refugees, told Agence France-Presse that 80 percent of the tens of thousands of North Koreans living in China are female.[13] The refugees typically arrive in China with no money or job prospects, and many end up as prostitutes or bought brides, beholden to pimps for whom the trade in women has become increasingly lucrative.[14] Observers say a refugee woman for sale brings in ten times the money she did just twenty years ago.[15]

Asia's thriving sex trade cannot be blamed on the gender imbalance alone. In recent years economic growth has also brought more personal and social freedoms, relaxed sexual mores, and a hyper-commercialization of nearly everything. Combine those three and you get a continent-wide realization that sex sells. But the gender imbalance is, at the very least, a contributing factor. The U.S. Department of State's annual *Trafficking in Persons Report* lists the dearth of women in Asia as one of the principal causes of sex trafficking in the region. "A major consequence of the widening gender imbalance is the increased demand for forced marriages and prostitution," Mark Lagon, director of the department's Office to Monitor and Combat Trafficking in Persons, told an audience of policymakers in Washington, DC, in 2008. "The lack of women contributes to greater demand for prostituted women and girls . . . fueling the demand for victims of trafficking."[16] Researchers at the Chinese Academy of Social Sciences echoed that finding in 2010 interviews in which they said forced prostitution and human trafficking have become "rampant" as a result of the country's gender imbalance.[17]

And while international trafficking gets more attention, Asia is also witnessing a flourishing trade in *intra*national trafficking, from western to eastern China and northeastern to northwestern India—a process that can be just as jarring for its victims. Like a kidnapped Vietnamese girl shuttled across the border in the dead of night, the purchased rural Chinese or Indian preteen often has minimal to no knowledge about where she will end up.

Historically, prostitution thrives in places where men outnumber women. In nineteenth-century France, brothels flourished in the wake of industrialization, which spawned an urban migration that left cities full of men.[18] A similar phenomenon occurred in 1930s Shanghai, where according to estimates from the time one in every thirteen women was a prostitute.[19] Today too, brothels in Asia have proliferated where the sex ratio is most skewed. Countrywide, China has a higher rate of prostitution than the United States, with 13 percent of men between the ages of twenty-one and thirty reporting they have been to a prostitute. In a recent analysis based on a 2000 Chinese health survey, economists Avraham Ebenstein and Ethans Jennings Sharygin found that percentage is even higher in counties with large populations of single men.[20] In Suining, the Jiangsu province town where I first interviewed parents about sex selective abortion, locals now refer to one stretch of downtown simply as *ji'nü jie*—Prostitute Street. Prostitutes even work the town's surrounding farmland, their lipstick stark red against the muted greens and browns of the rice paddies and wheat fields.

Sex workers who enter the profession out of choice, meanwhile, recognize that the skewed sex ratio is good for business. As demand for their services rises, they are starting to organize. In July 2010 prostitutes in the Chinese city of Wuhan took to the streets with red umbrellas—the symbol used by defenders of sex workers' rights around the world—to protest government crackdowns on prostitution and circulate a petition calling for its legalization. "This kind of suppression will never last," wrote one of the protesters, who goes by the moniker Hooligan Sparrow, on her blog. "With the gender ratio out of proportion, sexual constraints on single [men] have created enormous social demand."*[21]

——— ⚭ ———

While the proliferation of prostitutes in China is especially striking, anti-trafficking workers stress that gangs sell women into both sex work and marriage, and the majority of trafficked women end up as bought brides, invisible farmers' wives disappeared into village routine. According to one local NGO report, ninety percent of Burmese women trafficked to China end up in forced marriages.[22] The bulk of North Korean women, too, are purchased by men seeking wives.[23] Nguyen and Doan, of the IOM, say they have heard of Vietnamese women sold into marriage to men living as far away as Inner Mongolia. Forced marriage has become common enough in Asia that it has joined female genital muti-

---

*She has a point. At moments throughout history, governments have encouraged prostitution as a means of placating men in high sex ratio societies. The British government once sent a ship of female convicts, many of them prostitutes, to frontier Australia to mollify male settlers.

lation, domestic abuse, and marital rape as a basis on which a woman can petition for political asylum in the United States.[24]

For a woman smuggled across provincial or national borders, then, fate could mean servicing dozens of men a day, or it could mean simply answering to one man, bearing his children, and struggling to adapt to life in a strange place cut off from friends and family. After looking into it, I wondered whether there was much difference.

In a village on the outskirts of Suining, I meet Zhang Mei, a thirty-seven-year-old village woman clad in men's pants and a black-and-white polka-dot shirt that billows around her thin frame. Zhang is from distant Yunnan province, from a poor mountain region near the border with Tibet, an area that has less in common with Suining than Tennessee does with Alaska. Her neighbors say she ended up in the village twenty years ago, after a long journey in which a trafficker took her east to deliver her into marriage. She had no idea where she was headed beyond the vague promise that she would find work there, and yet she had some faith in the trafficker, for she hadn't been kidnapped. Her parents had sold her.[25]

The trip east was not altogether bad. The trafficker took her through Kunming, Yunnan's capital, and her glimpse of that provincial outpost marked her first time in a city. Zhang remembers visiting the department store Yiliang General Merchandise, which for her represented modernity and all its promises. Someone snapped a photo of her outside, and in the surviving image her hair falls over one shoulder and flows down her chest in a shiny black wave, nearly reaching her waist. After arriving in Suining, however, she cut it. Urban glamour would elude Zhang, whose fate was to remain in the village, work the land, and have babies.

The man who became her husband was gentle, but fifteen years her senior, undeniably ugly, and one of the poorest residents of the village. She learned that she had to work hard to make ends meet, and that she could not leave, even for a short trip home. Today Zhang copes with lifelong detention by gambling at raucous village *majiang* games, burying herself in soap operas (on the afternoon of my visit, she watches one called *Women Don't Cry*), and praying. Like Liao Li, she belongs to the state-sanctioned Three Self church. "I carry some burdens," she tells me, as we sit on the couch in her one-room home. "If I didn't pray, I would keep them all in my heart."

Her family sends a steady stream of photos from Yunnan, allowing her to trace the growth of her sisters' children, the march of weddings, and the lunar new year reunions back home. She keeps those snapshots locked in a small drawer. The image that dominates her house in Suining, displayed just above the television, is an enlarged photo of her and her husband taken on their wedding day. The couple stands against a misty airbrushed backdrop, both clad in white. The groom is short, with big ears and hen eyes; the bride is solemn and pale, with a face coated in white powder. She looks like a bewildered ghost.

Perhaps the most perverse detail is that Zhang has, in a sense, repeated history. Soon after she married, she found herself under pressure to have a son. One came on the third try, after two girls. But as the children grew, her husband complained it cost too much to educate their daughters, and since it is sons that matter in Suining, he sent one of the girls back to Yunnan to be raised by Zhang's parents: a return, one generation later, of a lost girl. Later I wonder how far the parallel will extend—whether as the girl matures, she will be ushered onto the same path as her mother and sold into marriage to a stranger, sight unseen.

Zhang was an early migrant, arriving as Suining's sex ratio at birth was just starting to skew. But others soon followed. At the time of my visit, the sleepy village of a few hundred people was home to four women from Yunnan. Yunnan women are renowned across China for their cheapness, obedience, and availability. Google the characters for "Yunnan bride," and you will pull up thread upon thread of forum posts in which men trade their experiences in acquiring wives from China's poor southwestern province. According to provincial police statistics, over one thousand women and children are trafficked out of Yunnan every year. The actual total is probably much higher than that, as the fact that parents frequently sell their daughters makes cases difficult to track.[26]

In 2004 the International Labor Organization launched an anti-trafficking program in southwestern China in collaboration with the government-run All-China Women's Federation. Over several years, educators canvassed in the very mountains where Zhang Mei's traffickers bought her, distributing leaflets warning recipients about the dangers of leaving with the first person who approaches them on the street. The leaflets were rendered in cartoons—Yunnan's illiteracy rate is among the highest in China—and targeted at young women, for whom television, the Internet, and glowing reports from friends who have already left make the outside world irresistible.[27] But Zhu Hui'e, a former journalist and Yunnan native who oversaw the program, tells me getting the message across was a challenge. Ambitious teenagers realize the opportunities available to them if they stay in their villages are limited, and so the smartest women are in fact the most susceptible to trafficking. "Young people want to leave," she says. "There is nothing for them to do in the village after they grow up."

And Yunnan is merely the preferred source of women for now. In one Chinese forum thread on bride buying I read a commentator scoffed, "It's old-school to go to Yunnan to buy." A Yunnan girl averages around ¥5,000 ($760)—around the same price as a girl from Vietnam. In Shandong province, the bride buying expert claimed, women can be bought for a mere ¥3,000 to ¥4,000 ($460–$610).[28] While Taiwanese and Korean marriage agencies coat their deals in language that helps men pretend their marriages are not transactions, in rural China go-betweens do not worry about coming across as crass. The matchmakers lining the streets of Ruili, along Yunnan's border with Myanmar, tout Burmese girls as a bargain: *half price!*[29]

A similar trade is flourishing in India, which, like China and Vietnam, has a long history of human trafficking. The flow of women from poor areas in the east to the male-dominated northwest began centuries ago, says Ravinder Kaur, a sociologist at the Indian Institute of Technology in Delhi who studies the issue. The Rajputs—the same caste that practiced female infanticide under British rule—routinely kidnapped young girls for marriage, and nineteenth-century colonial officers recorded dozens of cases of trafficked women and girls each year.[30] But domestic trafficking has steadily increased in recent years, to the point that Kaur says she now regularly sees "women who are duped into marrying much older or poorer men and meet with disappointment or end up leading a very hard life, with little acceptance by the host community."[31] Exacerbating the problem is the fact that regional differences can be stark in India, and for women migrants raised in insular eastern villages, the northwest might as well be another country. Often women arrive with no way of communicating with their husbands or in-laws. Just outside of Delhi, Kaur met a bride from Bengal who confessed she struggled to understand her mother-in-law's orders. The older woman punished her for her incomprehension by beating her.[32]

Once, Kaur tells me, a woman's adjustment to her new community was complicated by the fact that locals whispered about both her and the family that was so desperate to find their son a wife that they had to buy one. As the ranks of migrant women have swelled and residents have come to see trafficked brides as normal, though, the gossip has dissipated. "There is social acceptability of these marriages now due to the dire need for women," she says. Elaborate rituals have arisen to help families conceal the essential oddity of the new marriages. Traditionally in India, it is the bride's family that should pay the groom's upon marriage, not the other way around. Today, that has been reversed—the groom buys the bride—but families pretend they are following the old ways. Often, the groom gives the bride's parents a symbolic sum of money, and the bride's parents then hand the money right back to him, as if they had scraped for a dowry for their daughter for years instead of sold her.

For women struggling to acclimate to new families and castes, increased social acceptance is a positive change. But the normalization of sex and marriage trafficking, like the East Asian marriage agency industry, also makes it possible for people living in areas where sex selection is widespread to ignore its consequences. The need for women, Kaur laments, "isn't having the effect we wish it would have of leading to less sex selective abortion."

In some areas, locals have come up with solutions to the shortage of women that will probably never be considered normal. In one bizarre but sadly recurring scenario, a woman is trafficked to a high sex ratio region to marry one man, only to learn she must sleep with his brothers as well. Polyandry—marriage to multiple men—was once practiced in parts of China and India as a way for families to avoid splitting up their land among their sons. But it was never widespread. Today most Asians frown on such arrangements, and those parents who do buy a woman for multiple men typically try to hide the fact from their neighbors. Still, polyandry has become common enough that it is reflected in the fees paid for trafficked women. A woman who is expected to sleep with several brothers draws a higher price. [33]

In yet other grim cases, the only wives who can be found are prepubescent girls. India has long been home to a preponderance of child marriages, accounting for 40 percent of the world total, and the recent deluge of single men has encouraged this trend—particularly in the northwest, where sex selection is most rampant.[34] Every April in Rajasthan, girls are routinely married in the annual festival Akha Teej, some of them mere infants.[35]

In China too child marriage is on the rise. The once extinct practice of buying an infant or young girl and raising her alongside her future husband—a custom euphemistically called *tongyangxi*, or "foster daughter-in-law"—has reemerged.[36] By cornering the marriage market early on, parents can rest easy, without worrying about how they will save enough money to help their son attract a good wife later on. But finding young girls can be a challenge today, and so many "foster daughters-in-law" are in fact stolen. Chinese public security officials estimate thousands of baby girls are snatched from their parents every year—so many that police have set up an online registry called *Baby Come Home*, along with a DNA database where parents can go to report missing babies.[37] Parents of daughters in some corners of the world face an unenviable choice: sell their girls to traffickers and send them off to join the female underclass, or guard the girls closely to protect them from kidnappers.

Trafficking across borders is at least monitored by international organizations like IOM. Women at risk of being transported from one region to the next have fewer people looking over them. Once the women arrive at their destination and are assigned to a husband or a pimp, they are completely on their own. Unlike a Vietnamese bride living in Taiwan or South Korea, a woman from northeast India brought to the northwest receives no assistance, no legal representation or handbooks explaining her rights, no language or cultural training.

Preventing the flow of women from sending villages is another challenge, another area underfunded and underresearched. A few months after I met Zhu Hui'e, she closed down the International Labor Organization's Yunnan office because her budget had run out. That was around the same time Zhang Mei, the trafficked Suining wife, sent one of her daughters back to Yunnan to be raised by the parents who had sold her.

Women are not the only ones victimized by traffickers. Desperation to find a wife makes men, and the parents who are so often involved in marriage negotiations, vulnerable as well. In 2008 police in Haryana, a high sex ratio state near Delhi, arrested two forty-year-old women who had posed as marriage brokers in a scheme to rob local families. After arranging a marriage, the women would wait for the couple to settle in and then split with the bride, who was in on the plan, along with the family's valuables. Police interrogators discovered the brokers headed up a gang of young women, which explains why that particular area had seen close to a dozen cases of runaway brides—or what the Indian press dubbed "fake wives"—over the previous year.[38] In 2009, Chinese villagers were taken in by a remarkably similar ruse. That year, police in a town in Shaanxi province documented eleven cases of runaway bought brides. There too they suspect the women belonged to a gang. Three of the brides arrived within months of each other, claiming to be friends from the same region of China. They fled on the same day, making off with thousands of dollars in bride-price.[39]

A society in which girls are kidnapped off the street, in which a young bride may turn out to be a con artist, is not a nice place to live, of course. But the increase in trafficking and prostitution brought on by the sex ratio imbalance affects more than security. It can also transform a community in less obvious ways. The commoditization of sex and marriage means families with more money have a better chance of finding wives for their sons. As a result, as women have grown scarcer and competition for brides has increased the amount of money and other assets parents stash away has spiked—and often these assets are more substantial than the Mao pins Suining father Wu Pingzhang collects for his twin boys' marriages. Shang-Jin Wei, an economist at Columbia University's business school, says China's skewed sex ratio at birth contributes to its astronomical household savings rate, which has nearly doubled over the past two decades and is now among the highest in the world.[40] That squirreling away of money, in turn, reverberates internationally: the high savings rate fuels Chinese demand for U.S. government bonds.

Other scholars believe the proliferation of surplus men will lead to a rise in the incidence of sexually transmitted diseases. China is already one of the most closely watched places in the world for HIV and AIDS.

While infection rates there have not yet reached epidemic level, they have risen sharply over the past few decades, particularly among key risk groups, so that in 2008 AIDS passed tuberculosis and rabies to become the leading killer among infectious diseases in the country.[41] Paralleling this increase has been a change in the makeup of China's HIV-positive population. HIV was once primarily transmitted through intravenous drug use, but increasingly it is spread through sex. With prostitution on the rise and Chinese men less likely than American men to regularly use condoms, those infected through sex now account for an estimated 44 percent of all HIV-positive people in China.[42] Ebenstein and Sharygin, the economists who examined prostitution in China, say as more surplus men come of age that share will go up. If current prostitution rates remain steady, they have calculated, China's skewed sex ratio at birth will contribute to a 2–3 percent increase in the number of men who pay for sex—a change that, in turn, means the "[HIV-] infected population will increase precipitously over the next thirty years."[43]

It isn't just that lifelong bachelors are more likely to frequent prostitutes. Surplus men also constitute what public health researchers call a "bridging population"—a group that transfers the virus from high-risk to low-risk people. In his teens and twenties, a surplus man may contract HIV from a sex worker. Later he may buy a woman from Vietnam or North Korea—a woman who would not otherwise be at risk for HIV—and transmit the virus to her, and in turn to their children. Bridging populations contributed to the spread of HIV in sub-Saharan Africa, and today Asian surplus males, according to a group of American and Chinese medical researchers writing in the journal *AIDS* in 2005, are "fundamental to the future of the HIV epidemic."* The AIDS researchers say the continent's gender imbalance demands nothing short of a rethinking of public health work in Asia: "Prevention strategies that emphasize traditional measures—condom promotion, sex education, medical training—must be reinforced by strategies which acknowledge surplus men and sex

---

*It isn't just AIDS that is on the rise in Asia. Syphilis—a disease that was nearly eradicated in China fifty years ago—has become the most common communicable disease in Shanghai, prompting a group of medical researchers writing in the *New England Journal of Medicine* to call it "a major scourge lurking in the shadows."

workers," they write. "As this demographic shift occurs, it will be impera-
tive to appreciate the evolving sexual risk of . . . young, unmarried
males."[44]

———oഞ്ചൊ———

When the taxi screeched to a halt at the border and Tran Tuan Dung
spotted the checkpoint staffed by uniformed patrol guards, he thought the
girls were finally safe. For the past few kilometers the thugs had trailed
close behind the taxi, but now the motorcycle's driver, seeing the checkpoint, pulled an abrupt U-turn and sped off, perhaps figuring it was better
to lose a few prostitutes than to risk the wrath of the authorities. Tran
breathed a sigh of relief. The chase was over, and his group had won.

But now they had other things to worry about. The taxi driver pulled
up to the Chinese exit bureau station, where an officer motioned for the
girls to hand over their passports and visas. There was no translator on
duty, so Tran couldn't explain why the girls lacked any sort of identification, and when he couldn't produce papers for them, the guard balked.
Arguing in Vietnamese was no use, and the next thing Tran knew, he,
his colleague, and the two trafficked girls were in the back of a squad car,
heading for a military base to be detained as illegal immigrants.

Eventually justice prevailed. The military base had a translator on
staff, and once officers there heard Tran's story they assured him his
group would be protected. The next day, Tran led a band of around fifteen officers, a mixture of military and police personnel, back to the
brothel where he had found Lam. He watched from the squad car, film-
ing the scene from his point-and-shoot camera, as the officers stormed
the brothel and marched out with the madam and pimps. The men who
had chased the taxi weren't there, but Tran took satisfaction in witnessing
the officers arrest the handful of men they did find. The bust also led to
more girls being freed. That day, the officers rescued another four Vietnamese girls who had been kidnapped and forced into prostitution in
Hochai.

Unlike many trafficking stories, the saga ended happily—for the most
part. The day after the brothel bust, Tran and his colleague returned to
Vietnam to avoid overstaying their visas, leaving Lam and the other girls

with the Chinese authorities, who promised them they would be well cared for until they could obtain papers. Back in Vietnam, Tran contacted the antipoverty NGO Oxfam, and the organization sent supplies and helped arrange papers for the girls so they could return to Hanoi. Two weeks later, the girls were reunited with their families.

The pimps and madam arrested during the bust went to prison. The Hochai police had let the brothels flourish for years, but now, in a minor public relations blitz, they claimed this single incident as a victory. Tran, for his part, became something of a celebrity in Hanoi's NGO community, and the recognition gave him a greater sense of purpose. His life, he tells me, now has more meaning.

For the girls who spent months as prostitutes, however, the return home was not so simple. To escape retaliation from their traffickers, they went into hiding. Several organizations now help conceal their whereabouts, and with support they may one day resume normal lives. But for Lam, the youngest, and the one who made the phone call that made the rescue possible, a complete return to normalcy will be more difficult. Sometime during months of sleeping with over a dozen men a day, she contracted HIV.

Chapter 13

THE BACHELOR

[A] fitthundreth might be sent of women, Maidens young and uncorrupt to make wives to the Inhabitants and by that meanes to make the men more settled and lesse moveable.

—VIRGINIA COMPANY OF LONDON ORDER REGARDING
THE SETTLEMENT OF JAMESTOWN, VIRGINIA, 1619[1]

If you are a little bored, a little lonely, a little defense-less, and you need a little excitement and a little risk taking; if you have the courage to face battle; if you are good at leading a team; if you are equally intelligent and brave; if you can face hardship and difficulty: you will never again have to fight alone.

—FLYER SOLICITING PARTICIPANTS FOR AN
AIR GUN BATTLE, SHANGHAI, CHINA, 2005[2]

Across cultures and throughout human history, violent acts are over-whelmingly committed by men. Male skeletons from hunter-gatherer times show more clubbing and stabbing wounds than female skeletons, and archaeologists believe that early on most killings were male-on-male affairs.[3] Tribal men—who make good research subjects because they haven't had violent images planted in their heads by mass media—tell researchers they dream about death and weapons more than do tribal women.[4] In the animal world too males are more belligerent than females, with the exception of the few species in which males are the principal caregivers and put their energy into rearing offspring rather than defending territory. And while today it may be politically incorrect to suggest that gender and violence are linked, crime statistics show that this particular stereotype is irrefutably true. Around the world, men are far more likely than women to be incarcerated; to commit armed robbery, aggravated assault, or murder; to be arrested for carrying weapons; and to be convicted of rape.[5]

Part of the answer for the gender divide lies in testosterone. A hormone found in both men and women, testosterone occurs in much higher amounts in men, and it is the release of testosterone in the first weeks of fetal development that lends a fetus male characteristics. Over the past few decades, behavioral scientists have used saliva tests to gauge testosterone levels in both sexes, charting how individuals with varying amounts of the hormone flowing through their bloodstream react to certain situations. The scientists have found that, contrary to popular belief, testosterone does not cause violence in humans. But if a person is already prone to aggression and certain cultural and environmental factors are in place, testosterone can elevate those aggressive tendencies, making the hormone an important predictor—what they call a "facilitative effect"—of whether he or she will resort to violence.[6]

Prison inmates of both genders incarcerated for violent crimes have significantly higher testosterone levels than those incarcerated for theft or drug offenses.[7] Among judo competitors, men with high levels of testosterone attack and threaten their competitors more often than do their low-testosterone counterparts.[8] The connection between testosterone levels and violence is also the reason that athletes who take anabolic steroids—which are essentially powerful doses of testosterone—are prone to bouts of what is popularly called "roid rage." The most famous recent case of a steroid-pumped man going haywire is that of professional wrestler Chris Benoit. In 2007 he strangled his wife, suffocated his seven-year-old son, and then hanged himself on a portable weight machine. An autopsy determined that Benoit had ten times the normal level of testosterone coursing through his veins at the time of the murders.[9]

Testosterone does not just facilitate violent crime, moreover. It is also associated with other antisocial acts like vandalism, aggression, risk taking, and violations of basic norms.[10] Men who test high for testosterone are more prone to buy and sell stolen property, incur bad debts, and be arrested for crimes other than traffic violations.[11] They are more likely to see military combat (though researchers don't know whether this is because high-testosterone men seek violence or because recruiters identify them as aggressive and single them out for battle).[12] High-testosterone men even smile less.[13] In a study of nearly 4,500 U.S. veterans, psychologist James M. Dabbs concluded that "individuals higher in testosterone more often reported having trouble with parents, teachers, and classmates; being assaultive toward other adults; going AWOL in the military; and using hard drugs, marijuana, and alcohol. They also reported having more sexual partners. The overall picture is one of delinquency, substance abuse, and a general tendency toward excessive behavior."[14]

But it isn't simply that some men have more testosterone than others. Hormone levels also fluctuate over a man's lifetime. It is these variations that matter when it comes to the world's surplus men.

There are two salient hormonal shifts. One is the gradual decline in testosterone that occurs with aging. The hormone peaks in the years following puberty and wanes as a man approaches old age.* The second is that between youth and retirement a man's hormones can rise or fall along with physical and emotional changes. Stress and weight gain, for example, are events that both correlate with drops in testosterone. Another is marriage. Taken together, these fluctuations mean that young unmarried men have, on average, the highest testosterone of any males.

Scientists have long known that married men have lower levels of testosterone than single men and that fathers have lower levels of testosterone than childless men.[15] For years, however, the reason for that difference

---

*Among those to note this phenomenon, interestingly, is Malcolm Potts, who served as IPPF's medical director in the late 1960s, at the time Planned Parenthood was looking into sex determination research. "Aggression is predominately an activity of young males," he wrote in the 2009 book *Sex and War,* which he coauthored with journalist Thomas Hayden. "Societies where the proportion of young males to older males is high are often particularly prone to conflict."

remained elusive. Without tracking men over time, it was impossible to prove causation, and so the researchers cautiously assumed that marriage is simply an effect of low testosterone—that low-testosterone men conform better to social roles and are therefore more likely to get married. But increasing evidence suggests that the opposite is also at play: that tying the knot and having babies can actually cause the amount of testosterone in a man's blood to decline.

In a study spanning ten years, researchers Allan Mazur and Joel Michalek tracked the testosterone levels of over two thousand Air Force veterans, logging both biological shifts and changes in the men's lifestyles. (Veterans make good subjects because many are enrolled in long-term government health surveys.) What the scientists found was telling: subjects' testosterone levels dropped when they married and increased when they divorced.[16]

This happened, the scientists concluded, because marriage reduces the exposure men have to incidents—barrooms brawls, for example—that connect to higher levels of testosterone. "Single men spend more time in male company than do married men, and they are more likely than married men to encounter confrontations and challenges," according to Mazur and Michalek. "Lacking the social support of a wife, they are more likely to face situations in which they must watch out for themselves, acting defensively and adopting protective postures. These are precisely the kinds of situations in which testosterone elevates."[17]

By contrast, when a man marries or has children his body seems to broker an evolutionary trade-off: it relinquishes some of the hormones that enable him to compete with other men in exchange for becoming a loving mate and parent—both roles that help him carry on his genes.[18]

Behavioral scientists still have a number of unanswered questions about aggression, but it is clear that married men commit fewer crimes than single men, and that this is particularly true for men in the prime of adulthood.[19] Without factoring marriage into the equation, young men are far more likely than older men to commit murder.[20] Add marriage in, though, and the contrast is stark: bachelors between the ages of twenty-four and thirty-five are three times as likely to murder another man as a married man of the same age.[21]

The testosterone studies can tell us a bit about our current demographic quandary. They can tell us why an excess of 160 million men will look very different from an excess of 160 million women.* They can tell us why it matters that the world's surplus men are young. They give us specific indicators—crime, murder, delinquency—that suggest how the failure of one generation to marry can affect an entire society. What the testosterone studies cannot foretell is the effect of gathering tens of millions of young bachelors in one place for years on end. Nothing can predict that because it has never happened before. But history can provide some guide.

———— ∞ ————

In the founding myth of Rome, the ancient city-state to which we owe much of modern government, architecture, and language, the twins Romulus and Remus grew up wild on the banks of the river Tiber, suckled by a she-wolf and fed by a woodpecker. This rugged upbringing made them strong and assertive, and by adulthood they commanded a motley assortment of followers, mostly shepherds and outlaws, with whom they dreamed of starting a city.

The twins disagreed about where to locate the new settlement, however, and a fight ensued during which Romulus killed Remus. His power secure, Romulus then established the city-state in his chosen location, naming the settlement after himself, in 753 BC.

The new king's first order of business was to attract inhabitants to supplement his fledgling group of outcasts. "To help fill his big new town, he threw open . . . a place of asylum for fugitives," the historian Livy wrote six centuries later in The Early History of Rome. "Hither fled for refuge all the rag-tag-and-bobtail from the neighboring peoples: some free, some slaves, and all of them wanting nothing but a fresh start. That mob was the first real addition to the City's strength, the first step to her future greatness."[22] But the new arrivals who made up the "mob" were mostly men, and Romulus soon realized that a population

---

*Incidentally, societies in which women substantially outnumber men are hardly progressive paradises. As long as a patriarchal power structure endures, women become valued, in the words of sociologists Marcia Guttentag and Paul F. Secord, as "mere sex objects," while men "have opportunities to move successively from woman to woman or to maintain multiple relationships with different women."

of fugitives, though useful for defending his city, did not bode well for its longevity. "Rome was now strong enough to challenge any of her neighbours," Livy continued, "but, great though she was, her greatness seemed likely to last only for a single generation. There were not enough women, and that, added to the fact that there was no intermarriage with neighbouring communities, ruled out any hope of maintaining the level of population."

By this point Romulus had appointed a hundred senators, who wisely advised him to focus on the shortage of women before getting on with the business of conquering Europe. The king sent out ambassadors to neighboring city-states to see whether they might be willing to provide a few brides. But Rome's wary neighbors lacked empathy for Roman men. A few snickered that if Romulus were so intent on recruiting females he should open up the city to female criminals as well as male ones. When the ambassadors related this message to Romulus, he grew angry. "A clash seemed inevitable," Livy wrote.

Instead of attacking the neighboring kingdoms straightaway, though, Romulus bluffed. Putting on a cheerful front, the king spread word that he was planning a huge festival, replete with lavish entertainment, to honor the god Neptune.

On the day of the party families from neighboring cities flooded Rome's streets, curious to see the new city. No sooner had the women and children arrived than Romulus's hoard of bachelors pounced. "At a given signal all the able-bodied men burst through the crowd and seized the young women," Livy recounted. "Most of the girls were the prize of who-ever got hold of them first . . . By this act of violence the fun of the festival broke up in panic."

Days later, the men who lost their wives and daughters to the Romans returned to exact vengeance. Some foes Romulus's men eliminated easily. The Sabines, however, proved more vicious, and after sneaking into the city and seizing its citadel, they launched a surprise attack and set about killing Roman men in what became one of the first battles of the budding empire.

The toll to both sides would have been much higher, according to Livy, had not the Sabine women intervened, brokering an uneasy peace between the men who raised them and the men who kidnapped them as wives. Rome hardly registered on neighboring states' radar, and yet its gender imbalance had already led to a bloody battle.

While the tale of Rome's origins is apocryphal—we know that if Romulus existed he was probably not raised by a she-wolf—it nonetheless suggests that anxiety about the pernicious effects of a shortage of women appeared early in Western civilization. Millennia after Romulus's fateful party, the tale continued to captivate artists and writers. Nicolas Poussin and Pablo Picasso both rendered the "rape" of the Sabine women on canvas, and sculptors inspired by the story carved flailing women out of marble.* But Rome's story is only the earliest example of a skewed sex ratio affecting regional stability. It was followed by many others.

In 1976 demographers working with funerary inscriptions and ancient texts reconstructed birth records for fourth-century BC Athens. The city-state was not far from Rome, of course, but by then Romulus had been dead for several centuries, and his legacy could hardly explain why the scholars found a sex ratio of between 143 and 174 males for every 100 females.[23] Other mitigating factors might explain the gap, to be sure: men and boys were probably overrepresented in classical registration records. But the high sex ratio the demographers uncovered fit with accounts of early Athenians practicing infanticide. The scholars concluded that despite the problems inherent in relying on classical records, men significantly outnumbered women in early Athens.[24]

If that sex ratio is accurate, then it helps explain the low status of women in Athenian society. Men kept their wives and daughters as property, mostly confined within household compounds, and when women did go out they were expected to stick to a strict code of propriety. Girls married at puberty, female adultery was punished severely, and marriage by capture was common.[25] It is more difficult to say whether the dearth of women contributed to the bloodshed that characterized Athens in the fourth and fifth centuries BC, when the city-state was decimated by the Peloponnesian and Corinthian wars. But it is clear that, as in legendary Rome, a shortage of women resulted in women being treated as chattel.

*In this context "rape" refers to kidnapping, not sexual assault.

The closer we get to the present, the more pronounced these themes become. Genealogies spanning two centuries of nobility in medieval Portuguese reveal a sex ratio of 112 males for every 100 females. The imbalance—assumed to be the result of elite parents selectively neglecting their daughters—was exacerbated by the fact that many high-status women languished in convents. Over the two hundred years in question, the anthropologist James L. Boone has found, the number of elite Portuguese men who produced no surviving children doubled.[26]

With marriage out of the question, aristocratic men found other ways to amuse themselves. Many entered a period of condoned vagabondage shortly after adolescence, roaming the country in groups and preying on unsuspecting villagers. King João I quickly realized the preponderance of restless unmarried men posed a threat to his empire, however, and the surplus males figured into his decision to launch military campaigns in North Africa. "Landless elite males, mainly younger sons, participated in and were a main impetus behind Portuguese expansion into Africa and India," writes Boone.[27]

More recently, anthropologist Lionel Tiger has argued that an abundance of single young men in Afghanistan—where women are not scarce but strict gender segregation means they may as well be—contributes to the spread of terrorism there.[28]* But to truly understand the history of single men and violence, we might look at America.

The United States is the most violent industrialized nation in the world. America's reported homicide rate is ten times the rate found in Japan, eight times the rate in Norway, four times the rate in Italy, and three times the rate in Canada.[29] In the rest of the developed world, our school shootings, beleaguered ghettos, and Wal-Mart gun counters are seen as curiosities. According to United Nations public health data, the United States

---

*To make matters worse, Afghanistan is on the short list of countries that could soon show sex ratio imbalances. At the moment sex selective abortion is rare because fertility remains relatively high, but some scholars believe once Afghans start having fewer children, they will turn to ultrasound and abortion in larger numbers.

counts more murders per capita than several war-torn or impoverished countries, including Somalia, Israel, Peru, Morocco, and Lebanon.[30] Murder rates for males between the ages of fifteen and twenty-four are even more startling. In that high-testosterone demographic the United States leaves all other developed nations in the dust.[31] How did the world's major superpower become so unsafe?

Over the years many explanations have been offered up for the American love affair with violence. Some trace it back to the country's settlement by criminals, dissidents, and heretics. Others say violence has its roots in the bloody revolution that marked America's birth and the civil war that ravaged the country soon after. In still other accounts the slave trade makes an appearance, as does European settlers' inhumane treatment of the native people they encountered in the New World; Americans were brutal toward others, and toward each other, from the very beginning. Recently, however, historians have put forth another explanation: the United States is torn by violence today because the geographical and industrial frontier zones that shaped so much of American identity were predominantly settled by men.

The most obvious of those zones was the Wild West, our celebrated mid-nineteenth-century haven of fortune seeking and vice. The West took shape out of the American desire for a new frontier, for land that could be tamed and for rudimentary cities where men could remake themselves, and it was not nearly as glamorous as the dashing cowboys and overnight riches of Hollywood westerns now make it appear. Traveling across the country back then was grueling and unforgiving, with diseases claiming many along the way. Those willing to take the risk were typically poor southerners desperate for work, men interested more in survival than in unbridled opportunity.

If these men were lucky and arrived in good health, they found jobs that demanded raw strength and endurance: mining, cattle driving, and lumbering. After working long hours, they returned to squalid camps, where they subsisted on diets of salted meat, white flour, and lard. Scurvy was a common scourge; many men in the camps died from poor nutrition.[32] Another price migrant men paid was bachelorhood. Women were reluctant to undertake the difficult journey west, and as a result the American frontier was largely male.

A sex ratio map of the United States in 1870 looks like one of China today. In a large swath of America, including most of the land west of the Mississippi River, there were over 125 males for every 100 females in the total population. California had a sex ratio of 166. In Nevada it was 320; in Idaho, 433. Western Kansas counted an astounding 768 males for every 100 females.[33] Unlike present-day China, the nineteenth-century United States balanced out with pockets in the East in which women outnumbered men. (As women in Manhattan can attest, eastern cities have remained predominantly female up to the present. A few years ago, a widely circulated "singles map" calculated using census data showed there were 210,000 more single women than single men in New York City.)[34] But it was the frontier that arguably had the largest impact on America's character.

The economy of the West developed to serve the largely male population. Gambling houses, saloons, and pornographic publications flourished. Alcohol consumption raged, and prostitutes were in such high demand that the prices charged by the West's abundant brothels soared.[35] In 1880, the historian David Courtwright has calculated, the mining town of Leadville, Colorado had a saloon for every 80 residents, a casino for every 170 residents, and a brothel for every 200 residents. (Many western towns openly tolerated prostitution in the belief that access to prostitutes would prevent men from assaulting "respectable" women.)[36] Each of Leadville's churches, by contrast, served five thousand people.[37] According to Courtwright, Leadville was a sort of Neverland where "the demographic circumstance of many peers and few wives and children made for a world of arrested male adolescence."[38]

Not that everyone wanted it that way. The men of the Wild West certainly tried to marry. As in Asia today, matchmaking thrived, and by the end of the Gold Rush the marriage age for women on the frontier had fallen to the point that they could no longer be called women. Some married at age twelve or thirteen. (Eastern brides were typically eighteen or nineteen at the time of their weddings.)[39]

Some men took Native American lovers; tribes "lent" out native girls to white men in exchange for food or sold them outright. As it does today, keeping a bought woman frequently entailed abuse. The Wyoming hunter known as Mountain Bill Rhodes explained to one observer:

"The girl, when sold to a white man, is generally skeary for a while and will take the first chance to run away. Should you take her again, and whip her well, and perhaps clip a little slice out of her ear, then she will stay."[40] For the most part, though, American settlers, unlike Spanish colonists to the south or French traders to the north, did not marry native women. Their particular Anglo-Saxon breed of racism precluded intermixing, and so many men remained single.[41]

Testosterone, recall, carries a "facilitative effect" that can increase aggression in combination with cultural and environmental factors. One of the most important of those additional factors is whether a man belongs to a culture that puts a premium on honor. This is one reason murder rates in America have long been higher in the South, where settlers descended from Scottish Lowlanders and warring English border clans, than in the North, where people trace their roots to uptight Puritanism. In studies that test how quickly men snap when insulted, southerners hit the point of boiling blood well before their northern counterparts.[42] So it is significant, then, that many of America's western migrants were southern.[43]

By the late nineteenth century the West's murder rate was dozens of times what it was on the East Coast. Leadville counted 105 murders per 100,000 residents in 1880—compared with a mere 5.8 per 100,000 in Boston.[44] In Tombstone, Arizona, the journalist Clara Spalding Brown observed: "When saloons are thronged all night with excited and armed men, bloodshed must needs ensue occasionally."[45] But the men of the Wild West didn't just kill each other. They also assaulted the few women who weren't employed in sex work—in this regard a liberal attitude toward prostitution proved ineffectual—and ravaged Native American tribes, killing thousands of California's original residents.[46] According to the French missionary Edmond Venisse, who ministered in the area, much of this violence was utterly senseless. Some men, he wrote with dismay, "kill Indians just to try their pistols."[47]

Observers at the time categorically blamed the violence on the lack of women. In 1855 social crusader Hinton Helper wrote that a "very important cause of this wild excitement, degeneracy, dissipation, and deplorable condition of affairs, may be found in the disproportion of the sexes—in the scarcity of women." Helper believed this relationship was so absolute that only "an influx of the chaste wives and tender mothers that bless our other seaboard" could reduce the violence in the West. Without women, he continued, "vice only is esteemed and lauded, virtue is treated as an idle dream, an insulting pretence of superiority, or a stupid folly beneath the notice of men of sense."[48] Reformer Eliza Farnham, meanwhile, opined that because they lacked wives, "thousands of men have not only forfeited character, but abandoned all pretension to it; and tens of thousands have stained themselves by deeds, at the contemplation of which they would have shuddered before coming here."[49] Her solution, launched in the wake of the Gold Rush, was to organize a ship of a hundred "upstanding Yankee women," over age twenty-five and bearing letters of recommendation from their preachers, to sail around Cape Horn at the tip of South America to San Francisco, where they might set about civilizing the place.[50]

In the end Farnham's bride ship was a bust. When she arrived in San Francisco with just two women in tow, according to chronicler Chris Enss, "hundreds of angry bachelors nearly started a riot."[51] With few other women settlers forthcoming, the chaos continued. By the 1930s, when the western sex ratio finally began to level out, whole Native American tribes had been decimated, many white men and women killed, and swaths of pristine land destroyed.[52] The legend of the Wild West, moreover, was enshrined in American culture. The generations of Americans that followed would replay that myth on the big screen again and again, internalizing images as children and acting them out as adults. In the sex ratio imbalance of the frontier lay the seeds of a nation's violence.

But what lessons does America's case hold for India, Azerbaijan, and Vietnam—for parts of the world with very different cultural traditions and civilizations extending back thousands of years? It turns out Asia has it own tradition of young, unattached men from cultures that value honor wreaking havoc on society.

———— ∞ ————

In early-nineteenth-century China, a series of grain shortages led rural families to kill infant girls. In one northeastern peasant community residents killed an estimated one-fifth to one-quarter of all daughters.[53] The Qing dynasty nobility practiced female infanticide as well, though to a lesser degree and for different reasons.[54] By the middle of the century the country counted many more men than women.

Some of those men went abroad. Between 1840 and 1911, 10 million Chinese migrated overseas, many of them men bound for California, where they worked on the railroads or in restaurants and laundries.[55] (As it turned out, migration did not yield better access to women. After 1875, exclusionary U.S. immigration policies prevented Chinese women from joining the men, and many of America's early Chinese immigrants ended up living in all-male communities that spawned what became known as Chinatown vice.) But most men stayed home, where the adult sex ratio remained dispiritingly high. Rich men exacerbated the problem by hoarding women—some had dozens of concubines—with the result that throughout the nineteenth century between 10 and 20 percent of all Chinese men could not find wives.[56]

In the 1850s, as the power of the Qing dynasty weakened, charismatic leaders took advantage of the preponderance of unattached men to mount a series of insurrections. The unrest started in what is now northern Jiangsu province, not far from Suining, where government figures from 1874 give a sex ratio of 163 males for every 100 females.[57] As in the Wild West, though, it wasn't enough simply that many men had no hope of marrying. Chinese interactions are shaped by something that, if not explicitly honor, is quite close to it: an emphasis on "face." For men, face—a prestige derived from an individual's position in relation to others—is closely tied to certain societal roles. "Face is essentially an attribute of married men who have families to protect and obligations to fulfill," writes the anthropologist James L. Watson. Unmarried men, by extension, do not command much respect. Even the Chinese term for bachelor, *guanggun*—"bare branch" or "bare stick," in reference to the man's inability to add to his family tree—suggests incompetence. "Bachelors remain perpetual adolescents who cannot play a full role in society," Watson continues. "An unmarried youth can have no face."[58]

Then, as now, the men who remained bachelors were the ones with less money and status, men at the bottom of the social pecking order.* "A bachelor," the anthropologist Claude Lévi-Strauss once quipped, is only "half a human being."[59] He was describing the Bororo, a native tribe in

---

*Today this phenomenon is exacerbated by bride buying and sex trafficking. By 2030, scholars predict the provinces in China's lowest income quintile will have 50 percent more bachelors over age 30 than provinces in the richest quintile.

central Brazil, but he just as easily might have been detailing the status of a bare branch in Asia. A *guanggun* can, however, try to scrounge up a bit of respect by publicly challenging the face of other men.

By the mid-nineteenth century central China was in turmoil. Many of the area's criminals were bare branches.[60] Bandits looted peasant homes, men walked the streets brandishing weapons, and gangs vied for spheres of influence. In 1851 lawlessness came to a head when the Yellow River flooded valuable cropland, giving rise to still more poverty and unrest. Many desperate men joined the Nian, a loose group of rebels that preyed on local families by stealing their grain and animals. The historian Jonathan Spence writes that a "profound imbalance in the region's sex ratios" made of the Nian rebels

> a rootless and volatile group capable of swinging into action with a raiding party at any time. The settled local communities tried to guarantee some security by establishing small protective militias, walled villages, and crop-watching associations, but the Nian nevertheless launched raids to seize crops from nearby villages, to rob the transport vehicles of government salt merchants, to kidnap wealthy landlords for ransom, or even to attack a local jail where a fellow Nian gang member was being held.[61]

Lacking an ideology beyond unfocused discontent, the Nian nonetheless became a full-fledged rebellion by 1855, with smuggler Zhang Luoxing emerging as lord of the alliance. Other Nian leaders took more formidable nicknames: Big Cannon Chang, Water Pipe Wei, and Cat-Eared Golden King of Hell Wang.[62]

By the summer of 1855 the Nian had severed the Qing's lines of communication between north and south. As they tightened their control over central China they swiped women, who could be "sold outright, or ransomed in exchange for horses."[63] Virgins were particularly attractive targets, as families would pay a premium if the rebels returned their daughters, their hymens intact, before nightfall.[64] Disorder intensified, and in the mid-nineteenth century a Chinese poet wrote of the area: "Children carry swords, adults shoulder guns, and desperadoes gather by the hundreds to kill in broad daylight."[65]

Meanwhile, a charismatic failed scholar named Hong Xiuquan was rounding up *guanggun* to the south. Hong was a curious figure, the sole intellectual in a family of farmers who, after failing the civil service examination several times, fell ill and rose from his sick bed convinced he was the younger brother of Jesus.[66] Hong had studied under an American Southern Baptist missionary, but in the interpretations of the Gospel he passed on to his followers a lot was lost in translation. (In Hong's writings, the Ten Commandments included a ban on smoking opium.)[67] He peppered his slapdash faith with statements blaming the dearth of women on the Qing's Manchu rulers. "The Manchu demon devils have taken all of China's beautiful girls to be their slaves and concubines," read one manifesto. "Thus three thousand beautiful women have been ravished by the barbarian dogs, one million lovely girls have had to sleep with the malodorous foxes; to speak of it distresses the heart, to talk of it pollutes the tongue."[68] Not surprisingly, such rhetoric struck a chord among bare branches.

By the end of 1851 Hong had amassed over sixty thousand recruits. No sooner did the men become believers than Hong put their faith to the test. The prophet Isaiah, he informed his followers, had called on them to revolt and break away from the Manchus to form the Taiping Tianguo, or Heavenly Kingdom of Great Peace.[69] But the Taiping Rebellion, as historians now call it, was anything but peaceful. Spence describes it "one of the most deadly and protracted rebellions in Chinese history."[70]

As the Taiping rebels advanced north toward the imperial capital of Nanjing, they were aided by the devastation wrought by the Nian, which was leaving a power vacuum in central China.[71] The cities they encountered along the route fell quickly and easily. Still they ransacked the already suffering communities, looting homes.[72] Hong's forces took Nanjing, a regal city that at several points throughout Chinese history had been the imperial capital, on March 29, 1853, declaring it the center of his new empire. In the days that followed, his forces summarily killed, stabbed, or drowned all of the Manchus they encountered there, down to young children and babies.[73]

Hong quickly assumed the trappings of an emperor, donning extravagant yellow robes and taking concubines, and for the next eleven years he ruled China. But he was an emperor in appearance only. Under his rule attention to administrative matters fell by the wayside, and the Heavenly Kingdom essentially remained a military state. Upon Hong's death in 1864, Manchu troops stormed Nanjing and resumed control of the city. The rebels who didn't die in the city's capture gathered together and, violent to the very end, set themselves on fire. "Such a formidable band of rebels," wrote an incredulous witness, "has been rarely known from ancient times to the present."[74]

After the Manchus regained power, they were justifiably paranoid that China's bare branches would continue to cause trouble. In an effort to tame what historian Matthew Sommer terms a "dangerous underclass of surplus males," the state unveiled a series of increasingly moralistic policies, criminalizing prostitution and sodomy and executing offenders.[75] The Qing had been weakened by decades of turmoil, however, and it would only be a matter of time until the empire fell once and for all. After the dynasty finally collapsed in 1912, scholars pointed to the destabilizing force of the Nian and Taiping rebellions decades earlier—and to the bachelors who made those rebellions possible.

⸻ ∞ ⸻

Since the days when Hong Xiuquan ruled Nanjing as Heavenly King, the city has become the capital of Jiangsu province and less an imperial showcase than a center for Communist administration. But in one important sense it has not changed all that much.*

Today's surplus men do not organize full-scale rebellions. Their activities are not altogether that different, however. In present-day Nanjing men come together under the auspices of the Patriot Club, a band of hobbyists occupying a patch of woods hidden high in the hills of a city park who are obsessed, above all, with guns.

I visit the club's headquarters on a sunny spring day, following the directions I've been given to turn onto a path at the edge of a picnic area and

---

*Nanjing's skewed sex ratio, the legacy of decades of sex selective abortion, is exacerbated by a large population of male migrant workers.

trek up a steep hill. As the camphor trees that dot the grounds thicken into forest, I notice that nailed at haphazard angles to the trees around me are handcrafted signs carved out of rough chunks of wood, in the style favored by American summer camps, and printed with red characters that read "Look Out" and "Defend the Motherland." The warnings continue up the hill, a new one appearing every few steps, building the suspense to an almost comical level. "Heighten Vigilance." And then, again, "Look Out." The path steepens until I am holding onto small trees for support. Finally I emerge through a gap in the trees into a dirt clearing.

The clearing is encircled by olive green army tents and inhabited by nearly a dozen young men in stiff camouflage fatigues, who are milling around and kicking up clouds of dust. At a green table that appears to have been swiped from the picnic area below, a handful of men load white pellets into metal cartridges and slide the cartridges into mock M-4s and AK-47s. On the edge of the clearing, meanwhile, two others test their guns on signs splattered with fake blood spots, screaming "Waaaaa!" when the pellets hit their mark. Another man stands in the shadow of a ramshackle clubhouse, firing pellets into the woods without bothering to take aim. Still others adjust their kneepads, slide thick plastic masks over their faces, or secure camouflage fanny packs around their waists.

The clearing is a cacophony of yelling, swearing, and laughter, and most of the men are too preoccupied with their preparations to register a foreigner standing on the periphery. They don't have time, either, for within minutes someone signals for them to scramble into action. Moving in unison, they slam their guns to their chests, snap into a line, and march, in a stylized jog—legs bowed, fanny packs bobbing up and down—into the surrounding trees. About ten yards from the picnic table, the first man hits the ground. Within a few minutes of dispersing, the men open fire.

It is a Saturday afternoon, and the park below is thronged with families. Tottering young children, their faces smeared with ice cream, are watching their parents fly kites. Like most public spaces in China, the park gets heavy use. Every morning old people gather in the picnic area to carve tai chi movements out of the air, their feet sliding elegantly over the tiles. Later in the day they return with their pet birds in tow to chat and pass the time. From what I can tell, the visitors little suspect that a few hundred meters above them young men with illegal replica machine guns are darting through the woods, unleashing pellets on each other. And indeed with its primitive campground, slapped-together clubhouse, and acres of tangled, overgrown woods, the Patriot Club may seem a fringe group operating in isolation. It is anything but.

Across China today there are many clubs like the Patriot Club: the Shanghai Band of Brothers, the Guangzhou Fight Men, Chongqing's Green Beret. The aspiring warriors who make up their membership call the battles they wage "war games," a term that belies the seriousness they assign them. War games can easily consume a man's weekends and vacations and take over his workday mind as well; the Chinese Internet is overrun with forum threads in which players discuss weapons and strategy. A serious player owns fatigues, long underwear, a bulletproof vest, several camouflage T-shirts, a rucksack, a bandolier, a helmet, a walkie-talkie, a two-liter water bag, and several guns.[76]

As the Nanjing woods resound with the staccato *ping-ping-ping* of pellets loosed in bursts of rapid fire, I find myself alone in the clearing with a man who sports the severe flat top and narrowed gaze of a seasoned general. He introduces himself as Mr. Zhang and tells me he opened the Patriot Club in 1997. Then he invites me to sit at the picnic table. Once I am settled on a bench he lays out the popularity of war games in the most straightforward of terms. "Guns are like soccer," he says. "Men just like them."

The weapon of choice for the Patriot Club members, as for many Chinese men, is the soft air gun, a mock weapon that shoots plastic pellets yet looks and feels real. War game players would prefer to collect real guns, were real guns easy to obtain in China.* But in some ways air guns are just as effective: they can take out an eye, penetrate internal organs, and lodge themselves in young bones. Occasionally they kill.[77]

The battle continues as Mr. Zhang and I sit at the table and watch. Just beyond the clearing three men are crouched down behind a pile of sandbags, their bellies flat on the ground, shooting at two opponents concealed by a collection of rotting wooden crates. Sometimes a pellet

---

*Even fake guns are illegal in China. But they can be smuggled in from Hong Kong with relative ease.

finds its way under a face mask or into the flesh of a player's unprotected neck and he gets hurt, Mr. Zhang says. But this is just a risk a soldier has to take, he adds. He gazes into the distance and muses, "You don't stop doing something because it's dangerous, do you?"

In fact I do. But Mr. Zhang's world is peopled by young unattached men, for whom the answer is an unequivocal *no*. Some nights in the park after the families and tai chi practitioners have gone home, Patriot Club members fight in the dark, prowling the woods with their weapons, an angry, testosterone-pumped horde with a collective death wish.

As the battle rages on, Mr. Zhang explains his players' lust for battle with the enthusiasm of a football coach discussing his star athletes. An otherwise reticent man, he is excited by the topic of guns, and I have trouble getting a word in edgewise until we are interrupted by a commotion behind the sandbags. A man leaps to his feet and shakes a fist in the air. "I died!" he shouts jubilantly.

Chapter 14

THE WORLD

It could have an imbalancing effect on the sex ratio and obviously would mean there'd be an increase in the ratio of males to females born. . . . If you want to continue this science-fiction business a little farther, you can then say this means you're going to have a lot more aggressive men running around.

—PRINCETON UNIVERSITY SOCIOLOGIST
CHARLES WESTOFF, SPEAKING TO
NEW YORK MAGAZINE ON
SEX SELECTION TECHNOLOGY, 1977[1]

On September 16, 2003, four hundred Japanese businessmen convened in the coastal city of Zhuhai, China, for a three-day conference that was only in the very loosest sense about business. They stayed at the Zhuhai International Conference Center Hotel, a gaudy luxury hotel with spacious conference and banquet facilities. They didn't get much use out of the facilities, though. Early on in their stay, the construction company that sponsored the conference staged a party at a separate location and hired five hundred prostitutes, for prices ranging from ¥800 (US$120) to ¥1,800 (US$270) each, to accompany the men.[2] Once the men had eaten and drunk their fill, they took the women back to their hotel—which appropriately sits on Lovers' Road—and reportedly groped them in the lobby before herding them into the elevators and ascending to their respective rooms.

Zhuhai is notorious for sex tourism, and it was hardly the first time that a group of men, or a group of foreign men for that matter, had hired prostitutes. "We see lots of Japanese," sex worker Coco Wang, one of the women hired that week, told a reporter.[3] But this particular group of Japanese had unfortunate timing: September 18, the last day of the conference, was the anniversary of the 1931 Japanese invasion of Manchuria. Nor did it help that Japanese soldiers had raped thousands of Chinese women during the 1937 Nanjing Massacre—an incident that remained remarkably vivid in popular memory, thanks to a budding youth nationalist movement that had seized on the trope of China as a raped woman.[4] And so for the growing number of young male patriots sniffing about for targets toward which they might direct their ire, the Zhuhai affair smelled like a deliberate insult.

Within days, tens of thousands of Chinese had gone online to vent their anger over the prostitution spree. The state press, and then the international press, jumped on the incident. "I saw one of the Japanese men lean across and put his hand in a girl's top and fondle her breasts," Chinese hotel guest Zhou Guangchuan told a reporter in the media blitz that followed.[5] The Chinese government, meanwhile, moved to punish the perpetrators, shutting down the International Conference Center Hotel for two months and doling out prison sentences to over a dozen Zhuhai pimps and prostitutes.[6] Two got life sentences.[7] The Ministry of Foreign Affairs issued a statement calling the conference antics "an extremely odious criminal case" and imploring Japan to do a better job of educating its people.[8] And in a final puff of bravado, the government asked Interpol to arrest the Japanese event organizers who had made the affair possible.[9]

Interpol did not. But the Japanese government did launch an investigation into the construction company that paid for the prostitutes and remind its citizens to obey the laws of other countries while abroad, leading critics to allege Japan caved to Chinese pressure.[10] Ultimately, the incident strained already fraught Sino-Japanese relations—and showed the influence a cohort of angry young men can wield over geopolitics.

Angry young men: the demographic, in fact, is called just that. *Fenqing,* the term used for China's restless, mostly male nationalists, literally means "angry youth."* Japan is a favorite target of *fenqing,* but other countries are occasionally singled out as well. The nationalists coalesced in May 1999 around the NATO bombing of the Chinese embassy in Belgrade, an event that they roundly blamed on the United States.[11] That month young people marched on two dozen cities, setting fire to a U.S. consul's residence and stoning KFC and McDonald's franchises where American consulates were lacking.[12] Since then, *fenqing* have become a persistent political force, taking aim at a range of victims—even, on occasion, the Chinese government.

The influence wielded by different nationalist factions varies. Some angry young men don't get much further than online forums, and others exclusively pursue activities that involve women and weapons: harassing an actress who appeared in a Beijing fashion magazine wearing a dress imprinted with the imperial Japanese flag, for example, or submitting to the adrenaline rush of war games.** (The members of the Patriot Club, as its name might suggest, are mostly *fenqing.*) But some have made world politics their game, and this group can be set off by even the driest of developments. One morning in 2005 shortly after Japan made a bid for a permanent seat on the United Nations Security Council, I awoke to find several thousand *fenqing* marching down my normally sleepy Shanghai street, throwing eggs at the local sushi restaurant and shouting "Japanese pigs get out!" It is such outpourings of rage that threaten to undermine regional stability.

In recent decades the rule of the Chinese Communist Party has hinged on maintaining record-breaking economic growth. A little newfound wealth goes a long way: in exchange for prosperity, Chinese refrain from questioning outmoded Communist doctrine. Basing political legitimacy on rapid development entails a delicate balancing act, however, for it means the government has to fatten middle-class pocketbooks and

---

Fenqing is pronounced FUN-ching.

**Fenqing* responded to actress Zhao Wei's alleged offense by posting doctored nude photos of her on the Internet, pelting her house with bricks, mobilizing survivors of the 1937 Nanjing Massacre (Zhao received a letter of protest signed by one thousand septa-and octogenarians), and smearing her face with feces.

simultaneously placate the poor in the face of widening economic inequality. To bolster its power Beijing falls back on nationalism. One reason for the rise of *fenqing* is that today's young people were brought up to be angry. Shortly after the Tiananmen Square protests drove home for officials the potential threat posed by reform-minded youth, the Chinese government unveiled a series of jingoistic history books.[13]

But often *fenqing* activism seems more the outgrowth of some ill-defined rage than it does of strict patriotism. Men today "are under too much pressure," Wu Gang, a former boxer who opened the Rising Sun Anger Release Bar on the bank of Nanjing's Yangtze River to cater to what he saw as a simmering rage, tells me. "They need a way to release it." Wu's venue—a sort of above ground commercial fight club—provides men the chance to do just that. For the price of a few drinks customers can pay to pummel one of the bar's hired hands.

Government officials, for their part, are keenly aware that nationalism is a double-edged sword: at moments in Chinese history patriotic movements have turned pro-democratic. They also know that the particular strain of unrest fueled by sex ratio imbalance can—as with the Nian Rebellion—take a decidedly anti-establishment tone.

And sometimes China's *fenqing* seem on the verge of violence. In 2006 a foreign English teacher living in Shanghai began blogging about his exploits with Chinese women. The Blogspot journal was not exactly in good taste. ("She jumped and quivered, sighed and open-mouthed pressed against me," wrote the teacher, who went by the moniker Chinabounder, in one entry.)[14] But nor was it the sort of thing consumers of Internet media typically take seriously. That changed when psychology professor Zhang Jiehai launched a bloodthirsty "Internet manhunt"—a nationalistic attempt to crowd-source knowledge and pinpoint the teacher's identity.

"The IMMORAL FOREIGNER plays around with Chinese women," declared Zhang, a young goateed man with a piercing gaze, in a wanted ad he posted on several popular Chinese websites.* "How can we let him commit such wanton perverse acts?"[15] Zhang's *fenqing* followers tried the wayward English teacher in Internet chat rooms and found him guilty—

---

*On staff at the prestigious Shanghai Academy of Social Sciences, Zhang nonetheless stretches the bound of what might be considered scholarship. In a later project he cataloged the desires of foreign women.

and might have punished him severely had their virtual chase succeeded. "Let's kill the animal," one sleuth suggested on Zhang's blog.[16]

When I catch up with the sociologist in a Shanghai coffee shop to discuss the outcome of his manhunt, he has just come out with a book entitled *I Am Angry: The True Story Behind the Immoral Foreigner Incident.* He alludes to being disappointed that the chase did not yield more direct action. "Does this Chinabounder type of man still run around China? Did anyone lower foreigners' salaries?" he says. He stubs out his cigarette and looks at me. "Did anyone beat up foreigners in the street?"[17]

The growing importance of China's *fenqing* suggests one way in which male surpluses might reverberate beyond the borders that contain them. And yet it is difficult to predict to what degree 2030 China—or 2030 India, Albania, or Georgia for that matter—will resemble the Wild West. Unlike bride buying, polyandry, or even a sudden spike in prostitution, rising violence and unrest cannot so easily be pinned on a skewed sex ratio at birth. Crime rates across the continent, to be sure, have soared over the same period that the share of males in the young population spiked. Between 1992 and 2004, China's crime rate nearly doubled.[18] In India from 2003 to 2007, meanwhile, rape cases surged by over 30 percent and abductions by over 50 percent, prompting the government to unveil female-only trains in several cities.[19] But the past few decades have also brought rapid economic development and societal change to Asia. How much of the increase in crime is correlation, and how much causation? How much of it, in other words, is connected to excess testosterone?

There are ways to arrive at preliminary answers, however. One method is to break down incidences of crime and disorder by region and time period. In 2007 a group of economists at Chinese University of Hong Kong and Columbia University—among them Lena Edlund, the Korean-born economist who uncovered sex selection in the United States and who warns of a "female underclass"—did just that, looking at crime statistics from the past few decades for China. Helping their quest was a quirk in 1980s governance: enforcement of the one-child policy at the provincial level involved a time lag. Early on in the policy's lifespan, the central government handed over responsibility to local governments, and some of those provinces enacted strict controls earlier than others, which meant an earlier drop in the birth rate—and spike in the number of boys born. This staggered enforcement meant teenage sex ratios increased in different years for different provinces, allowing the group to track whether provincial crime rates followed suit.[20]

The results were significant. Chinese provinces where the sex ratio at birth spiked earlier also had earlier crime waves. By applying complex formulas to this finding, Edlund and her colleagues found a clear link between a large share of males and unlawfulness, concluding a mere 1 percent increase in sex ratio at birth resulted in a five-to six-point increase in an area's crime rate.[21] "The increasing maleness of the young adult population" in China, they wrote, "may account for as much as a third of the overall rise in crime."

Fewer studies have been done in India, but there too the upswing in crime has not been evenly distributed. Rape, domestic violence, and "honor crimes" proliferated quickly in Haryana and Uttar Pradesh, which both have very skewed sex ratios.[22] In that last state, meanwhile, rising incidences of abuse and sex crimes have so aggravated a group of women that they now take justice into their own hands.[23] Donning magenta saris, the women band together into *gulabi,* or pink, gangs and brandish clubs against offending men.[24]

But the female vigilantes are treading in dangerous territory, for India's northwest has also become known for bloody killings. The best way to predict whether a certain part of India has a high murder rate, indeed, is to look at its sex ratio. Even a high poverty rate doesn't correlate as strongly.[25] Parents in the region have always worried about protecting their daughters, and particularly about guarding their chastity, but today they tell researchers their fears have escalated as the proportion of single men in the population has grown. "The dangers [facing young girls] are said to have further increased with the large numbers of young and not so young unmarried men, men with no outlet for their sexuality," reads a recent report by Delhi's Center for Women's Development Studies.[26]

Another way to get some sense of the impact millions of surplus men will have on societal stability is to look at the toll bachelorhood takes on a man's quality of life. Throughout Asia marriage and health are closely linked. Even after correcting for differences in age, education, and ethnicity, unmarried men in China are 11 percent less likely to describe themselves as being in good health than are married men.[27] The effects of this disparity accumulate over a man's lifetime, moreover. In both China and India, unmarried men have a lower life expectancy than their married counterparts.[28] A failure to marry, then, may negatively impact a man's physical health. And even before he reaches the age of marriage the gender imbalance may have a profound effect on his psychological health.

Thérèse Hesketh, a health researcher at University College London's Center for International Health and Development, is heading up a study in three provinces in China that aims to track, among other issues, the gender imbalance's psychological effects.[29] Hesketh is interested in cataloguing depression rates; she suspects boys may be affected by the knowledge they don't have potential partners waiting for them from childhood. "Are guys growing up knowing they're not going to get laid?" she says. "Do they sense that?" In addition to the fact that young single men have higher testosterone levels than their married counterparts, they may simply feel more hopeless or desperate.

That helps explain why in December 2007 Liu Guiming, head of the Chinese Society of Juvenile Delinquency Research, told delegates to a Beijing seminar that today's teens commit crimes "without specific motives, often without forethought."[30] And why in northwest India the Center for Women's Development Studies report revealed that "unemployment and drug addiction are taking a toll on an entire generation of young men."[31] And why China has lately been hit with the sort of senseless violence that was once America's domain. In 2004 and again in 2010 the country saw separate waves of attacks on elementary schools and child care centers in which crazed murderers went on rampages and bludgeoned and stabbed children to death.[32]

All of the killers were men; eight out of ten lived in eastern Chinese provinces with high sex ratios at birth; several were unemployed. One man told neighbors, before he was arrested and summarily executed, that he was frustrated with his life and wanted revenge on the rich and powerful.[33] Another apparently told police he was upset because his girlfriend had left him.[34]

The destabilizing effects of surplus men can be overstated. In the book *Bare Branches: The Security Implications of Asia's Surplus Male Population*, political scientists Valerie Hudson and Andrea den Boer argue that the gender imbalance in China and India poses a serious threat to the West. After accurately pointing out that societies in which young men vastly outnumber young women are typically violent, the two scholars go one step further and link an excess of men to despotism. "High-sex-ratio societies," they write, "are governable only by authoritarian regimes capable of suppressing violence at home and exporting it abroad through colonization or war."[35]

This supposition ignores the fact that India remains one the most vibrant democracies in the developing world, along with the fact that China's government, while now authoritarian, could look very different if young, agitated *fenqing* turn against it. (Indeed, pressure on the government to expand political and social freedoms has mounted, not decreased, in recent years.) Historically, a connection between sex ratio and governance style has never been so straightforward. Adolf Hitler came to power at a time when Germany had over 2 million more women than men as a result of the toll taken by World War I.[36] But assuming the necessity of authoritarian governance allows Hudson and den Boer to leap to their next conclusion, which is that the Asian giants might readily absorb the extra men into their militaries.[37] Chinese and Indian bachelors might be quarantined in remote areas, or sent abroad: "stationed far from cities, perhaps even on foreign assignments."[38]

Alarmist links between Asian demographic change and global political instability are nothing new. "The chances of war increase with each addition to the population," Paul Ehrlich wrote in *The Population Bomb* in 1968, "intensifying competition for dwindling resources and food."[39] To add drama, today the hordes threatening to overwhelm Western shores are no longer starving children and their parents; they are grown single men. But like Ehrlich's dire predictions of mass starvation and war, this new round of alarmism is poorly supported. Hudson and den Boer lack familiarity with the countries they write about, mostly basing their conclusions on English news reports and secondary sources. The scholars "don't go to China and don't go to India," says Hesketh, the British researcher who is overseeing the study on depression rates. "They sit in their offices. And they make what are to me inappropriate jumps."

But while the sex ratio imbalance may not bring on a new wave of fascism or swell Asia's armies to the point where full-scale war is inevitable, it will almost certainly threaten regional stability. "There is . . . evidence that, when single young men congregate, the potential for more organized aggression is likely to increase substantially," wrote Hesketh in a paper she published with coauthor Zhu Wei Xing in the *Proceedings of the National Academy of the Sciences* in 2006. "The effects of male surplus will be a major problem for several Asian countries over the next two to three decades."[40]

Among intellectuals in China, the rising power of *fenqing* is provoking fears of large-scale ruination. "What's truly horrifying is when a country is swayed by its angry youth," essayist Xiong Peiyun recently wrote in the magazine *Southern Breeze*. "It's reasonable to have a certain percentage of angry young people in the country, but if the management of the country is handed over to them, and the whole nation, including mild old men and women and innocent children, is forced to join the angry youth, then the consequences will be total chaos and disaster."[41]

But perhaps the best indication that something is amiss is the fact that Chinese and Indian leaders are themselves worried about the surplus men. After years of largely ignoring or dismissing the gender imbalance, officials in both countries have lately taken a genuine interest in the topic.

In 2008, in the first speech by an Indian leader on the topic, Prime Minister Manmohan Singh called the abortion of female fetuses a "national shame" with ramifications for all of Indian society. Sex selection, he avowed, was a "terrible onslaught on our civilization."[42] Across the border in China, similar ideas have taken hold among Singh's Chinese counterparts. Just a few years ago Chinese sources told me the issue of surplus men was too sensitive to discuss. Then the government shifted course. "In the past, everyone thought we didn't have a problem," demographer Gu Baochang says of the sex ratio imbalance. "Now they're starting to pay attention." At a symposium in August 2007, National Population and Family Planning Commission head Zhang Weiqing announced that the gender imbalance harbored a "hidden threat to social stability." Before long, officials had dropped the word "hidden."[43]

Commission officials, in fact, have been quietly looking into the sex ratio imbalance for years—ever since the late 1990s, when after years of unsuccessful lobbying two Chinese scholars finally convinced them to take sex selective abortion seriously. Zhu Chuzhu, one of China's first female demographers, had been documenting incidences of selective infanticide and abortion since the early 1980s. With Shuzhuo Li, a young Stanford-educated colleague at Xi'an Jiaotong University, she got through to the family planning commission at a key moment. Declining fertility rates meant that reducing population growth was no longer the most urgent priority. Commission officials were casting about for other population issues to concern themselves with.

China had forbidden sex determination in 1989, but the prohibition was poorly enforced. Zhu and Li convinced the government to make good on the law by cracking down on miscreant ultrasound technicians. Since they had done extensive fieldwork in areas with a high sex ratio at birth, they had several other ideas about how to combat gender imbalance. The plan they presented to the family planning commission included a mixture of carrots and sticks intended to boost the importance of girls.

The commission agreed to try out the program in a contained area. Care for Girls, as the project became known, first took shape in 1999 in Chaohu, a small city in Anhui province. For local officials in Chaohu, the immediate impetus for eradicating the gender imbalance was the prospect of unruly surplus men. "We realized the [skewed sex ratio's] influence on society could be vast," Cao Rongshan, Chaohu's family planning director, tells me. "We had to resolve the problem or it would bring societal instability." But in 1999 the sex ratio imbalance was considered so sensitive because of its connection to the one-child policy that Cao was one of the few local officials to consent to the campaign. Li and Zhu selected his city as the pilot for Care for Girls merely because he said yes.[44]

As the program launched, Chaohu's local family planning volunteers—mostly middle-aged retired women who live in the neighborhoods they serve—augmented their routine of birth monitoring and contraceptive distribution. The women began making pointed visits to newlyweds during which they distributed pamphlets explaining the concept of sex ratio at birth and emphasized the importance of having daughters. District family planning commission officials, meanwhile, offered microcredit loans to women, doled out cash grants to parents of girls—typically ¥200, or around $31, awarded shortly after a birth—and staged mandatory seminars for elderly women believed to be pressuring their daughters-in-law to have sons. Messages like "Boys and girls are both treasures" and "Caring for girls starts with me" went up on walls, replacing the likes of "You can beat it out! You can make it fall out! You can abort it! But you cannot give birth to it!"

But the family planning commission also began tightly monitoring ultrasound technicians. The effort even extended to the Chaohu district's expansive family planning office, where an official proudly showed me what he termed the Two-Lock System: the door to the room containing the ultrasound machine was outfitted with two handles, and no employee was allowed to possess keys to both of them at once. (How this works in a country where technicians administer ultrasound examinations out of the backs of their cars is beyond me. Still, the move may have helped send the message, at least symbolically, that sex selection is no longer tolerated.) According to family planning commission data and independent surveys, Chaohu's sex ratio at birth dropped from 125 in 1999 to 114 in 2002. Convinced of its effectiveness, the commission then scaled up Care for Girls to twenty-four other districts. Those areas too showed promising reductions in sex ratio at birth, collectively dropping from 134 in 2000 to 120 in 2005.[45]

But figuring out exactly what lessons to draw from Care for Girls is tricky. Demographers Zhu and Li say their program's short-term gains were likely the result of the crackdown on sex selective abortion, which explains why eliminating gender imbalance in cities that have not received the same level of oversight as Chaohu has been a much stiffer challenge. In 2006 Care for Girls was introduced nationwide, and the program has yet to produce a dent in the national sex ratio at birth. China lacks a broader political will to enforce the sex determination ban, and absent any sort of punishment simply doling out rewards to parents of girls is ineffectual. Given that the parents who abort female fetuses tend to be among the wealthier residents of their communities, the $31 offered for the birth of a girl is insignificant.

Critics, meanwhile, say that outside of demonstration zones like Chaohu Care for Girls has become a way for the National Population and

Family Planning Commission to justify its existence in an era in which Chinese have very few children by choice. Since the days of widespread forced abortions the commission has swollen to half a million workers, and yet it has become largely redundant. Its birth targets are no longer necessary: surveys show many Chinese now have one child willingly.[46] After learning their lesson in the early 1980s, moreover, organizations like the Ford Foundation—which sponsors Care for Girls—are no longer willing to fund coercive population measures.

Care for Girls, then, marks the government body's attempt to stay relevant by remaking itself as a catalyst for gender equality. "The Family Planning Commission is . . . curing the disease by treating the symptoms rather than the root cause," says Wang Feng, a demographer with the Brookings Institution in Beijing. "They're evading the more difficult, and the more fundamental, part, which is the [one-child] policy."[47] Chinese parents have every reason to view the commission's about-face with skepticism: the very agency that once tacitly condoned the abortion of female fetuses now encourages them to have daughters?

It isn't just China that is foundering in attempts to deal with its male surplus. India too is struggling to take meaningful action.

The country's 1994 Prenatal Diagnostic Techniques Regulations and Prevention of Misuse Act is extensive. The law forbids doctors from revealing fetal sex to potential parents, requires clinics to register their ultrasound machines, and empowers authorities to search clinics. But it took over a decade for state governments to finally begin enforcing it. In 2006 a Haryana doctor and his assistant were sentenced to two years in prison for violating the Prenatal Diagnostic Techniques Act—the first time a doctor in India was punished for sex selection.[48]

As the Manmohan Singh government made sex selective abortion an issue, a few more cases followed. The Indian Ministry of Health and Family Welfare sponsored a public information campaign extolling the virtues of daughters, and posters went up around India proclaiming "Indira Gandhi and Mother Teresa: Your daughter can be one of them."[49] (Indira Gandhi is an unfortunate choice for a strong female role model, of course, since the AIIMS experiments happened under her watch.) A grimmer attempt at driving home the message uses male and female cables to represent India's future marriage market: a dozen connector cables aim at a single receiver.

As in China, a few Indian states pay parents of girls. In the Indian iteration of this program, the state government invests a sum of money into a fund after a girl's birth that matures when she reaches the age of eighteen. Haryana, for its part, recently announced the ambitious goal of monitoring expectant mothers throughout their pregnancies.[50] But sex selection remains rampant, in part because law enforcement is sorely lacking. When a civil servant in the city of Hyderabad recently audited nearly four hundred local ultrasound providers, only 16 percent could provide complete addresses for their patients—making it impossible for authorities to track down women who had visited to the clinic to see whether their scans had led to abortions.[51]

Efforts to promote the value of daughters, moreover, are largely canceled out by a worsening quality of life for women in India. Communities in the northwest have, unfortunately, responded to the recent rise in crime by further restricting the behavior of young girls and women. In an ostensible attempt to reduce sexual harassment, several colleges in Uttar Pradesh recently banned female students from wearing jeans and other Western clothes.[52] In Haryana, meanwhile, parents worried about their daughters' safety are withdrawing the girls from school.[53] No one wants to bring a girl into a world plagued by kidnapping, sex crimes, and unrest. Left unaddressed, the gender imbalance snowballs.

The global sex ratio imbalance has inspired films (Indian director Manish Jha's *Matrubhoomi: A Nation Without Women*) and science fiction (Ian McDonald's story "An Eligible Boy," set in 2047 Asia), and as its effects become more apparent other works will probably follow. But the most perceptive analysis came in 1993, in the form of a novel by Lebanese writer Amin Maalouf.

In *The First Century After Beatrice* the world is divided, much like our own, into the wealthy North and the developing South. Drama unfolds

when the people of the South discover that a mysterious powder—
reminiscent of the "manchild pill" of Western scientists' 1970s fantasies—
ensures the birth of a son when ingested before sex. The South's sex ratio
at birth soon spikes.

Generations of inhabitants, the tale's scientist narrator recounts, are
"amputated of their future."[54] A few years down the line trafficking, violence, and general disorder reign. National governments give way to
warring clans, the men of the South transform into "mutants drunk
with violence," and the few remaining women are kept under siege as
"the precious property of their tribes, prizes fought over in bloody quar-
rels." A bustling traffic in kidnapped baby girls emerges, and parents of
the few existing daughters guard them closely.

But when news of mayhem reaches the North its residents are smug:

> Had not the North resolved its population problems? It had attained the
> desirable negative growth, with no surplus, no superfluity; what is more,
> opinion polls showed clearly that couples here had no preference be-
> tween boys and girls. No disproportion to be feared. The whole business
> could be discussed at leisure, like so many other things, everything
> would remain theoretical, nothing affecting them physically.

Only after sex selection reaches Germany and refugees from the
South begin to overwhelm northern borders does the North send in
peacekeeping troops. But by then, as you might guess, it is too late.

The real-world drama now imitating Maalouf's art also remains
mainly theoretical for many in the West. Even as UNFPA refrains from
taking a strong stance on sex selection, even as the U.S. government remains silent on the issue and women's groups sweep it under the rug, several key Western institutions are studying the global gender imbalance.
The American Enterprise Institute, a conservative think tank founded to
protect business interests after World War II, recently hosted a lengthy
seminar on the topic.[55] Years after it funded coercive population control
programs that helped spawn the sex ratio imbalance, the World Bank has
hired one of the leading experts on the topic, the Indian demographer
Monica Das Gupta, to research it. And according to a defense contractor I
spoke with, the U.S. military is keeping close tabs on China's surplus men.

(Whether military analysts fear hordes of conscripted bachelors attacking America or whether—like General William Draper so many years earlier—they are interested in regional stability in Asia I cannot say.)

But studying the imbalance from a distance is hardly the same as taking action. *The First Century After Beatrice* concludes with the narrator contemplating, as he approaches death, how his world degenerated so quickly. "Was everything that happened unavoidable?" he asks. "I think not, I still believe that other paths existed."

Chapter 15

THE BABY

There is always a well-known solution to every human problem—neat, plausible, and wrong.

—H. L. MENCKEN

In 2007 South Korea reported a normal sex ratio at birth for the first time in over twenty years, becoming the only formerly imbalanced country in the world to wipe out sex selective abortion. The experts wasted no time in rushing to interpret its success. By that point they had been weighing approaches to getting couples to have girls for several years. Here, suddenly, was a real-life case of a country that had seemingly achieved the impossible. And so they parsed the data for nuggets that might be useful elsewhere in the world, wrote papers, and gave interviews.

Monica Das Gupta, the demographer hired by the World Bank, took the lead in elucidating the South Korean case. In a paper published by the bank's Development Research Group in 2009, she concluded that South Korea's sex ratio at birth had balanced out because economic development and a wave of new gender-sensitive policies worked together to weaken sexist values. "Increased urbanization and education," Das Gupta and her coauthors wrote, "eroded the societal structures and values that underpinned son preference—and a change in social norms swept through the population, sharply accelerating the speed of the reduction in son preference."[1] South Korea's experience bodes well for China and India, Das Gupta asserted, since the Asian giants have more progressive gender polices in place than did Korea when it was at a similar level of development. "The good news," she wrote, "is that there seems to be an incipient turnaround in the phenomenon of 'missing girls' in Asia."[2]

This was a hopeful conclusion: not only was Asia's sex ratio at birth on the verge of balancing out, but cultural and social change had sufficed to make South Koreans desire girls in larger numbers. That meant punitive measures such as a crackdown on ultrasound providers would not be necessary—in China, India, or elsewhere.

What I had seen over two years of looking into sex selective abortion in Asia suggested the very opposite of an incipient turnaround. Most scholars I had interviewed believed in some version of Christophe Guilmoto's transition theory—that countries with sex ratio imbalances eventually reach a level of economic development at which couples no longer abort female fetuses. But they typically expected the transition cycle to last several decades. Sex selection, after all, had not yet reached the poorest parts of China and India, not to mention countries like Nepal and Bangladesh.

Still, it made sense to me that more gender-sensitive policies would reduce the number of couples who turned to technology to have a boy. I went to South Korea, then, expecting to hear about the country's transformation. I figured a new wave of gender equality, bolstered by widespread societal change and tolerant government policies, would be an easy thing to get people to talk about—perhaps even a point of national pride. So I am surprised to find myself, on day two, in a swank Seoul coffee shop listening to Catherine Min tell me she wishes she had a son. "Frankly speaking, I prefer boys," says Min, a midlevel telecom company manager in her early forties and the mother of a single daughter. She is wearing an angora sweater over a black turtleneck, and her face is impeccably made up, her hair shaped into a perfect bob. She speaks in fluent English. "I prefer boys," she says, sipping a mug of hot chocolate, "because I have experienced sexual discrimination myself." When I ask whether government policies had led to an improvement in the status of women, she looks at me quizzically.

Across town at the government-affiliated Korea Women's Development Institute, I put the same question to sociologist Whasoon Byun. She laughs heartily, then proposes that the notion that Korean women are significantly better off than they were ten or twenty years ago must have been put in my head by a man. According to the United Nations Development Program's indicators for gauging opportunities available to women, Byun points out, South Korea is doing dismally.[3] "Even as our society becomes better and better off, our gender empowerment measurement remains one of the lowest of any developed country," she says.

Indeed, Heeran Chun, the sociologist who spoke with me about Korea's history of abortion, bleakly summed up the standing of Korean women in a 2006 paper. "Women have lower socioeconomic status than men, and their lives are markedly restricted by the cultural values associated with Confucianism," she wrote. "Despite their greater longevity, South Korean women still report higher rates of morbidity and distress than men."[4] At our coffee shop meeting, Min concedes that more and more women in Seoul work, but she tells me powerful positions remain unobtainable. "The glass ceiling very clearly exists," she says. "And then we have to give birth to babies on top of it."*

Min did not decide to have a daughter—her own small contribution to Korea's balanced sex ratio at birth—because her country had suddenly become a nice place for females. She had a daughter, she says, because she and her husband had banked on having a son afterward. By the time they tried for a second baby, however, Min could not get pregnant. She was too old.

In that sense she typifies Korea's current generation of women, who for various reasons have fewer and fewer children—so few, in fact, that in 2005 Korea bottomed out with the lowest total fertility rate in the world, at an average of 1.08 children per woman. (The birth rate has since climbed, just barely, to 1.22.)[5] Many women spend their most fertile years single, then marry to discover child care options are scarce and education is prohibitively expensive. When I ask Min whether she has noticed the disappearance of sex selective abortion among her friends and acquaintances, she looks at me sadly. "Sex selective abortion," she

---

*In 2005 women made up only 6 percent of the country's corporate executives, political leaders, and senior managers.

says, "is a fortunate worry" for women to have. "Because at least they are fertile." She dabs at her eyes with a tissue. "To have an abortion you at least need to be able to get pregnant."

South Korea's situation is a perverse twist on the discovery Christophe Guilmoto had made in India years earlier. Then, the fact that couples were having fewer children concealed the detail that they were mostly having boys. Now, the fact that Korea's sex ratio at birth is balanced obscures the important detail that Koreans have almost no children, male or female. And when it comes to making up for decades of predominantly male birth cohorts and increasing the number of women in Korea, a balanced sex ratio at birth matters hardly at all if couples are not having babies.

South Korea's love affair with population control did not last forever. Democracy arrived in 1987, and with it came a more sensible approach to procreation. The new government promptly outlawed sex identification during ultrasound and amniocentesis.[6] In 1990 the Ministry of Health and Social Affairs stiffened penalties for doctors caught aiding women in sex selection and, in a series of highly publicized busts, suspended the licenses of eight doctors found to be violating the law. A few years later president Kim Young-sam's administration staged another public crackdown on sex selective abortion, hiring pregnant women to go undercover as patients seeking sex determination tests. Doctors who illicitly performed the tests were punished with one year in prison, up to $12,000 in fines, and the possible loss of their licenses.[7]

But it wasn't that the Korean government had suddenly become concerned about the status of women. Instead demographic change moved it to action. As the national population strategy shifted from small families toward more sustainable growth, sex selective abortion was no longer a useful silent partner in reducing the birth rate. More immediately, government advisers worried about a coming marriage squeeze.[8] In 1995 demographers projected that half of boys ages ten through fourteen would not be able to find female partners in their age range when they reached adulthood.[9] The public information campaign that accompanied the 1990s crackdowns centered not on the status of women and girls but on the future dearth of brides. A poster from the time shows a classroom dominated by pairs of little boys. One raises his hand and asks, "Teacher, if I do nice things can you find me a girl partner?"[10]

In the year after the 1990 crackdown, South Korea's sex ratio at birth fell from 117 to 113, and while it rose slightly after that, it would never be quite so skewed again.[11] The sex ratio at birth fell anew after the second wave of arrests in 1994, and it continued on a downward slump thereafter.[12] The crackdown was "temporarily effective," says Cho Young-Youl, the gynecologist who performed sex selective abortions. The sting operation approach might have eradicated the practice entirely, he adds, had the health ministry stuck with it. As it was, he says, government suppression was not sustained, so the arrests actually served as an advertisement for some doctors. Once they had paid their fines and done their time, these physicians started practicing under the table again, this time with a new coterie of patients seeking them out. Pregnant women knew "they could go to the clinics that were prosecuted to get the sex identified," Cho says.

But by the time the jailed doctors were back in business, they had fewer potential customers. After years of penalties for out-of-quota births, incentivized sterilizations, and forced abortions, Korean women had finally given in and stopped having children. In 1995 South Korea hit a total fertility rate of just over 1.6 children per woman, and the fertility rate continued to drop at a pace more rapid than even China's.[13] The country's once astronomical abortion rate had in turn fallen by 69 percent, from 64 abortions per 1,000 births in 1980 to 20 per 1,000 in 1996.

Doctors and demographers alike now cite the low pregnancy rate as the primary cause of South Korea's balanced sex ratio at birth. "Fertility decline has been too rapid," explains Doo-Sub Kim, a demographer at Hanyang University in Seoul and head of the Population Association of Korea. "So couples' number preference has become a little bit stronger than their sex preference."

Sex selection was always something Korean couples turned to for second or third births. Recall that in 1989, on the eve of the crackdown on ultrasound providers, the sex ratio for first births was 104, or close to perfect. As the birth rate plummeted, the basic idea—to keep a female fetus if one comes on the first try—endured. The few couples that do have more children today continue to screen for sex; for third births, Kim has found, Korea's sex ratio remains skewed toward males.[14] But for the most part second and third births have disappeared. Having even one baby has "become optional," explains Baik Eun-Jeong, an obstetrician with the Korean Medical Association. "[Couples] just want to have one child, no matter what—boy or girl. That is the most realistic reason for the sex ratio at birth normalizing."[15]

The World Bank paper I read, I quickly learn, is flat-out wrong. An "incipient turnaround" boosted by gender-sensitive policies is convenient in that it does not require strong action on the part of international institutions. If Asia's gender imbalance is on track to disappear, there is no need to acknowledge the role Western organizations played in causing it—like, for example, the $30 million the World Bank earmarked for population control in Korea during a period of entrenched coercion. And there is no need to delve into messy abortion politics and risk a difficult discussion about women abusing choice.

―――∞∞―――

If the Korean example is not a model for solving the world's gender imbalance, what does work? We have some evidence to go on. For its flaws, China's Care for Girls program did yield results in Chaohu, the pilot area where it was tried, much as South Korea's arrests of doctors in the early 1990s helped reduce the country's sex ratio at birth in the period immediately afterward. Taken together, those two cases are a sign that tougher measures can be effective—if countries can be convinced to move beyond isolated demonstration projects and sporadic bursts of arrests toward broad and consistent action.

Reproductive rights activists tend to fear any restrictions on abortion, and they often argue that a crackdown on sex selective abortion is unwieldy. Since women frequently visit one provider for an ultrasound and another for an abortion, how do you determine which women are aborting because they want sons, and which are doing it for other reasons?

One strategy is to focus on ultrasound providers and send in pregnant women as decoys, as South Korea has done—but do it routinely, over years, rather than processing only a few cases, and prosecute veiled references to sex ("Time to decorate the baby room in pink") as well as overt instances of sex determination. But since ultrasound technicians can be mobile, and exams done with handheld machines are difficult to track, more scrutiny needs to be placed on doctors who perform abortions as well. Because the technology currently available in most parts of the developing world can only reveal fetal sex in the second or third trimester, and because in countries with sizable gender imbalances abortion is typically highly accessible and available in the first trimester, there is a good chance a woman visiting a clinic for a late abortion is there because the fetus she is carrying is female.

"I'm a bit hard on doctors," says Thérèse Hesketh, the British health researcher overseeing the study on Chinese bachelors, who is herself a pediatrician. "You could say they don't know. But in China abortion is widely available and available early on. These happen at twenty weeks." Hesketh advocates getting tougher on violators. While "China will see very high and steadily worsening sex ratios in the reproductive age group over the next two decades," she and two coauthors recently wrote in the *British Medical Journal*, "enforcing the existing ban on sex selective abortion could lead to normalization of the ratios."[16]

Doctors could interview women coming in for second- or third-trimester abortions, as Rubena Moisiu did in her Albanian maternity hospital, to make sure they are not terminating because the fetus is female. They could even go so far as to screen the pregnancy themselves and investigate women carrying female fetuses more thoroughly—or risk being held accountable. (Here too sting operations are useful for catching offenders.) But without global pressure and attention, without any real action by women's health and population organizations, and without a UN agency doling out funds for fighting sex selection, nothing happens.

This is not to suggest there is no movement to stop sex selective abortion. There is. The Christian right—which has no problem with what Sharada Srinivasan calls the "A-word"—has seized on sex selective abortion. Conservative groups tally the number of female fetuses aborted in Asia. They call the UNFPA to task (although here they often go overboard, wrongly accusing the agency of complicity in a slew of sinister ventures). They circulate videos and carry out fund-raising drives. But their motives, of course, extend beyond eliminating sex selection. Beneath their impassioned cries lies the goal of reducing access to abortion around the world—starting in the United States.

The most vocal right-wing group to take on sex selection as an issue is the Washington, D.C.–based Population Research Institute. PRI is headed by Steven Mosher, the onetime Stanford University anthropology graduate student who in the early 1980s circulated photos of Chinese women forced to abort as late as seven months. What he witnessed in China fundamentally transformed his politics, he tells me: "It is one thing to be pro-choice in the abstract. It is another thing to witness a woman who is in the third trimester of pregnancy and carrying a baby well past the point of viability—in a good marriage and carrying a wanted child—be forced to abort that child." In the years following his expulsion from Stanford, the former fan of Paul Ehrlich converted to Catholicism, authored the book *Hegemon: China's Plan to Dominate Asia*, fathered nine children, and reinvented himself as an anti-abortion activist, with a focus on the global population control movement.[17]

His work paid off in 1995 when he was brought on to direct PRI, which shares a founder and some members of its board of directors with the notorious anti-abortion group Human Life International.[18] According to the mission statement posted on its website, PRI aims to "expose the relentless promotion of abortion" and "promote pro-natal and pro-family attitudes, laws, and policies."[19] The best way to do that, as Mosher sees it, is to chip away at abortion rights slowly but steadily. In 2008 he posited to supporters that sex selective abortion was the next logical battleground in the abortion war—not because it is inherently discriminatory and results in worsening status for women but because an "incremental approach" to restricting access to abortion is more politically workable than a flat-out ban. "I propose that we—the pro-life movement—adopt as our next goal the banning of sex-selective abortion," Mosher wrote in an article in the Population Research Institute's magazine. "By formally protecting all female fetuses from abortion on ground of their sex, we would plant in the law the proposition that the developing child is a being whose claims on us should not depend on their sex."[20]

A few months before Mosher's essay appeared, Lena Edlund's study revealing the occurrence of sex selection among Asian Americans had been published in the *Proceedings of the National Academy of the Sciences*. The numbers described in the study, you may remember, were not large. If anything the existence of sex selective abortion among Asian groups in the United States said more about the pull of fertility trends in Asia than it did about American abortion providers. But the study garnered significant media attention, and Mosher saw an opportunity. If he and his fellow activists could slip into U.S. law a prohibition on sex selective abortion, Mosher recognized, they might create a precedent for later restrictions.

The idea of using sex selective abortion as a pawn in the drive to ban all abortions dated to a 1994 article by Amherst College political scientist Hadley P. Arkes. In that work the conservative theorist outlined a calculated trajectory for activism.[21] "We seek simply to preserve the life of the child who survives the abortion," Arkes wrote. "From that modest beginning, we might go on to restrict abortions after the point of 'viability,' or we could ban those abortions ordered up simply because the child happens to be a female. We could move in this way, in a train of moderate steps, each one commanding a consensus in the public, and each one tending, intelligibly, to the ultimate end, which is to protect the child from its earliest moments."[22] Sex selection was barely on the radar in the West, and yet Arkes deftly saw that banning "abortions ordered up simply because the child happens to be a female" might prove useful in achieving the anti-abortion movement's ultimate goal of prohibiting any and all abortions. This was, politically speaking, a stroke of genius: it meant the pretext of gender discrimination could be put to work in curtailing women's rights.

If sincerity among the Christian right about the plight of women and girls in Asia quickly evaporates, however, political will does not. For the next fourteen years anti-abortion activists kept at sex selective abortion, and in 2008, the year Mosher's essay appeared, they scored an important victory when Arizona congressman Trent Franks introduced to the House of Representatives the Susan B. Anthony and Frederick Douglass Prenatal Nondiscrimination Act, which called for an all-out ban on sex selective abortion.* A climate change skeptic who advocates investigating civilian

---

*The act also included a ban on "race selective abortions," using high abortion rates among African Americans to argue that U.S. abortion clinic workers discriminate on the basis of race—a provision that adroitly played to the black community's memory of forced abortions in the 1970s.

Muslim groups, Franks is a dyed-in-the-wool Republican. In 2010 the *National Journal* ranked him as one of the most conservative members of the House of Representatives.[23] (He tied for first place.) For him the Prenatal Nondiscrimination Act—the movement's first attempt at using sex selection to "plant in the law," as Mosher put it, the notion that the fetus is human—was the culmination of decades of working against abortion rights.

The text of the Prenatal Nondiscrimination Act displayed a use of facts that was, at best, highly muddled. Nowhere did the bill mention that in the United States sex selective abortion has only been found to occur among Asian Americans. Instead it used vague language like "certain segments of the United States population."[24] At the press conference Franks held on Capitol Hill to mark the bill's introduction, he avoided any mention of Asians or Asia—and yet he used numbers drawn from the continent. His bill, he said, was being "put forth in the backdrop of over one hundred million little girls being aborted simply because they were little girls instead of little boys."[25] One hundred million presumably sounded better than a few thousand, the actual number of fetuses believed to have been aborted on the basis of sex in the United States.[26] But Franks's fudging would come to be highly typical of a campaign that uses abuses unearthed abroad to restrict rights at home.*

When the Prenatal Nondiscrimination Act failed to make it out of committee, anti-abortion activists were undeterred.[27] Franks's bill had, at the very least, put reproductive rights activists on the defensive. The activists persevered, moving on to the old American fallback strategy of taking the fight to the states, where they convinced anti-abortion state legislators to introduce clones of the Prenatal Nondiscrimination Act.

Here the movement has had more success. As this book goes to press, bans on sex selective abortion have been passed or are pending in nine states: Illinois, Pennsylvania, Oklahoma, Michigan, Minnesota, Georgia, New Jersey, Arizona, Mississippi, and Idaho. Arkes's early instinct proved

---

*Mosher also tells me that Christians, as a rule, do not practice sex selection, and that the reason the Philippines has no sex ratio imbalance is that its people are predominantly Roman Catholic. In fact abortion is illegal in the Philippines, and the country has a fertility rate of over three children per woman.

correct: sex selective abortion is a helpful pawn in the quest to ban all abortions. And it is a great target, in no small part, because it splits reproductive rights groups right down the middle.

———— ∞ ————

One of the few left-leaning organizations in the United States to take on sex selection is Generations Ahead, a fledgling Bay Area NGO. Sujatha Jesudason formed the organization in 2008 after realizing the politics of U.S. reproductive rights organizations sorely needed updating. "The issue of sex selection has become politicized and been pulled into the abortion debate," Jesudason explains to me when I stop by the organization's small office, a few sparely furnished rooms in depressed downtown Oakland. Jesudason has shoulder-length hair streaked with gray, and she is wearing a black T-shirt and jeans. Reproductive rights activists, she says, needed "an organization to really take the lead on [sex selection] and say this is how to do advocacy on it, this is how to do organizing on it, this is the policy that should be taken on it."

After Franks introduced the Prenatal Nondiscrimination Act Jesudason brought together representatives from twenty-five abortion rights groups for a day-long strategy session. But she soon realized it would be difficult to present a united front against the likes of Franks and Mosher, and not only because the conservatives were so much better funded. "People had really mixed feelings on sex selection," she recalls. Many of the activists at the session didn't believe it was unequivocally wrong. Some believed sex selection was wrong only when it discriminated against girls; selecting *for* girls was another matter.

With the National Asian Pacific American Women's Forum and Asian Communities for Reproductive Justice, Generations Ahead published a toolkit to prep activists for possible dissension emerging around the issue. One scenario asks participants to imagine their organization's response to a ban on sex selective abortion being introduced in their state legislature. Staff members are divided, the toolkit explains. Viewpoints range from "Any restriction on abortion is antithetical to women's rights" to "As a South-Asian woman, I am very concerned about the issue of sex selection" to "This issue is too complicated, we should side-step this altogether." If there is a right answer, the toolkit does not identify it, and indeed most feminist groups have let the last viewpoint win out. To date, neither the National Organization for Women nor NARAL Pro-Choice America has taken a stance on sex selection.

Apart from misleading rhetoric about the nature of sex selection in America and language comparing abortion to killing, the Prenatal Non-discrimination Act is not such a bad law—were it to be enacted in the countries that actually need it. The bill allows for up to five years in prison for doctors and other health professionals who perform sex selective abortions and one year for staff members who know about the procedures and fail to report them. Women seeking sex selective abortions are not themselves held liable.[28] But the act—like its state-level offspring—is not intended for developing countries with high abortion rates. It is meant for the United States, where a woman seeking an abortion already has to jump through a number of hoops.

Whether such a law is necessary in the United States is less clear. Some say that for bans to be effective abroad we need to criminalize sex selection at home. "Ethically it's a good idea to say that we're not going to tolerate sex selective abortion," says Joseph Chamie, the former United Nations Population Fund head, who now directs the Center for Migration Studies in New York. "It's wrong. It does damage to the society. We need to have balance. If we do not give any circumstances under which abortion can be denied, then the logical conclusion is women have a right if the fetus is female to abort it."

Jesudason, on the other hand, maintains it is possible to address sex selective abortion and yet keep abortion rights in America intact. One thing is clear: if the left does not develop a sophisticated stance on the issue soon, progressives will soon be backed into a corner by the right's drive to criminalize sex selective abortion in America. "Not only will [anti-abortion groups] lead the discussion, but most reproductive rights and feminist groups will find themselves opposing bills because they are anti-abortion legislation," says Jesudason. "We want to make sure that they don't position themselves just as abortion groups but also as groups fighting for gender rights."

In 2005 South Korea's government abruptly broke with the past and started promoting childbirth.[29] Signs of the country's rapidly graying population had by that point become pervasive. Businesses catering to an older clientele had cropped up along the streets of Seoul; on my way to meet Catherine Min, the mother who yearns for a son, I passed a cheery advertisement for an "Anti-Aging Café." Obstetrics clinics had been converted into assisted-living facilities.[30] And children had become scarce. Projections released by the Korean National Statistic Office showed that unless the birth rate were to suddenly increase, by 2026 one-fifth of Koreans would be over age sixty-five—a figure that made South Korea one of the world's "super-aging societies."[31] A generation after logging record-breaking abortion rates, the country was displaying the fastest rate of population aging in human history.[32] Unless they took prompt action to increase the birth rate, government officials believed, their country would soon face labor shortages, a pension crisis, and a general economic slowdown.

The initial government plan called for $37 billion over five years to increase the birth rate.[33] In the next cycle of funding President Lee Myung-bak's government increased that to $67 billion and set the goal of boosting the total fertility rate to the OECD average of 1.7 children per woman by 2020.[34] Demographers who had once advised the government on how to decrease the birth rate turned their attention to increasing it, while the Korean Medical Association—whose members previously abetted the population control drive by performing sex selective abortions—launched a campaign extolling the merits of babies.[35]

Some of the measures that followed were long overdue.[36] Paid maternity leave was increased to ninety days, with an optional unpaid parental leave of up to twelve months, and the government increased spending on child care and benefits for working mothers.[37] Other initiatives bordered on absurd. The Korean Ministry of Health, Welfare, and Family Affairs, for example, mandated that the lights in its office building be turned off at 7:00 PM once a month in a highly publicized drive to encourage employees to go home and make babies.[38] Municipal district governments in Seoul, meanwhile, began staging matchmaking events for young singles.[39]

But South Korea's extensive birth drive is not working. According to a recent report from the organization Population Action International,

"Financial incentives are having little impact on Korea's extremely low fertility rates, and concern is rising that a shortage of new workers is already slowing the rate of business creation."[40] The birth campaign's largest impact, indeed, seems to be a further curtailment of women's rights. After years of promoting abortion as birth control, the Korean government has turned against abortion—all abortions, not just those done because the fetus is female.

Abortion has always been illegal in South Korea, except in cases where the mother's health is in danger. The government never bothered to legalize terminations because it didn't have to: in the years when foreign funding for population control flowed into the country abortion became so common that most people didn't even realize it was illegal.[41] But after decades of Korean clinics openly flouting the law, Lee has suddenly begun enforcing it, staging highly publicized sting operations and imprisoning offending gynecologists.

Lee has never been a particularly popular president, but with the anti-abortion campaign he has, for once, broad political support. In a recent case brought to court in the city of Ulsan, a judge stripped a doctor of his license after he performed a first trimester abortion on a teenage girl—a situation many would see as exactly the sort in which abortion is appropriate—and set an alarming precedent by ruling "a fetus' life is exactly the same as a person's life, and deserves the full benefit and protection of the law."[42] Even doctors have joined the anti-abortion drive. In 2009 a group of physicians branched off from the Korean Medical Association to form the anti-abortion Korean Gynecological Physicians Association. Shim Sang-duk, the obstetrician who founded the group, has said the move wasn't prompted by religion. He was simply tired of aborting as many babies as he delivered.[43]

Worried the backlash against abortion is endangering women's health, Korean feminists have organized.[44] Reports are circulating of pregnant women working second jobs in order to afford payoffs to doctors willing to risk arrest.[45] The country's abortion rate is, in fact, lower than it has been in decades. But to the supporters of the crackdown that fact matters very little. They are, after all, living with the nasty aftermath of decades of misdirected abortions—tens of thousands of surplus men, an influx of uneducated foreign wives, and a graying population brought on, in part, by a decrease in the number of mothers. A failure to address sex selective abortion earlier has led to feminists' worst nightmare: a ban on all abortions.

That is the real lesson that South Korea holds for China, India, and the many smaller countries where sex ratio imbalances have appeared—and really it is a lesson for family planning organizations and feminist groups as well. Failing to address a problem because it is too politically dicey today can come back to haunt you tomorrow.

Catherine Min, for her part, has become an advocate of early pregnancy. "I give advice to my colleagues," she says. "I tell them they shouldn't wait." Her concerns have, however, become less relevant as technology makes it possible for women to have children into their forties and fifties. In vitro fertilization is coming into vogue in Seoul, with dozens of fertility clinics opening in the past few years.[46]

And while sex selective abortion has all but disappeared among the elite, who dismiss it as a crude tool of the 1990s, many parents maintain an interest in manipulating the sex of their children. Abortion, it turns out, is no longer necessary for that. "These days because of IVF technology parents have a lot of different embryos to choose from," says Sohyun Kim, a doctor who runs a small clinic in a tony part of Seoul. "They ask for the ones they don't want"—the embryos of the undesired sex—"to be eliminated. The girls can be erased. And the boys remain."

EPILOGUE

Have you always dreamed of having a precious daughter, but ended up with rough-and-tumble sons instead? . . . Find support and get advice from other parents who are trying to beat Mother Nature's odds.

—BABYCENTER.COM[1]

Oh, the visions they had of pink ruffles and big blue eyes, blonde curls and shopping trips for grad dresses, trips to the mall for fancy hair-dos and manicures! How proud they would be some day to walk that daughter down the aisle and marry her off to a handsome man who would provide brilliant, blue-eyed grandchildren for them. Well, I was blue-eyed, but that's where it stopped.

—BRIARPATCH MAGAZINE, 2005[2]

This story does not end in Korea. It ends in Los Angeles, in a posh clinic on Ventura Boulevard called Fertility Institutes.

A proud old road in the San Fernando Valley lined with tall palm trees, Ventura Boulevard is known to Los Angeles residents for its shopping,

and on my way to Fertility Institutes I pass a Bed, Bath, & Beyond, a Land
Rover dealer, a Pilates studio, a spa, and a number of small boutiques nes-
tled into cute Spanish-tiled complexes. The clinic occupies the fourth
story of a bland office building, across the street from an outdoor mall. I
picture a woman fitting in an appointment between a manicure and an
afternoon coffee date.

Seventy percent of the patients who visit L.A.'s most notorious fertility clinic come for sex selection. "Be certain your next child will be the
gender you're hoping for," promises the Fertility Institutes website. "No
other method comes close . . . PGD offers virtually 100% accuracy."[3]
Preimplantation genetic diagnosis, or PGD, is an add-on to in vitro fertilization, which an increasing number of Americans now use to have
children. Once the woman's—or a donor's—eggs have been retrieved
and fertilized with a man's sperm and the resulting zygotes have completed the cell division that yields eight-celled embryos, a single cell is
removed from each embryo and tested for defects, disabilities, or a propensity toward certain diseases.

But lab technicians can also identify sex chromosomes and separate XY
embryos from XX ones, thereby screening for sex—the first nondisability
or nonmedical condition to be turned into a choice. PGD thus attracts
Americans who are perfectly capable of having babies the old-fashioned
way but are, like parents in Delhi and Tirana, hell-bent on having a child
of a certain sex. So determined are they that they're willing to submit to the
diet of hormones necessary to stimulate ovulation, a price tag ranging
from $12,000 to $18,000, and IVF's low success rate to get one.* Decades
after America's elite pushed sex selection on the developing world, they
have taken it up themselves.

Fertility Institutes' sex selection program is the work of Dr. Jeffrey
Steinberg, who founded the clinic in 1986. A squat, balding man who exudes a jovial confidence, he ushers me into his spacious corner office and
talks as if he has all the time in the world, peppering his stories with
Hollywood gossip. (To wit: the producers of the show *CSI* once stopped

---

*According to the Centers for Disease Control and Prevention, only around 40
percent of IVF cycles in the United States for women under thirty-five result in
live births. The rate is even lower among older women.

by the clinic to evaluate a sperm cryopreservation tank's potential as a weapon.) Back in the 1980s, Steinberg tells me, he began offering in vitro fertilization to couples who were having trouble conceiving on their own. When PGD became available in the early 1990s, he started screening embryos for chromosomal disorders like Down syndrome.

Then he started screening for single-gene disorders like cystic fibrosis.

Then he offered sex selection to couples with a history of sex-linked disease.

Finally he began offering the procedure to couples with no history of disease.

Patients had been calling seeking no-questions-asked sex selection, and Steinberg sensed an opportunity. In 2003 he had a publicist announce his clinic would be offering sex selection for social reasons, as nonmedical sex selection is sometimes called. "The media response was crazy," he says. "The patient response was crazy. We had twenty [phone] lines light up. We said, 'Well, okay. This is something.'"

Before long Steinberg was at the center of a media blitz reminiscent of America's 1960s enthusiasm for ultrasound. Two blond babies, identical but for their diapers—one wore pink and the other blue—graced the cover of *Newsweek*: "Girl or Boy? Now You Can Choose." "The brave new world is definitely here," proclaimed the article.[4] In the weeks that followed Steinberg appeared on *60 Minutes*, CNN *Sunday*, and *Good Morning America*.

Not everyone has been enthusiastic about Steinberg's work. Critics point to a litany of ethical issues: that preimplantation sex selection is available only to the rich, that it gives parents a degree of control over their offspring they shouldn't have, that it marks the advent of designer babies. But on the whole, acceptance of sex selection in the United States is growing—particularly in contrast to Europe, where social sex selection is largely illegal. "Americans," Steinberg tells me, "are not intimidated by the technology." Nor are we averse to commercialized, made-to-order health care. "Gender selection is a commodity for purchase," he has said. "If you don't like it, don't buy it."[5]

But fertility doctors who perform preimplantation sex selection also defend it on another ground, and that reason explains why at Fertility Institutes everything is pink. The wall on which the clinic's name is mounted, in a soft cursive script, is magenta. The mat in the framed collage of baby photos hanging on the wall is coral. The laboratory workers examining biopsied embryos under the microscope wear fuschia scrubs. For the most part Americans, like Asians and Eastern Europeans, have a particular preference in babies. And when doctors justify sex selection they point to that preference: what happens in America is different because it is not driven by patriarchy—in America, we want girls.

⊶∞⊷

While the fertility doctors who perform preimplantation sex selection take care to distinguish it from sex selective abortion, in many ways the technology's story is the same. Like in utero sex determination, PGD was developed to help couples carrying debilitating diseases have healthy children. Geneticist Mark Hughes introduced PGD in the United States in the early 1990s by screening embryos for conditions like cystic fibrosis. Sex chromosomes were easy to identify, but like the Danish scientists who pioneered sex selective abortion in 1955, Hughes didn't believe there would be significant demand for casual sex selection. Presented with a choice between the arduous certainty of PGD and the pleasurable unpredictability of sex, he said, "most people would rather have sex."[6]

And yet, as with sex selective abortion, sociologists, bioethicists, and doctors knew better. They noted acute interest among Americans in pre-pregnancy methods of sex selection early on. "There is a mass-market potential," sociologist Amitai Etzioni wrote in the pages of Science in his 1968 attempt to halt sex selection research. "The demand for the new freedom to choose seems well established."[7] Seventeen years later, as the technology was being perfected, bioethicist Helen Bequaert Holmes cautioned: "The desire to determine the sex of one's child is widespread and every child is 'at risk' for this trait. In the advance of the discovery of . . . accurate methods that are likely to be popular, bioethicists ought to prepare by serious consideration of the ethical issues."[8]

While Americans on the whole have never shown much interest in sex selective abortion, we have long tried to manipulate reproduction. Way back in 1899, we bought copies of Suggestion: The Secret of Sex, in which Clarence Wilbur Taber proposed that men put their wives into a trance before sex in order to plant in their minds the notion that they would conceive a son.[9] The early 1900s brought a slew of competing titles, including *Will It Be a Boy?*, *The Causation of Sex in Man,* and *The Key to Sex Control,* which looked at the supposed influence of the mother's diet on the sex of the baby.[10] In 1970 Dr. Landrum B. Shettles introduced what he billed as an effective and scientific method of at-home sex selection in the best-selling *Choose Your Baby's Sex.* By using certain sexual positions and timing the moment of conception, couples, Shettles proposed, might influence the sex of the resulting child. Studies have since proven Shettles's hypothesis wrong, but questionable scientific foundations did not prevent a generation of women from interrupting intercourse to take their basal body temperature.*[11]

But many 1980s bioethicists did not share Helen Bequaert Holmes's view that sex selection needed to be regulated. At the time a laissez-faire approach to reproductive technology reigned—in no small part because of abortion politics. Soon after the birth of IVF baby Louise Brown in 1978, a debate over the ethics of sex selection broke out. Many scholars found the practice objectionable; genetics expert Tabitha Powledge called it "the original sexist sin." And yet despite their qualms bioethicists were loath to advocate outlawing the practice, in part because reproductive rights in America rested on the state not intervening in childbearing decisions.[12] Because the Supreme Court's decision in *Roe v. Wade* legalizing abortion cited the right to privacy, selecting a baby's sex became simply another private decision. PGD went to market unobstructed.

Mark Hughes, who unveiled embryo screening to help couples avoid passing on devastating diseases, soon became one of social sex selection's most vociferous critics. "I went into medicine and into science to diagnose and treat and hopefully cure disease," he told *60 Minutes* correspondent Vicki Mabrey. "Your gender is not a disease, last time I checked."[13]

But the technology's spread has been difficult to stop. While Jeffrey Steinberg is the world's most visible sex selection doctor, many other

---

*The do-it-yourself appeal of the Shettles method has endured, and today the book is still in print. The 2006 edition even addresses the sex ratio imbalance in the developing world for readers who may be concerned about tampering with evolution—before roundly dismissing its effects as insignificant.

fertility doctors quietly offer the lucrative service. A 2006 survey of American fertility clinics that perform PGD by the Genetics and Public Policy Center at Johns Hopkins University found 42 percent of responding clinics give patients the option of screening sex for social reasons.[14] And with 1 out of every 100 babies in the United States born through IVF and the number growing every year, those clinics reach a mushrooming customer base.

Across Los Angeles in Pasadena, Huntington Reproductive Center Fertility offers a more subdued answer to Fertility Institutes. Most of the patients who gather in HRC Fertility's nondescript beige waiting room are classic fertility cases, says Dr. John G. Wilcox, who has slick hair with a side part and a perfect California smile. But "there is definitely growing demand" for sex selection, he adds, "as more and more people become acclimated with the knowledge that they have the ability to control reproduction in this way." HRC Fertility started offering sex selection only five years ago, and it already accounts for almost 10 percent of the center's business.

Fertility doctors like to say PGD is 99.9 percent accurate, and indeed cases of technicians misdiagnosing an embryo's sex are few and far between. The accuracy rate can be misleading because the possibility that a couple will produce no viable embryos, or only embryos of the "wrong" sex, is always high. But a technique now in FDA trials may increase the chances of parents getting what they want the first time around. MicroSort, as the technique is called, entails spinning semen in a centrifuge to separate X-and Y-carrying sperm before releasing the sperm in petri dishes with eggs. (Sperm sorting, which was originally developed with Department of Agriculture money for livestock breeding, relies on the fact that X-carrying sperm contain more genetic material and are therefore heavier than Y-carrying sperm.)[15] Couples can also turn to MicroSort alone, which has a lower success rate than PGD but is far cheaper and can be combined with artificial insemination, without the invasive hormones and egg harvesting required by IVF.

PGD already allows potential parents to screen for genes associated with conditions that develop later in life and can be treated if caught early: breast cancer, colon cancer, Alzheimer's. (Some fertility clinics call this "pruning the family tree.")[16] Screening for less debilitating conditions—a propensity toward obesity, for example—is not far off.[17] But as the first add-on sought by couples with no preexisting medical problems, sex selection is a boon for fertility doctors, opening up their services to the entire population.

At the moment wealthy Americans are the only ones who can afford PGD's steep price tag. Genetics & IVF Institute, the Fairfax, Virginia, clinic overseeing the MicroSort trials, sought interested couples by placing advertisements in the *New York Times* Style section.[18] But—again as with sex selective abortion—the practice could trickle down to the middle class as it becomes cheaper and more accessible. In surveys of prospective American parents over the past ten years, 25 to 35 percent say they would use sex selection techniques if they were readily available; presumably that means affordable and less invasive.[19] America's early-twentieth-century texts have already been replaced with reproductive technology guides like *Guarantee the Sex of Your Baby* and *Chasing the Gender Dream*. As this book goes to press, the second link that comes up when I google "sex selection" (after the Wikipedia entry) is not an article on the plight of the female sex in Asia but an entry on About.com titled "Girl or Boy? Sex Selection Techniques for Everyone Before Pregnancy."[20]

And like doctors in Asia who perform sex determination tests and sex selective abortions, America's practitioners of sex selection say refusing to do it is not an option. "If you don't do it," Wilcox tells me, patients "will look for another clinic that will."

Only the language surrounding America's breed of sex selection is different. Americans don't talk about gender preference. We say "family balancing," a term that implies couples have an inherent right to an equal number of boys and girls. We talk about "gender disappointment," a deep grief arising from not getting what we want. The author of *Guarantee the Sex of Your Baby* explains sympathetically: "The pain that these mothers feel when they fail to bear a child of the 'right' sex is more than just emotional angst. The longing and desire that they hold in their hearts can translate into real physical pain."[21] A recent *Elle* article on what women refer to in online forums as simply "GD" describes San Diego writer and party planner Stephanie Lewis, who went on Prozac after giving birth to twin boys because she wanted a girl. "I stayed in my room," Lewis is quoted as saying. "I drew the drapes. I felt like a funeral should be held."[22]

While it is often said that Asian parents who select for sex do so out of sexism, the rhetoric surrounding American fertility treatments suggests parents who seek out social sex selection are either rationally planning their families or shielding themselves from depression. "I didn't want to be in a disappointed state where I try for a boy and then end up with a girl again," a patient of Jeffrey Steinberg tells me when explaining her reason for undergoing multiple cycles of IVF in order to get a child of the preferred sex. "I didn't know how my emotions would be to a girl."

She is in the minority of PGD patients who use the technology to select for male embryos. (She spoke with me on condition of anonymity. She and her husband don't plan to tell their son how he was conceived.) For the most part parents going through PGD or sperm sorting dread having a boy. Girls are the goal for 80 percent of HRC Fertility's patients and 75 percent of the sperm sorting patients Genetics and IVF Institute takes on.[23] After examining these preferences, Hanna Rosin recently declared in an *Atlantic* cover story—provocatively titled "The End of Men"—that "the traditional order has been upended."[24]

In fact the traditional order has only been upended in the United States, where a shift in gender preferences barely makes a dent in the global imbalance. And examining why American parents want girls suggests that in one crucial way things have not changed all that much.

———— ❧ ————

Often American parents seeking daughters list the reasons you might expect. Mothers talk of princess parties, of ballet lessons, of girls who are, above all, feminine. When Dr. Sunita Puri surveyed Bay Area couples undergoing PGD for sex selection—most of them white, older, and affluent—ten out of twelve wanted girls for reasons like "barrettes and pink dresses."[25] "I'm not going to buy a boy a purse and I'm not going to take him shopping for clothes," Mallory Stout, a twenty-four-year-old mother and homemaker in the Chicago suburbs who is considering going through PGD to get a girl, tells me.[26]

Not all parents have visions of pink. Some mention that girls do better in school, and on this point the research backs them up: girls are more likely to perform and less likely to misbehave, while boys have lately become the source of a good deal of cultural anxiety. Others mention more noble goals. They talk about raising strong daughters; women speak of having the close relationship they had—or didn't have—with their own mother. For gay and lesbian parents gender is often more complex but still very important. Some gay male couples tell researchers they want daughters out of the belief girls will endure less teasing for having gay fathers. Lesbian couples, on the other hand, may worry about socializing and caring for boys.[27]

But when it comes down to it these reasons have one thing in common: Americans who select for sex are intent on having girls because of preconceived notions of how a girl will turn out. Bioethicist Dena S. Davis writes that people who take pains to get a child of a certain sex "don't want just the right chromosomes and the attendant anatomical characteristics, they want a set of characteristics that go with 'girlness' or 'boyness.' . . . If parents want a girl badly enough to go to all the trouble of sperm sorting and artificial insemination, they are likely to make it more difficult for the actual child to resist their expectations and follow her own bent."[28] In that sense American parents seeking a girl are no different from the Indian couple that selects for a son with the expectation he will turn into an upstanding heir. "It's not like [parents in the developing world] who are doing this thing are somehow weird," says Marcy Darnovsky, director of the Center for Genetics and Society, a Berkeley NGO focused on human genetic and reproductive technologies. "We're doing it, too. So let's look in the mirror, folks."[29]

Decades ago, the population control movement abstracted baby making into a matter of governance, turning people into numbers. Parents in developing countries were taught that small families were successful and well educated—that the *quality* of their children was inversely proportional to the *quantity*, as if children were factory goods. Today our concerns about population have come full circle. South Korea is the most extreme case of a rapidly aging society, but it's a harbinger of what is to come. Half of the countries in the world are at or below replacement-level fertility.[30] European policymakers concerned about graying populations have unveiled tax breaks and benefits to attract young, skilled immigrants. In the United States, where the fertility rate remains slightly higher, we are starting to talk about how population growth fuels innovation.[31] Even among environmentalists, the focus has shifted from overall population numbers to carbon footprint: an American baby makes a much larger impact on the world than a Bangladeshi one. But while the idea of government population control now sounds passé, we have not relinquished the notion that reproduction should be controlled; instead, we have shifted it to our own families. In China and California alike, mothers have become their own eugenicists.

⟶⟶⟶

Technologies like PGD are perhaps the best proof that fighting sex selection isn't simply a matter of addressing gender stereotypes. Imagine the United States adopting a pro-boy campaign along the lines of the educational campaigns that are now common in Asia. Posters would show boys in soft situations—curled up on their beds reading, perhaps, or lying in grassy fields braiding chains of daisies. Boys can be good students and confidantes, the posters would stress. Or perhaps we would focus on debunking our idealized notions of girls. We might circulate images showing girls knee-deep in mud or careening down hills on dirt bikes. "You May Not Get the Daughter You Want," a poster might caution.

Needless to say, it wouldn't work. As long as a technology is legal and available people find a way to use it, and allowing dubious fertility treatments encourages frivolous parenting decisions. And not just in America. California's fertility clinics also see significant numbers of Brits, Australians, and Canadians—along with wealthy Indians and Chinese. (Jeffrey Steinberg claims his patients include some of China's most renowned celebrities.) The United States has become a mecca for PGD patients because we have remarkably permissive policies. Even when it comes to cutting-edge technologies whose effects we barely understand, America is driven by the notion of choice.

According to the website BioPolicyWiki, nonmedical sex selection is prohibited in thirty-six countries.[32] The United Kingdom, which has a designated commission that considers the ethical implications and potential societal effects of new reproductive technologies before they go to market, has released a forty-four-page report detailing the potential harm PGD and sperm sorting might cause if legalized.[33] The United States, by contrast, has only the Food and Drug Administration, whose mandate is to evaluate new technologies on the basis of safety and efficacy, not ethics. (Incidentally, the FDA has intervened in the Fertility Institutes' work on safety grounds.)[34] The American Society for Reproductive Medicine, the industry organization for fertility doctors, endorses sperm sorting for "family balancing" reasons and has waffled on the issue of social sex selection during PGD, most recently opposing it.[35]

But the ASRM stance is only a guideline: fertility clinics are not required to follow it. Nor do U.S. clinics have to report patients' reasons for undergoing PGD to the Centers for Disease Control and Prevention, the government body that monitors the fertility industry.[36] American fertility clinics are sorely in need of a regulatory agency along the lines of Britain's Human Fertilisation and Embryology Authority, as its ethics commission is called, says Darnovsky at the Center for Genetics and Society: "Everything is left to the market. And that has caused a lot of unfortunate practices to take hold."

The American health care lobby, indeed, has not lost sight of the fact that fertility treatments now account for a multibillion-dollar industry.[37] The money involved has fractured the one group that might be expected to fight for more regulation of reproductive technologies. Conservatives who object to screening or discarding embryos on religious grounds are rivaled in strength by those who favor letting market forces govern health care.[38]

With the right divided, hope may come from an unlikely source: the reproductive rights community. It was cutting-edge reproductive technologies that prompted Sujatha Jesudason to found Generations Ahead, the Oakland NGO that advocates around sex selection. Preimplantation sex selection was just one issue. Also of concern was surrogacy; surrogate mothers tend to be poor, while the couples that hire them are typically wealthy. And what about the rights of egg donors? What about the technological modification and commercialization of a process that is central to womanhood? Or the inequality brought on by making fertility treatments accessible only to the rich? "The reproductive rights movement in the United States . . . has used an individual choice framework," Jesudason says. "If you apply that political framework to reproductive and genetic technologies, then you essentially go down this path of an individual deciding to do whatever she thinks is best for her." By linking preimplantation sex selection and sex selective abortion, Jesudason hopes to finally convince other reproductive rights organizations to take a stand, both on the tragedy sweeping the developing world and the smaller, more insidious changes taking place at home.

Bioethicists have mostly abandoned choice and privacy as starting points for thinking about reproduction. These days they talk about a framework that balances the rights of women with the rights of her potential children. Central to the new approach is the premise that every individual has the right to an "open future"—instead of having expectations foisted on him or her even before birth. Preimplantation sex selection, some theorists now conclude, prioritizes the needs of one generation over another, making having children more about bringing parents satisfaction than about responsibly creating an independent human being.

That seems a good starting point for thinking about sex selective abortion as well. A woman should have the right to terminate a pregnancy, but she should not have the right to shape the individual represented by that pregnancy to her own whims. As my brother and I hit adolescence, my mother taped the Kahlil Gibran poem "On Children" to the refrigerator to remind herself to let us choose our own destiny:

> Your children are not your children
> They are the sons and daughters of Life's longing for itself
> They come through you but not from you,
> And though they are with you yet they belong not to you.[39]

Or as gynecologist Puneet Bedi put it in the maternity ward at Delhi's Apollo Hospital: "You can choose whether to be a parent. But once you choose to be a parent you cannot choose whether it's a boy or girl, black or white, tall or short."

———— ❦ ————

The sex ratio imbalance has long been an urgent—and yet assiduously ignored—problem. But it recently got a lot more urgent. Along with mail-order blood tests like Baby Gender Mentor, preimplantation technologies are quietly spreading throughout the developing world, where they are finding a market among couples interested in selecting sex discreetly, without in-laws or neighbors knowing. South Korea is leading the way in

Asia, as the interest in IVF among Seoul's elite suggests. But other countries are quickly catching up. Sex selection via PGD is now offered in China, India, Cyprus, Thailand, Jordan, Egypt, Brazil, and Russia. (Nonmedical sex selection is outlawed in Russia, but a Russian medical tourism provider I spoke with says he routinely flies U.S. couples looking to select sex using PGD to Moscow for discount treatments.)[40] Fertility Institutes has opened an office in Guadalajara, Mexico. More worrying still, in some of those countries abortion is neither widely available nor legal: in Egypt PGD introduces sex selection to a population that did not have access to it before.

It took millions of dollars in funding from U.S. organizations, along with thousands of fieldworkers and a good number of mobile clinics, for sex determination and abortion to catch on in the developing world. Today people freely cross borders for life-shaping medical technologies and dissemination occurs much more quickly, without encouragement from the World Bank. With that change comes a new responsibility. Americans can't do much about what medical technologies are legal in Egypt. But we can do a better job of stemming initial demand for those technologies, which are born in places like Ventura Boulevard. Certainly the attitude that the sort of selection that occurs in Fertility Institutes laboratories is somehow inherently different from what happens in Indian abortion clinics is hubristic. American exceptionalism has already caused its fair share of destruction.

At stake with preimplantation sex selection, moreover, is much more than the global balance of males and females, as if that weren't enough. If you believe in the slippery slope, then sex selective embryo implantation pushes us a little further down it. "You can just anticipate what the arguments will be," says Darnovsky. "If we let people choose this important thing about their child—what sex it is—why would we object to them boosting their intelligence or IQ by twenty points?" Embryo selection on the basis of intelligence is not yet available but may not be far off. "From a technology perspective we can test anything," PGD creator Mark Hughes recently said. "The issue becomes what is considered serious enough to warrant such testing and who decides that."[41]

For now, Jeffrey Steinberg decides. In 2009 he announced on the Fertility Institutes website that the clinic would soon offer selection for eye color, hair color, and skin color. (This last he dubbed "complexion.") He might have gone through with it, too, had the advertisement not set off an uproar. The press descended, the Vatican issued a statement criticizing the "obsessive search for the perfect child," and couples who had used PGD for medical reasons balked, fearing frivolous use of reproductive technology would turn public sentiment against cases like theirs.[42] It turned out Americans had more problems with selecting for physical traits than they did with sex selection, and Steinberg retreated.

But he remains optimistic. "The timing was off is all," he tells me as we sit in his office, discussing the future of reproduction against a backdrop of palm trees. "It was just premature. We were ahead of our time. So we said, 'Okay, fine. We'll put it on the back burner.'" In the meantime, he says, couples obsessed with blue or green eyes continue to call the office. As he waits for public opinion to change, he keeps their names on a mailing list.

ACKNOWLEDGMENTS

In the beginning this was a zygote of an idea, a small plan for a magazine article on the effects of China's sex ratio imbalance. Ted Genoways at the *Virginia Quarterly Review* believed in that idea and provided me the space in which to explore it. He was also invaluable in encouraging me to look beyond sex trafficking and bride buying toward the other, less obvious ways in which sex selection can transform a society. His curatorial voice stayed with me as the article grew into a book.

Ariana Lindquist collaborated with me on that early assignment and turned out to be the best photographer I could have hoped for. Ariana introduced me to the Suining families whose experiences formed the backbone of my reporting, and her deeply humanistic photos pushed my writing to new levels. After we completed the article she continued to volunteer relevant details and read over drafts of chapters. I know few who are as dedicated to their work.

I am indebted to the editors who let me take time away from my regular correspondent gigs to write this book, particularly Beth McMurtrie at *The Chronicle of Higher Education* and Richard Stone at *Science*. Others commissioned and shaped articles that found their way into the preceding pages: Britt Peterson, then at *The New Republic*, and Ben Austen, then at *Harper's*. And I am obliged to those editors whose assignments sustained me, both economically and intellectually, over the past three years: Paul Adams, George Black, David Malakoff, Mike May, Michael Moyer, John Parman, Samir Patel, Jennifer Ruark, Greg Veis, and Jacob Ward.

This would perhaps be a very different work without the enthusiasm of Gillian MacKenzie, my agent, who loved the idea of a global book from the start and gave astute input in the proposal phase. She has been an excellent shepherd for the project.

Gillian also found the book a great home. The early and insightful guidance of Clive Priddle, my editor at PublicAffairs, nudged me in the right direction. Other editors who worked on the book but have since left the house include Morgen VanVorst and Lindsay Jones. Chrisona Schmidt copyedited, and Melissa Raymond, along with Sandra Beris of Perseus Books, saw the pages through to the printing stage. Katherine Schreiber diligently fact checked the manuscript and provided helpful suggestions along the way. All remaining errors are mine.

Various friends and family members read and commented on drafts. Thank you to Laura Danielson, Glenn Ford, Doris Klein, Jessica Pulver, and Renee Witlen for your insights and corrections. Rebecca Catching provided an extra set of eyes at the proofreading stage.

In my research on the population control movement I relied heavily on historian Matthew Connelly's amazingly thorough—and very well-written—account, *Fatal Misconception*. I appreciate his help in generously suggesting sources and sending relevant documents along the way. Also valuable were the librarians at Smith College's Sophia Smith Collection—particularly Amy Hague, who expertly pointed me in the direction of relevant files in the Planned Parenthood Federation of America boxes—and the guardian of the Center for Women's Development Studies archive in Delhi. (I wish I knew your name.) Finally, I drew on the deep website maintained by the Rockefeller Archive Center, along with the oral histories available on the Sophia Smith Collection and Truman Library websites.

Again and again I turned to demographers in the course of reporting this book. Some of them did not make it into the final draft. S. Irudaya Rajan graciously hosted me in Kerala, and Isabelle Attané spoke with me in Paris. Cai Yong was crucial in shaping my understanding of the one-child policy. Other scholars and activists who helped me grasp this topic include Mary E. John and Ratna Sudarshan in Delhi.

My reporting would have been a lot lonelier—and the book that resulted less detailed—were it not for friends who housed and guided me in various cities around the world: Mr. and Mrs. Shiv Suri in Delhi, Nana Eun-A Seo in Seoul, Amanda Hong in Taipei, Tracey Suen in London, Zac Wyman in Paris, Dayna and Ember Frank and Angela Kim in Los Angeles, James Luke David in San Francisco, and Megan Shank and Adam Feeney in New York.

Friends—and sometimes friends of friends—introduced me to sources and helped set up interviews: Jennifer Cheng, Yoonhee Cho, Gia Dinh, Karen Hyun, Christian Laudet, and Shravya K. Reddy. Ahead of my trip to South Korea I turned to Soyeon Gun, who translated my emails and made calls on my behalf. Arriving in Seoul, I relied on the expert translation of Ashley Sunya Yoon.

The writing process would have been a lot less fun without that motley club of book lovers from Sam Freedman's superb book seminar at Columbia School of Journalism: Gal Beckerman, David Biello, Shoshana Guy, Allan Jalon, and Kavitha Rajagopalan. Thanks to Sam for teaching me how to craft a proposal and for giving advice as I took a first stab at one. And thanks to Paul Hendrickson at the University of Pennsylvania for teaching me how to write—and observe—before that.

Two chapters of the book grew out of a late-night conversation with Adam Minter. A mentor and a close friend, Adam urged me not to shy away from difficult topics—and provided a fine example in his own reporting on China.

Also instrumental was the fiercely intelligent Laurel Kilgour. From suggesting bioethics readings to connecting me with potential sources to sending meticulous line-by-line edits on a draft, she was singularly helpful. I lucked out in the cousin department.

And I am grateful to the various friends and family members who related their experiences of pregnancy, abortion, IVF, and egg donation or let me sit in on intimate ultrasound exams and doctors' appointments. You know who you are.

Others who contributed ideas or otherwise helped along the way include Parisa Yousef Dorst, Isaac Stone Fish, Ken Kostel, Hien Le, Renee Reynolds, Dawn Stover, and Jiyoung Yoon.

This is a book about family, and I would be remiss if I didn't mention my own. Jake Hvistendahl, my brother, and Barrs Lang, my near-brother, taught me about sex ratio imbalance before anyone else. (In our household generalizations about testosterone didn't always hold true, and it was often I who terrorized them.) In addition to being a loving guardian for a few important years of my life, Hongyu Lang gave me my first Chinese lessons. My father was the original reporter and has always encouraged me in my work. Yet another generation back, I owe a lot to the feisty Joan Danielson and to the minister-turned-novelist Dave Danielson, for showing me how to seize life and love writing (two often contradictory acts), and to English professor Marion Hvistendahl, for teaching me about both the rules and wonders of language early on.

Most of all I thank Aksel Çoruh, for providing balance—both gender and the other sort—in my own life, and for being the double in my happiness.

NOTES

PROLOGUE

1. Nicholas Bakalar, "Sex Ratio Seen to Vary by Latitude," *New York Times*, April 20, 2009, http://tinyurl.com/4l5rhmo.

2. Bart K. Holland, *What Are the Chances? Voodoo Deaths, Office Gossip, and Other Adventures in Probability* (Baltimore, MD: Johns Hopkins University Press, 2002), 17.

3. "Johann Peter Süssmilch," German National Library catalogue, http://d-nb .info/gnd/118814834.

4. Charles Darwin, *The Descent of Man* (Amherst, NY: Prometheus, 1998), 218.

5. Darwin, *Descent of Man,* 221.

6. Darwin, *Descent of Man,* 268.

7. Veronica di Mambro, "The University of Cambridge Eugenics Society from 1911," *Galton Institute Newsletter,* June-September 2003, http://tinyurl.com/ 23o5vml.

8. Guillaume Chapron, quoted in "French Male Bears in Immediate Need of More Females," ScienceDaily, October 29, 2009, http://tinyurl.com/4zruv82.

9. Dena S. Davis, *Genetic Dilemmas: Reproductive Technology, Parental Choices, and Children's Futures* (New York: Routledge, 2001), 91.

10. M. Ruth Nentwig, "Technical Aspects of Sex Preselection," in *The Custom-Made Child? Women-Centered Perspectives,* ed. Helen B. Holmes, Betty B. Hoskins, and Michael Gross (New York: Humana Press, 1981), 181.

11. Aristotle, *On the Generation of Animals* (Whitefish, MT: Kessinger, 2004), 99, http://tinyurl.com/4tcpsv7.

12. Menachem Mendl Brayer, *The Jewish Woman in Rabbinic Literature* (Jersey City, NJ: KTAV, 1986), 2:208.

13. Forum Against Sex Determination and Sex Pre-selection, "Using Technology, Choosing Sex," 92, http://tinyurl.com/4wd6huz.

14. Olivia P. Judson, "Killing the Sex Ratio," *Nature*, December 8, 1994, 503.

267

CHAPTER 1

1. Amartya Sen, "More Than 100 Million Women Are Missing," *New York Review of Books*, December 20, 1990, http://tinyurl.com/4zxe2s6.

2. South India Fertility Project, http://tinyurl.com/4gfjb8v.

3. Christophe Z. Guilmoto, "Characteristics of Sex-Ratio Imbalance in India, and Future Scenarios" (paper presented at Fourth Asia Pacific Conference on Reproductive and Sexual Health and Rights, 2007), 9, http://tinyurl.com/4okjqdu.

4. Guilmoto, "Characteristics," 9.

5. Singapore and Taiwan figures from Elspeth Graham, "Son Preference, Female Deficit and Singapore's Fertility Transition," in *Watering the Neighbour's Garden*, ed. Isabelle Attané and Christophe Z. Guilmoto (Paris: CICRED, 2007), 89–106.

6. India figure from "Field Listing: Sex Ratio," in *CIA World Factbook 2010*, http://tinyurl.com/576yck; China figure from Shuzhuo Li, "Imbalanced Sex Ratio at Birth and Comprehensive Intervention in China" (paper presented at the Fourth Asia Pacific Conference on Reproductive and Sexual Health and Rights, 2007), 7.

7. Attané and Guilmoto, *Watering*, ix.

8. Christophe Z. Guilmoto, "Sex Ratio Imbalance in Asia: Trends, Consequences, and Policy Responses" (paper presented at Fourth Asia Pacific Conference on Reproductive and Sexual Health and Rights, 2007), 1, http://tinyurl.com/4ldcpgd.

9. Since fewer women lead to fewer births, factoring a skewed sex ratio at birth into global population projections yields low estimates for the total population twenty-five or fifty years out, and UNPD officers are, perhaps justifiably, wary of underestimating total population figures. Christophe Guilmoto, interview by author, Paris, August 11, 2009; Joseph Chamie, phone interview by author, January 19, 2011.

10. The total population of the United States, as of July 2010, was 310 million. Just under 160 million of those people are female. "North America: United States," in *CIA World Factbook 2010*, http://tinyurl.com/2l9rcv.

11. "World," in *CIA World Factbook 2010*, http://tinyurl.com/yrmnyw; and "Population," http://tinyurl.com/6cgwbj.

12. Christophe Guilmoto, interview by author, Paris, August 11, 2009. Also see "Field Listing: Sex Ratio," in *CIA World Factbook 2010*, http://tinyurl.com/576yck.

13. Guilmoto, "Characteristics."

14. Guilmoto, interview by author, August 11, 2009.

15. Mara Hvistendahl, "No Country for Young Men," *The New Republic*, July 9, 2008, http://tinyurl.com/48m844m.

16. Guilmoto, interview by author, August 11, 2009.

17. South Korea joined the OECD in 1996. See "Countries: Korea," *OECD Observer*, http://tinyurl.com/4j7tazh.

18. Sen, "More Than 100 Million."

19. M. Giovanna Merli and Adrian E. Raftery, "Are Births Underreported in Rural China? Manipulation of Statistical Records in Response to China's Population Policies," *Demography*, February 2000, 109–126. P. N. Mari Bhat, "On the Trail of 'Missing' Indian Females: Search for Clues," *Economic and Political Weekly*, December 28, 2002, 5105–5118.

20. Emily Oster, "Hepatitis B and the Case of the Missing Women," *Journal of Political Economy* 113, no. 6 (2005), http://tinyurl.com/4lqxylv.

21. Emily Oster et al., "Hepatitis B Does Not Explain Male-Biased Sex Ratios in China," http://home.uchicago.edu/~eoster/hbvnotecon.pdf.

22. Christophe Guilmoto, phone interview by author, November 9, 2010.

23. Christophe Z. Guilmoto, *The Sex Ratio Transition in Asia*, Center for Population and Development Working Papers Series (Paris: CEPED, 2009), 5.

24. "Asia's Declining Fertility," South Asia Research Institute for Policy and Development, December 20, 2006, http://tinyurl.com/47pv4na. Also see *Population and Social Integration Section Fact Sheets*, United Nations Economic and Social Commission for Asia and the Pacific (Bangkok: UNESCAP), http://tinyurl.com/46o2e4z.

25. Guilmoto, *Sex Ratio Transition*, 33.

26. "Country Comparison: Total Fertility Rate," in *CIA World Factbook 2010*, http://tinyurl.com/3yur88.

27. Guilmoto, *Sex Ratio Transition*, 9.

28. Guilmoto, "Characteristics," 8.

29. Richa Sharma, "Gender Imbalance Highest Among Affluent: Study," *Headlines India*, December 15, 2008, http://tinyurl.com/29kyb3h.

30. Guilmoto, *Sex Ratio Transition*, 8.

31. France Meslé, phone interview by author, December 16, 2008.

32. France Meslé, Jacques Vallin, and Irina Badurashvili, "A Sharp Increase in Sex Ratio at Birth in the Caucasus. Why? How?" in *Watering*, 73–88.

33. "Brides and Prejudice in China," *China Daily*, August 23, 2010, http://tinyurl.com/4abld7z.

34. Attané and Guilmoto, *Watering*, 3.

35. "HIV Funding Priority Shift Call," BBC, May 9, 2008, http://tinyurl.com/23csdbq.

CHAPTER 2

1. Suining's story is detailed in Mara Hvistendahl, "Half the Sky: How China's Gender Imbalance Threatens Its Future," *Virginia Quarterly Review*, Fall 2008, 188–215.

2. Guilmoto, *Sex Ratio Transition*, 33.

3. Hvistendahl, "Half the Sky." Figures adjusted to 2011 currency rates.

4. Barbara Miller, "Female-Selective Abortion in Asia: Patterns, Policies, and Debates," *American Anthropologist*, December 2001, 1087.

5. China's household per capita income was around ¥7,200 in 2006. Marcos Chamon and Eswar Prasad, *Why Are Saving Rates of Urban Households in China Rising?* IMF Working Paper (International Monetary Fund, June 2008), http://tinyurl.com/67xt3rx.

6. Twins, which are exempted under the one-child policy in China, have become more common in recent years as couples take cheap fertility drugs in an effort to work around the law. James Reynolds, "Chinese Challenge One-Child Policy," BBC, May 25, 2007, http://tinyurl.com/277w77y; also see Michael Sheridan, "Fertility-Drug Twins Beat China's One-Child Law," *The Times* (London), February 27, 2005, http://tinyurl.com/22olj4n.

7. "China Warned on Gender Imbalance," BBC, August 24, 2007, http://news.bbc.co.uk/2/hi/6962650.stm.

8. Hvistendahl, "No Country."

9. Hvistendahl, "Half the Sky."

10. Therese Hesketh and Zhu Wei Xing, "Abnormal Sex Ratios in Human Populations: Causes and Consequences," *Proceedings of the National Academy of Sciences*, September 5, 2006, 13272, http://tinyurl.com/67p5g2b.

11. Guilmoto, interview by author, August 11, 2009.

12. Michelle Goldberg, *The Means of Reproduction: Sex, Power, and the Future of the World* (New York: Penguin, 2009), 191.

13. Center for Women's Development Studies, *Planning Gender, Planning Families: Addressing the Adverse Sex Ratio* (Books for Change, 2008), 64.

14. Danièle Bélanger, "Sex-Selective Abortions: Short-term and Long-term Perspectives," *Reproductive Health Matters*, May 2002, 194.

15. Hvistendahl, "Half the Sky."

16. Hvistendahl, "Half the Sky."

CHAPTER 3

1. *India: Achieving Rapid and Inclusive Growth, Sustainable Development*, http://tinyurl.com/2g2fjgp.

2. "Women Shoot Past Men Across the Spectrum," *Economic Times*, June 22, 2009, http://tinyurl.com/29ftnpo.

3. Ranjit Devraj, "No Stopping Reserved Seats for Women in Parliament," IPS News, March 8, 2010, http://tinyurl.com/ylz4zs9.

4. Didi Kirsten Tatlow, "For China's Women, More Opportunities, More Pitfalls," *New York Times*, November 25, 2010, http://tinyurl.com/23er2xf.

5. Matthew Connelly, *Fatal Misconception* (Cambridge: Harvard University Press, 2008), 213.

6. Connelly, *Fatal Misconception*, 119–120.

7. Connelly, *Fatal Misconception*, 114.

8. Connelly, *Fatal Misconception*, 162.

9. Matthew Connelly, "Population Control in India: Prologue to the Emergency Period," *Population and Development Review*, December 2006, 633.

10. Connelly, "Population Control in India," 636.

11. Connelly, *Fatal Misconception*.

12. U.S. Office of Technology Assessment, *World Population and Fertility Planning Technologies: The Next Twenty Years* (Washington, D.C.: U.S. Government Printing Office, 1982), 108.

13. Connelly, "Population Control in India," 657. Also see Kristin L. Ahlberg, *Transplanting the Great Society: Lyndon Johnson and Food for Peace* (Columbia: University of Missouri Press, 2008).

14. Connelly, *Fatal Misconception*, 263.

15. Barbara B. Crane and Jason L. Finkle, *Organizational Impediments to Development Assistance: The World Bank's Population Program* (Princeton: Princeton University Press, 1981), 519.

16. Edward Goldsmith et al., "Preface: A Blueprint for Survival," *Ecologist*, January 1972, http://www.theecologist.info/page34.html.

17. "Treading Lightly: Does Mankind Need More Than One Planet?" *Economist*, September 19, 2002, http://www.economist.com/node/1337251.

18. Connelly, *Fatal Misconception*, 264.

19. Goldberg, *Means of Reproduction*, 71.

20. Seungsook Moon, *Militarized Modernity and Gendered Citizenship in South Korea* (Durham, NC: Duke University Press, 2005), 81.

21. Connelly, *Fatal Misconception*, 181, 265.

22. John Shields Aird, *Slaughter of the Innocents: Coercive Birth Control in China* (Washington, D.C.: AEI Press, 1990), 6.

23. Mara Hvistendahl, "Has China Outgrown the One-Child Policy?" *Science*, September 17, 2010, 1458.

24. Hvistendahl, "Has China Outgrown," 1458.

25. Mara Hvistendahl, "Of Population Projections and Projectiles," *Science*, September 17, 2010, 1460.

26. Susan Greenhalgh, *Just One Child: Science and Policy in Deng's China* (Berkeley: University of California Press, 2008), 130.

27. Greenhalgh, *Just One Child*, 127.

28. Song maintained, when interviewed by anthropologist Susan Greenhalgh, that he first met Olsder in 1978. I base this date on my interview with Olsder.

29. Hvistendahl, "Of Population Projections."

30. Greenhalgh, *Just One Child*, 133.

31. Hvistendahl, "Of Population Projections."

32. Greenhalgh, *Just One Child*, 152.

33. Hvistendahl, "Of Population Projections."

34. Greenhalgh, *Just One Child*, 154.

35. Hvistendahl, "Has China Outgrown," 1458–1459.

36. Mary-Jane Schneider, *Introduction to Public Health*, 2nd ed. (Sudbury, MA: Jones & Bartlett, 2006), 428.

37. Sukanya Hazarika, Public Health Foundation of India, interview by author, Delhi, June 29, 2009. See also Muhammad Yunus, *Banker to the Poor:*

Micro-Lending and the Battle Against World Poverty (New York: PublicAffairs, 2003), 134.

38. Phillip B. Levine and Douglas Staiger, "Abortion Policy and Fertility Outcomes: The Eastern European Experience," *Journal of Law and Economics,* April 2004, 229.

39. Timothy Heleniak, "Causes and Demographic Consequences of Fertility Decline in the Former Soviet Union and Central and Eastern Europe," *Marriage & Family Review,* January 2010.

40. Wolfgang Lutz, Warren Sanderson, and Sergei Scherbov, "The End of World Population Growth," *Nature,* August 2, 2001.

41. Christophe Z. Guilmoto, *The Sex Ratio Transition in Asia,* Center for Population and Development Working Papers Series (Paris: CEPED, 2009), 23.

42. http://www.indexmundi.com/albania/gdp_real_growth_rate.html

43. UNFPA, "Guidance Note on Prenatal Sex Selection," 2010, http://tinyurl.com/62hz39h.

44. These results have not yet been checked against Albanian census data.

45. Manuela Bello, email correspondence with author, June 29, 2010.

46. Half of pregnancies ended in abortion: United Nations Population Division Department of Economic and Social Affairs, "Albania," in *Abortion Policies: A Global Review* (United Nations, 2002), http://tinyurl.com/2eg6lpb. Percentage of women using contraception: Flora Ismaili, interview by author, Tirana, Albania, July 5, 2010.

47. Cost of ultrasound: Flora Ismaili, interview by author. Available from 1990s onward: Louise Grogan, email correspondence with author, July 9, 2010.

48. Flora Ismaili, interview by author.

49. Manuela Bello, email correspondence with author.

50. Douglas Almond and Lena Edlund, "Son-Biased Sex Ratios in the 2000 United States Census," *Proceedings of the National Academy of the Sciences,* April 15, 2008, 5681–5682, http://tinyurl.com/2f5e3db.

51. Almond and Edlund, "Son-Biased Sex Ratios."

52. "U.S. Birth Rate: Still Fueling Population Growth," online discussion, Population Reference Bureau, March 22, 2007, http://tinyurl.com/29memvr.

53. Lisa Wong Macabasco, "Why the Abortion Rate Among Asian-American Women Is So High," *Hyphen,* September 2, 2010; regarding the 18 percent abortion rate among whites, see http://tinyurl.com/2cvo3l2.

CHAPTER 4

1. Roger Jeffery, Patricia Jeffery, and Andrew Lyon, "Female Infanticide and Amniocentesis," *Social Science and Medicine* 19, no. 11 (1984): 1207–1212.

2. Indraprastha Apollo Hospitals, New Delhi, http://tinyurl.com/48sn6x3. Jay Solomon, "India's New Coup in Outsourcing: Inpatient Care," *Wall Street Journal,* April 26, 2004.

3. "Doctor Sought over Illegal Scans," BBC, December 5, 2007, http://tinyurl.com/2mf8oe.

4. Elisabeth Bumiller, *May You Be the Mother of a Hundred Sons: A Journey Among the Women of India* (New York: Fawcett Columbine, 1990), 113.

5. U.S. Office of Technology Assessment, *World Population and Fertility Planning Technologies: The Next Twenty Years* (Washington, D.C.: U.S. Government Printing Office, 1982), 99.

6. Chai Bin Park and Nam-Hoon Cho, "Consequences of Son Preference," 79.

7. Bumiller, *May You Be the Mother,* 115.

8. Vibhuti Patel, "The Political Economy of Missing Girls in India," in Tulsi Patel, ed., *Sex-Selective Abortion in India: Gender, Society, and New Reproductive Technologies* (Sage: 2007), 300.

9. Connelly, *Fatal Misconception,* 357.

10. Jeffrey R. Immelt, Vijay Govindajaran, and Chris Trimble, "How GE Is Disrupting Itself," *Harvard Business Review,* October 2009, 8.

11. Immelt, Govindajaran, and Trimble, "How GE Is Disrupting Itself," 8–9.

12. Peter Wonacott, "India's Skewed Sex Ratio Puts GE Sales in Spotlight," *Wall Street Journal,* April 18, 2007.

13. See Robin Elise Weiss, "Telling Your Baby's Sex by Ultrasound," http://tinyurl.com/5uyq9an.

14. Paul Glader, "Mindray Eyes U.S. As West Looks East," *Wall Street Journal,* September 14, 2010, http://tinyurl.com/39aw9ez.

15. Laura Lederer, "'Missing Girls' in Asia: Magnitudes, Implications, and Possible Responses" (panel discussion, American Enterprise Institute, Washington, D.C., September 17, 2008).

16. Wonacott, "India's Skewed Sex Ratio."

17. Wonacott, "India's Skewed Sex Ratio."

18. Kum Sung: Heeran Chun, interview by author, Seoul, December 14, 2009.

19. Rubena Moisiu, interview by author, Tirana, Albania, July 5, 2010.

20. "Google, Microsoft Pull Sex Ads After India Legal Threat," AFP, September 18, 2008.

21. Nell Boyce, "Revisiting the Baby Gender Mentor," NPR's *Morning Edition,* February 27, 2006, http://tinyurl.com/63urvrc.

22. Nell Greenfieldboyce, "Critics Question Accuracy of Fetus Sex Test," NPR's *Morning Edition,* September 29, 2005.

23. Julie M. Donnelly, "Acu-Gen Biolab Files for Ch. 11 Bankruptcy," *Mass High Tech,* December 17, 2009, http://www.masshightech.com/stories/2009/12/14/daily59-Acu-Gen-Biolab-files-for-Ch-11-bankruptcy.html.

CHAPTER 5

1. Barbara D. Metcalf and Thomas R. Metcalf, *A Concise History of Modern India,* 2nd ed. (Cambridge: Cambridge University Press, 2006), 62.

2. Duncan's appearance: James Douglas, *Bombay and Western India: A Series of Stray Papers* (London: Samson Low, Marston & Company, 1893), 175. Reputation: C. Collin Davies, "Review of *Jonathan Duncan and Varanasi* by V. A. Narain," *English Historical Review*, 1962.

3. John William Kaye, *The Administration of the East India Company: A History of Indian Progress* (London: Richard Bentley, 1853), 553.

4. Jonathan Duncan, letter to Lord Cornwallis, October 2, 1789, in *Selections from the Duncan Records* (Benares: Medical Hall Press, 1873), 134.

5. Philip Woodruff, *The Men Who Ruled India: The Founders* (Oxford: Alden, 1953), 179.

6. Kaye, *Administration of the East India Company*, 554; see also Duncan, letter to Lord Cornwallis, 134.

7. Kaye, *Administration of the East India Company*, 556.

8. L. S. Vishwanath, *Female Infanticide and Social Structure: A Socio-Historical Study in Western and Northern India* (Delhi: Hindustan Publishing Corporation, 2000), 8.

9. L. S. Vishwanath, "Efforts of Colonial State to Suppress Female Infanticide: Use of Sacred Texts, Generation of Knowledge," *Economic and Political Weekly*, May 9, 1998, 1104–1112.

10. Kaye, *Administration of the East India Company*, 557.

11. John Wilson, *History of the Suppression of Infanticide in Western India Under the Government of Bombay: Including Notices of the Provinces and Tribes in Which the Practice Has Prevailed* (Cornell University Library, 1855), 43.

12. Kaye, *Administration of the East India Company*.

13. Frederick Wilse Bateson, *The Cambridge Bibliography of English Literature: Index, Volume III* (London: Cambridge University Press, 1940), 907.

14. Kaye, *Administration of the East India Company*, 549.

15. Kaye, *Administration of the East India Company*, 549.

16. Kaye, *Administration of the East India Company*, 558.

17. Infant deaths from Lionel Rose, *The Massacre of the Innocents: Infanticide in Britain, 1800–1939* (London: Routledge, 1986). *Journal of Social Science* from historian Hilary Marland, University of Warwick, quoted in "Infant-killing and the Victorian Mother," BBC News, June 15, 2003, http://tinyurl.com/34658x5.

18. Kaye, *Administration of the East India Company*. 545.

19. Census results given are from 1901.

20. Vishwanath, "Efforts of Colonial State to Suppress Female Infanticide."

21. Kaye, *Administration of the East India Company*, 555.

22. Kaye, *Administration of the East India Company*, 552.

23. Vishwanath, *Female Infanticide*, 123.

24. Vishwanath, *Female Infanticide*.

25. Vishwanath, *Female Infanticide*, 95.

26. L. S. Vishwanath, "Female Infanticide, Property, and the Colonial State," in *Sex-Selective Abortion in India*, ed. Tulsi Patel (Sage, 2006), 270.

27. Philip Gourevitch, *We Wish to Inform You That Tomorrow We Will Be Killed with Our Families: Stories from Rwanda* (New York: Picador, 1999).

28. L. W. G. Malcolm, "Sex-Ratio in African Peoples," *American Anthropologist,* n.s., October-December 1924, 464.

29. Kaye, *Administration of the East India Company,* 552.

30. Charles Darwin, *The Descent of Man* (Amherst, NY: Prometheus, 1998), 263.

31. Darwin, *Descent of Man,* 264.

32. Darwin, *Descent of Man,* 267.

33. C. A. Bayly, *Indian Society and the Making of the British Empire* (London: Cambridge University Press, 1990), 7.

34. Metcalf and Metcalf, *Concise History.*

35. Metcalf and Metcalf, *Concise History,* 91.

36. Peter Marshall, "British History in Depth: The British Presence in India in the 18th Century," BBC, October 15, 2010, http://tinyurl.com/nt2ncc.

37. Bernard S. Cohn, "The Initial British Impact on India: A Case Study of the Benares Region," *Journal of Asian Studies,* August 1960, 429.

38. Metcalf and Metcalf, *Concise History,* 79.

39. Bernard S. Cohn, "Structural Change in Indian Rural Society 1596–1885," in *An Anthropologist Among the Historians and Other Essays* (Delhi: Oxford University Press, 1987), 183; quoted in Vishwanath, *Female Infanticide and Social Structure,* 133.

40. Vishwanath, "Female Infanticide," 274.

41. Vishwanath, *Female Infanticide and Social Structure,* 133–134.

42. Puneet Bedi, interview by author, Delhi, July 2, 2009.

43. Vishwanath, *Female Infanticide and Social Structure,* 98.

44. Vishwanath, *Female Infanticide and Social Structure,* 50.

45. Heeran Chun, interview by author, Seoul, South Korea, December 14, 2009.

46. "Sex-selection: A Brain-bending Intersection of Ideals," http://tinyurl.com/35v263d.

47. *The Missing Daughters of India/Sex Selection: The Issue; and What You Can Do* (brochure distributed by UNFPA India office).

48. Mark Landler, "A New Gender Agenda," *New York Times Magazine,* August 18, 2009, http://tinyurl.com/358ttun.

49. Steven W. Mosher, "Opinion: Ban Sex-selective Abortions, in the U.S.," August 28, 2008, http://tinyurl.com/5vw7sp8.

50. Institute for Social Development Studies, "New 'Common Sense': Family-Planning Policy and Sex Ratio in Viet Nam" (paper presented at the Fourth Asia Pacific Conference on Reproductive and Sexual Health and Rights, 2007), 9.

51. Elisabeth Bumiller, *May You Be the Mother of a Hundred Sons: A Journey Among the Women of India* (New York: Fawcett Columbine, 1990), 115.

52. Tina Rosenberg, "The Daughter Deficit," *New York Times Magazine,* August 19, 2009, http://tinyurl.com/2vmbncq.

53. Institute for Social Development Studies, "New 'Common Sense,'" 7.

54. William Saletan, "Fetal Subtraction," *Slate,* April 3, 2008, http://tinyurl .com/37l7fxa.

55. Goldberg, *Means of Reproduction,* 194, 196.

56. "Gujarat Miniser's Motorbike Campaign Against Female Foeticide," *Indian Health News,* April 20, 2006, http://tinyurl.com/4huq53j.

57. "Anand Jon's Sister Lends Support to Save Girl Child Campaign in India," *ThaIndian News,* October 14, 2009, http://tinyurl.com/2vexmga.

CHAPTER 6

1. Connelly, *Fatal Misconception,* 165–166.

2. Puneet Bedi, phone interview by author, July 14, 2010.

3. Connelly, *Fatal Misconception,* 310.

4. Connelly, *Fatal Misconception,* 171.

5. Puneet Bedi, phone interview by author, July 14, 2010.

6. Sabu George, interview by author, Delhi, July 3, 2009.

7. Ishwar C. Verma et al., "Prenatal Diagnosis of Genetic Disorders," *Indian Pediatrics,* May 1975, 384.

8. Puneet Bedi, phone interview by author, July 14, 2010.

9. Sabha Hussain, "Population Policy," *Social Scientist,* October-November 1985, 25.

10. Verma et al., "Prenatal Diganosis."

11. William Grimes, "Sheldon J. Segal, Who Developed Contraceptives, Dies at 83," *New York Times,* October 20, 2009, http://tinyurl.com/33qvawm.

12. Soma Hewa and Darwin H. Stepleton, *Globalization, Philanthropy, and Civil Society: Toward a New Political Culture in the Twenty-first Century* (New York: Springer Science/Business Media, 2005), 62–63.

13. Connelly, "Population Control in India," 649.

14. Connelly, *Fatal Misconception,* 216.

15. "In Memoriam: Christopher Tietze," *Studies in Family Planning,* May-June 1984, 152.

16. Stephen Miller, "Sheldon Segal, Leading Developer of Contraceptives, Dies at 83," *Wall Street Journal,* October 21, 2009, http://online.wsj.com/article/ SB125616647908300053.html.

17. Connelly, *Fatal Misconception,* 199.

18. *Annual Report for 1966,* The Rockefeller Foundation (New York: Rockefeller Foundation, 1967).

19. Connelly, "Population Control in India," 646.

20. Connelly, *Fatal Misconception,* 217; Connelly, "Population Control in India," 651.

21. Connelly, "Population Control in India," 634.

22. Connelly, "Population Control in India," 646, 656.

23. Roger Jeffery, "New Patterns in Health Sector Aid," *Economic and Political Weekly,* September 11, 1982, 1500.

24. Hewa and Stepleton, *Globalization, Philanthropy, and Civil Society,* 63.

25. Sheldon J. Segal, *Under the Banyan Tree: A Population Scientist's Odyssey* (Oxford University Press, 2003), 191.

26. Connelly, *Fatal Misconception,* 172.

27. S. N. Agarwala, "Social and Cultural Factors Affecting Fertility in India," in *Proceedings of the Seventh Conference of the IPPF,* 100–105, Series VIII, Box 202, Sophia Smith Collection, Smith College, Northampton, MA.

28. List of Conference Participants, International Conference on Planned Parenthood Program, February 10–16, 1963, Series VIII, Box 202, Sophia Smith Collection, Smith College, Northampton, MA.

29. S. N. Agarwala, "Social and Cultural Factors."

30. Rockefeller Foundation Archives Collection, Rockefeller Foundation Field Offices, Record Group 6.7–New Delhi, India, 1835–1976, Subgroup II–Medical and Natural Sciences Program," http://tinyurl.com/4f8sjjb.

31. Ford Foundation Grants Database, 1969 Grants, http://tinyurl.com/6xzsjan. Accessed June 15, 2010.

32. International seminar: B. Pastakia, "Doctors and Overpopulation," letter to *British Medical Journal,* May 6, 1972, 534. World Health Organization symposium: K. R. Laumas, *Recent Developments in Contraceptive Technology: Proceedings of an International Symposium Held on 18th and 19th October, 1974, at New Delhi* (Delhi: All-India Institute of Medical Sciences, 1974).

33. Roger Jeffery, "New Patterns in Health Sector Aid," 1498, 1500.

34. Connelly, *Fatal Misconception,* 318.

35. Connelly, *Fatal Misconception,* 324.

36. Goldberg, *Means of Reproduction,* 83.

37. Connelly, *Fatal Misconception,* 322.

38. 6.2 million: Connelly, *Fatal Misconception,* 323. Nazi totals: Ian Kershaw, *Hitler 1889–1936: Hubris* (New York: Norton, 2000), 487.

39. Kingsley Davis, "Asia's Cities: Problems and Options," *Population and Development Review,* September 1975, 83.

40. Connelly, *Fatal Misconception,* 321.

41. Connelly, *Fatal Misconception,* 321.

42. Connelly, *Fatal Misconception,* 310, 322.

43. Barbara B. Crane and Jason L. Finkle, "Organizational Impediments to Development Assistance: The World Bank's Population Program," *World Politics,* July 1981, 552.

44. Connelly, *Fatal Misconception,* 323.

45. Hussain, "Population Policy." Bumiller, *May You Be the Mother,* 113.

46. Barbara Miller, "Female-Selective Abortion in Asia: Patterns, Policies, and Debates," *American Anthropologist,* n.s., December 2001, 1091.

47. *CIA World Factbook;* Arjun Adlakha, *Population Trends: India,* U.S. Department of Commerce, Economics and Statistics Administration, Bureau of the Census, http://tinyurl.com/32gvsa5.

48. "China's Population to Peak at 1.4 Billion Around 2026," U.S. Census Bureau press release, December 15, 2009, http://tinyurl.com/45t2h8j.

49. Vina Mazumdar, "Changing Terms of Political Discourse: Women's Movement in India, 1970s–1990s," *Economic and Political Weekly*, July 22, 1995, 1872.

50. UNFPA, Ministry of Health and Family Welfare, and National Human Rights Commission, *Uphold My Reproductive Rights* (brochure distributed by UNFPA India office).

51. Vina Mazumdar, *Amniocentesis and Sex Selection,* Center for Women's Development Studies Occasional Paper Series (Delhi: Center for Women's Development Studies, 1994), http://tinyurl.com/6chg5zu.

52. Mazumdar, *Amniocentesis and Sex Selection.*

CHAPTER 7

1. John Postgate, "Bat's Chance in Hell," *New Scientist*, April 5, 1973, 14.

2. Buddy Hackett, Paul Erlich, Ben Wattenberg, *The Tonight Show,* August 13, 1970.

3. Connelly, *Fatal Misconception,* 258.

4. Paul R. Ehrlich and Anne H. Ehrlich, "*The Population Bomb* Revisited," *Electronic Journal of Sustainable Development* 1, no 3 (2009).

5. Ehrlich and Ehrlich, "*Population Bomb* Revisited."

6. Paul Ehrlich, *The Population Bomb* (London: Cox & Wyman, 1971), 1.

7. Ehrlich, *Population Bomb*, 85.

8. Connelly, *Fatal Misconception,* 259.

9. John Tierney, "Betting on the Planet," *New York Times Magazine,* December 2, 1990, http://tinyurl.com/4m7wwdq.

10. Connelly, *Fatal Misconception,* 259.

11. Ehrlich, *Population Bomb.*

12. Ehrlich, *Population Bomb,* 141.

13. "U.S. Population Tops 300 Million and Shows Accelerating Growth," PBS *Newshour,* October 17, 2006, http://tinyurl.com/26ynry3.

14. "Campaign Aims to Cut Size of U.S. Families," *Los Angeles Times,* August 11, 1971. Planned Parenthood Federation of America Papers, Series IV, Box 130, Sophia Smith Collection, Smith College, Northampton, MA.

15. On Berelson: John D. Rockefeller, "The Commission on Population Growth and the American Future," *Studies in Family Planning,* May 1972, 78.

16. Margaret Snyder, "A Summary of the Discussions," in "The Behavorial Sciences and Family Planning Programs: Report on a Conference," *Studies in Family Planning,* October 1967.

17. Vera Rubin, "Steven Polgar 1931–1978," *American Anthropologist,* n.s., March 1979, 79–84.

18. Hudson Hoagland, "The Control of Fertility: AAAS Symposium, December 27, 1968," *Science,* September 20, 1968, 1261; Landrum B. Shettles and

David M. Rorvik, *How to Choose the Sex of Your Baby: The Method Best Supported by Scientific Evidence* (New York: Broadway Books, 2006), 18.

19. Rubin, "Steven Polgar 1931–1978."

20. Deepankar Basu and Robert de Jong, "Son Targeting Fertility Behavior: Some Consequences and Determinants," *Demography*, May 2010, 521–536.

21. Charles F. Westoff and Ronald R. Rindfuss, "Sex Preselection in the United States: Some Implications," *Science*, May 10, 1974, 633.

22. "Family Planning Case Record," Planned Parenthood Federation of America Papers, Series VIII, Box 203 (Taiwan), Sophia Smith Collection, Smith College, Northampton, MA.

23. Gale Largey, "Sex Control and Society: A Critical Assessment of Sociological Speculations," *Social Problems*, Winter 1973, 314–315.

24. Chai Bin Park and Nam-Hoon Cho, "Consequences of Son Preference in a Low-Fertility Society: Imbalance of the Sex Ratio at Birth in Korea," *Population and Development Review*, March 1995, 59.

25. Edgar Snow, *Population Care and Control*, Report of the Victor-Bostrom Fund Committee and the Population Crisis Committee, Spring 1971, Planned Parenthood Federation of America Papers, Series VIII, Box 203, Sophia Smith Collection, Smith College, Northampton, MA.

26. Mindel C. Sheps, "Effects of Family Size and Sex Ratio of Preference Regarding the Sex of Children," *Population Studies* 17 (1963): 66–72.

27. Margaret Snyder, "A Summary of the Discussions," *Studies in Family Planning*, October 1967.

28. Connelly, "Population Control in India," p. 644.

29. Snyder, "Summary of the Discussions."

30. Jaswant Raj Mathur, petition to Alan F. Guttmacher for funding, April 1967, Planned Parenthood Federation of America Papers, Series VIII, Box 204, Sophia Smith Collection, Smith College, Northampton, MA.

31. Richard Day, memorandum to Alan F. Guttmacher, May 4, 1967, Planned Parenthood Federation of America Papers, Series VIII, Box 204, Sophia Smith Collection, Smith College, Northampton, MA.

32. Alan F. Guttmacher, letter to Dudley Kirk, May 23, 1967, Planned Parenthood Federation of America Papers, Series VIII, Box 204, Sophia Smith Collection, Smith College, Northampton, MA.

33. Kenneth A. Lawrence, letter to Alan F. Guttmacher, July 21, 1967, Planned Parenthood Federation of America Papers, Series VIII, Box 204, Sophia Smith Collection, Smith College, Northampton, MA.

34. William D. McElroy, "Biomedical Aspects of Population Control," *BioScience*, January 1969, 23.

35. Arno G. Motulsky, "Brave New World?" *Science*, August 23, 1974.

36. Postgate, "Bat's Chance in Hell," 12–16.

37. Bernard Berelson, "Beyond Family Planning," *Science*, February 7, 1969, 533–543.

38. Connelly, *Fatal Misconception,* 257.

39. Matthew Connelly, "Controlling Passions," *Wilson Quarterly,* Summer 2008, 63.

40. Alexandra Minna Stern, *Eugenic Nation: Faults and Frontiers of Better Breeding in Modern America* (Berkeley: University of California Press, 2005), 202.

41. Frederick S. Jaffe, "Scientific Foundations of Population Policy with Particular Attention to Population Growth and Distribution in the U.S." (notes on meeting held at the Population Council, New York, March 6–7, 1970), Planned Parenthood Federation of America Papers, Series IV, Box 109, Sophia Smith Collection, Smith College, Northampton, MA.

42. "The 1970 Meeting of the Population Association," *Population Index,* July-September 1970, 319.

43. Arthur A. Campbell and Bernard Berelson, "Contraceptive Specifications: Report on a Workshop," *Studies in Family Planning,* January 1971, 14–19.

44. Campbell and Berelson, "Contraceptive Specifications."

45. "Child Health Institute Population Research Center Now Shaping Up Rapidly; Initial Research Areas Pinpointed as Advisory Cmte. Staff Are Named," National Institutes of Health Memo, December 4, 1968, Planned Parenthood Federation of America Papers, Series IV, Box 130, Sophia Smith Collection, Smith College, Northampton, MA.

46. "In Memoriam," *Studies in Family Planning.*

47. Campbell and Berelson, "Contraceptive Specifications," 18.

48. Helen Bequaert Holmes, "Sex Preselection: Eugenics for Everyone," in *Biomedical Ethics Reviews: 1985,* ed. James M. Humber and Robert F. Almeder (Clifton, NJ: Humana Press, 1985), 57.

49. Gregg Easterbrook, "Forgotten Benefactor of Humanity," *The Atlantic,* January 1997, http://tinyurl.com/345m4y6.

50. P. R. Ehrlich et al., "Checkerspot Butterflies: A Historical Perspective," *Science,* April 18, 1975, 221–228.

51. Center for Conservation Biology: Books by Paul R. Ehrlich, www.stanford.edu/group/CCB/Staff/books.htm.

52. Paul Ehrlich, interview by author, Stanford, CA, April 30, 2010.

53. Paul R. Ehrlich and Anne H. Ehrlich, "*The Population Bomb* Revisited," *Electronic Journal of Sustainable Development* 1, no. 3 (2009).

54. "Editorial: Obama's Mad Science Adviser," *Washington Times,* August 16, 2009. http://www.washingtontimes.com/news/2009/aug/16/obamas-mad-science-adviser/.

CHAPTER 8

1. Charles Thorpe, *Oppenheimer: The Tragic Intellect* (Chicago: University of Chicago Press, 2006), 177.

2. Murray L. Barr, "A Morphological Distinction Between Neurons of the Male and Female," *Nature,* April 30, 1949, 676–677.

3. Barr, "Morphological Distinction," 676.

4. Ruth Schwartz Cowan, "Women's Roles in the History of Amniocentesis and Chorionic Villi Sampling," in *Women and Prenatal Testing: Facing the Challenges of Genetic Technology*, ed. Karen H. Rothenberg and Elizabeth J. Thomson (Columbus: Ohio State University Press, 1994), 37.

5. "Dr. Murray L. Barr," Canadian Medical Hall of Fame, http://www.cdn medhall.org/dr-murray-barr.

6. Barbara L. Drinkwater, ed., *Women in Sport* (Oxford: Blackwell Science, 2000), 184–185.

7. Cowan, "Women's Roles," 37.

8. Cowan, "Women's Roles," 37.

9. Cowan, "Women's Roles," 38.

10. Joan Rothschild, *Dream of the Perfect Child* (Bloomington: Indiana University Press, 2005), 77.

11. Cowan, "Women's Roles," 38.

12. Joseph Woo, "A Short History of the Development of Ultrasound in Obstetrics and Gynecology," Collège Français d'Echographie Foetale, http://www .cfef.org/archives/bricabrac/histoiredesultrasons.pdf.

13. Glen Wade, "Human Uses of Ultrasound: Ancient and Modern," *Ultrasonics* 38 (2000): 1–5.

14. George D. Ludwig and Francis W. Struthers, "Considerations Underlying the Use of Ultrasound to Detect Gallstones and Foreign Bodies in Tissue," Naval Medical Research Institute, National Naval Medical Center, June 16, 1949, http:// www.ob-ultrasound.net/ludwig_june_1949.html; Joseph Woo, "Dr. George D. Ludwig, Pioneer in Medical Ultrasound," http://www.ob-ultrasound.net/ludwig .html.

15. Woo, "Short History."

16. Joseph Woo, "Wright and Meyer Articulated Arm Scanner," http://tinyurl .com/4mfprcv.

17. Donald Fleming, "On Living in a Biological Revolution," *The Atlantic*, February 1969, http://tinyurl.com/39jpxjk.

18. "Ultrasound Device Takes Guessing Out of Pregnancy," *Pittsburgh-Press*, November 9, 1971; Edward Edelson, "Knowledge Is Key to Happy Childbirth," *Los Angeles Times*, December 7, 1975; Lee Edson, "A New Eye into the Womb: Ultrasonics," *New York Times*, July 9, 1972; Joseph Woo, "Short History."

19. "Control of Life: Audacious Experiments Promise Decades of Added Life, Superbabies with Improved Minds and Bodies, and Even a Kind of Immortality," *Life*, September 10, 1965.

20. See, for example, Willard Gaylin, "We Have the Awful Knowledge to Make Exact Copies of Human Beings; The Frankenstein Myth Is Real," *New York Times*, March 5, 1972.

21. Amitai Etzioni, "Sex Control, Science, and Society," *Science*, September 13, 1968, 1109.

22. Amitai Etzioni, phone interview by author, December 21, 2010.

23. Etzioni, "Sex Control," 1110.

24. John Brigham, Janet Rifkin, and Christine G. Solt, "Birth Technologies: Prenatal Diagnosis and Abortion Policies," *Politics and the Life Sciences*, February 1993, 33.

25. Brigham, Rifkin, and Solt, "Birth Technologies," 33.

26. Cowan, "Women's Roles," 41.

27. Brigham, Rifkin, and Solt, "Birth Technologies," 35.

28. Tietung Hospital Department of Obstetrics and Gynecology, "Fetal Sex Prediction by Sex Chromatin of Chorionic Villi Cells During Early Pregnancy," *Chinese Medical Journal* 1 (1975): 117–126; Audrey Milunsky and Jeff M. Milunsky, *Genetic Disorders and the Fetus: Diagnosis, Prevention, and Treatment,* 6th ed. (Oxford: Wiley-Blackwell, 2010), 161.

29. Brigham, Rifkin, and Solt, "Birth Technologies," 35.

30. Cowan, "Women's Roles," 41. Milunsky and Milunsky, *Genetic Disorders,* 161.

31. Cowan, "Women's Roles," 38.

32. Jane M. Friedman, "Legal Implications of Amniocentesis," *University of Pennsylvania Law Review*, November 1974, 92–156.

33. Patricia McCormack, "Prenatal Medicine Brings Up Moral Questions," *Star-News,* June 2, 1976.

34. P. K. Lynch, "Women: The Next Endangered Species?" *Mademoiselle*, May 1977.

35. Connelly, *Fatal Misconception,* 265–266.

36. Goldberg, *Means of Reproduction,* 81.

37. "Nafis Sadik: Former UNFPA Executive Director, UN Under-Secretary General," http://tinyurl.com/4eugdgb.

CHAPTER 9

1. Quoted in Jing-Bao Nie, *Behind the Silence,* 82.

2. William H. Draper Jr., interview by Jerry N. Hess, transcript of audio recording, January 11, 1972. Harry S. Truman Library and Museum, http://tinyurl.com/6evzwy; Connelly, *Fatal Misconception,* 186.

3. Phyllis Tilson Piotrow, interview by Rebecca Sharpless, transcript of audio recording, September 16, 2003, Population and Reproductive Health Oral History Project, Sophia Smith Collection, Smith College, Northampton, MA. www.smith.edu/library/libs/ssc/prh/prh-narrators.html.

4. Draper oral history, http://tinyurl.com/6evzwy.

5. Draper oral history, http://tinyurl.com/6evzwy.

6. Piotrow oral history, 22.

7. Irene B. Taeuber, "Fertility and Research on Fertility in Japan," *Milbank Memorial Fund Quarterly*, April 1956, 129–149.

8. Goldberg, *Means of Reproduction,* 47. See also Deborah Oakley, "American-Japanese Interaction in the Development of Population Policy in Japan, 1945–1952," *Population and Development Review* 4, no. 4 (December 1978), 617–643.

9. UNFPA, "The State of World Population 1999—Chapter 3," http://tinyurl .com/5umtz3l.

10. Connelly, *Fatal Misconception,* 141.

11. Phyllis Tilson Piotrow, *World Population Crisis: The United States Response* (New York: Praeger, 1973), 38.

12. Betsy Hartmann, *Reproductive Rights and Wrongs: The Global Politics of Population Control* (Boston: South End, 1995), 105, http://tinyurl.com/6fzbc73.

13. Concern among policy elite: Connelly, *Fatal Misconception,* 186.

14. Food aid conditional: Connelly, *Fatal Misconception,* 231.

15. Connelly, *Fatal Misconception,* 243.

16. Connelly, *Fatal Misconception,* 244

17. For more background on this law, see the works of Indian scholar Malini Karkal.

18. Connelly, *Fatal Misconception,* 244.

19. George H. W. Bush, foreword, in Piotrow, *World Population Crisis,* vii–ix.

20. "The NSSM 200 Directive and the Study Requested," Stephen D. Mumford, Population-security.org, http://tinyurl.com/2tuodh. Also see Goldberg, *Means of Reproduction,* 47–48.

21. Nie, *Behind the Silence,* 213.

22. "Religions: Hinduism and Abortion," BBC, http://tinyurl.com/6j5alcn.

23. Brian Peter Harvey, *An Introduction to Buddhist Ethics: Foundations, Values, and Issues* (Cambridge: Cambridge University Press, 2000), 316.

24. Nie, *Behind the Silence,* 73.

25. Nie, *Behind the Silence,* 6.

26. Seungsook Moon, *Militarized Modernity and Gendered Citizenship in South Korea* (Durham, NC: Duke University Press, 2005), 81.

27. Mark Clifford, *Troubled Tiger: Businessmen, Bureaucrats, and Generals in South Korea* (Armonk, NY: East Gate, 1998), 36.

28. Draper oral history, http://tinyurl.com/6evzwy.

29. Jae-Mo Yang, "An Overview of Family Planning in Korea (1961–1978)," *Yonsei Medical Journal* 20, no. 2 (1979): 186.

30. Yu-ling Huang, "The Population Council and Population Control in Post-War Asia," Rockefeller Archive Center Research Reports Online, 2009, www.rock arch.org/publications/resrep/huang.pdf; Yu-ling Huang, email to author, February 3, 2011.

31. P. J. Donaldson, D. J. Nichols, and Ehn Hyun Choe, "Abortion and Contraception in the Korean Fertility Transition," *Population Studies,* July 1982, 229.

32. John A. Ross and Oliver D. Finnigan, "Within Family Planning—Korea," *Demography* 5, no. 2 (1968): 685.

33. Jae-Mo Yang, "An Overview of Family Planning in Korea (1961–1978)," *Yonsei Medical Journal* 20, no. 2 (1979), 188.

34. John A. Ross et al., "Korea and Taiwan: Review of Progress in 1968," *Studies in Family Planning,* April 1969, 8.

35. S. M. Keeny, George Cernada, and John Ross, "Korea and Taiwan: The Record for 1967," *Studies in Family Planning*, April 1968, 4.

36. Keeny, Cernada, and Ross, "Korea and Taiwan," 2.

37. Keeny, Cernada, and Ross, "Korea and Taiwan," 9.

38. Edward S. Mason et al., *The Economic and Social Modernization of the Republic of Korea* (Cambridge: Harvard University Asia Center, 1980), 390.

39. Ross and Finnigan, "Family Planning," 685.

40. Paul Hartman, "Medical Referral System and Mobile Services," *Studies in Family Planning*, August 1966, 1012.

41. Keeny, Cernada, and Ross. "Korea and Taiwan," 5.

42. Hartman, "Medical Referral System," 10.

43. Hartman, "Medical Referral System," 12.

44. Moon, *Militarized Modernity*, 84; Hartman, "Medical Referral System, 10.

45. Ross and Finnigan, "Family Planning," 680.

46. "Seoul National University, "Vasectomies in Experimental Animals, 1963," Population Council, Grant File, Regular, Box 53; "Seoul National University, Korea, Fertility Studies," Population Council, Grant File, Regular, Box 59; and "Seoul National University, Population Research and Training Center," Population Council, Grant File, Regular, Box 65, Rockefeller Archive Center, Sleepy Hollow, NY. Also see Huang, "Population Council," 16.

47. Hartman, "Medical Referral System," 12.

48. Hartman, "Medical Referral System," 11.

49. Kyung Shik Chang, George C. Worth, and Peter H. Michael, "Korea (South)," *Studies in Family Planning* 5, no. 5 (May 1974): 153.

50. Paul W. Kuznets, "Review of *Economic Development, Population Policy, and Demographic Transition in the Republic of Korea*," *Population and Development Review*, June 1982, 404–407.

51. Ross and Finnigan, "Family Planning," 687.

52. Heeran Chun, email to author, December 3, 2010.

53. Targets fell short: John A. Ross et al., "Korea and Taiwan: Review of Progress in 1968," *Studies in Family Planning*, April 1969, 1.

54. Sung-bong Hong and Christopher Tietze, "Survey of Abortion Providers in Seoul, Korea," *Studies in Family Planning*, May 1979, 163.

55. Hong and Tietze, "Survey of Abortion Providers," 161–163.

56. Teenagers outnumbering children: "The Shape of Things to Come: Country Case Study South Korea," Population Action International, http://tinyurl .com/5wkmnnb. Replacement rate: Doo-Sub Kim, "Theoretical Explanations of Rapid Fertility Decline in Korea," *Japanese Journal of Population*, June 2005, 10, http://tinyurl.com/6du454a.

57. Barbara B. Crane and Jason L. Finkle, "Organizational Impediments to Development Assistance: The World Bank's Population Program," *World Politics*, 1981, 552; Heeran Chun, email to author, November 28, 2010.

58. Norimitsu Onishi, "A New Korean Goal: Having a Big Family," *New York Times*, August 22, 2005, http://tinyurl.com/4jsfpa3.

59. "Republic of Korea: Intensified Drive to Curb Population Growth," National Security Council Bureau of Intelligence and Research, February 9, 1984. Executive Secretariat, NSC Records, Subject File, Box 82, Reagan Presidential Library, Simi Valley, CA.

60. Sang-Yong Song, "The Hwang Woo-Suk Scandal Hasn't Ended," *Journal of Korean Bioethics Association*, December 1, 2007.

61. Ross and Finnigan, "Family Planning," 689.

62. The lack of an anti-abortion movement at the time also explains why—unlike with forced abortions in China—today few Westerners know about the abuses committed in Korea.

63. C. H. Yen et al., "Taiwan," *Studies in Family Planning*, May 1974, 165–169.

64. Warren C. Robinson, *The Global Family Planning Revolution: Three Decades of Population Polices and Programs* (Washington, D.C.: World Bank, 2007), 304, http://tinyurl.com/69emmvx.

65. Geoffrey McNicoll, "Policy Lessons of the East Asian Demographic Transition," *Population and Development Review*, March 2006, 2.

66. D. M. Potts, "The Implementation of Family Planning Programmes," *Proceedings of the Royal Society of London*, December 10, 1976, 221.

67. Tyrene White, *China's Longest Campaign: Birth Planning in the People's Republic, 1949–2005* (Ithaca: Cornell University Press, 2006), 109.

68. "Abortion or Starvation: China Plan to Cut Population," *Sydney Morning Herald*, September 20, 1973.

69. William H. Draper Jr., "Table Tennis and Family Planning," The Victor-Bostrom Fund and The Population Crisis Committee magazine, Spring 1971, Planned Parenthood Federation of America Papers, Sophia Smith Collection, Series VIII, Box 203, Smith College, Northampton, MA.

70. Edgar Snow, "Mao Skeptical," *The Victor-Bostrom Fund and The Population Crisis Committee* magazine, Spring 1971, 10, Planned Parenthood Federation of America Papers, Series VIII, Box 203, Sophia Smith Collection, Smith College, Northampton, MA.

71. Edgar Snow, "Population Care and Control," *The Victor-Bostrom Fund and The Population Crisis Committee* magazine, Spring 1971, Planned Parenthood Federation of America Papers, Series VIII, Box 203, Sophia Smith Collection, Smith College, Northampton, MA.

72. Draper, "Table Tennis and Family Planning."

73. *Family Planning Perspectives*, May-June 1975.

74. Connelly, *Fatal Misconception*, 340.

75. Benjamin Viel, "Trip Report: Three Weeks in China, September 23–October 15, 1977," February 8, 1978, 12, Planned Parenthood Federation of America Papers, Series VIII, Box 203, Sophia Smith Collection, Smith College, Northampton, MA.

CHAPTER 10

1. Connelly, *Fatal Misconception*, 343.

2. Bernard D. Nossiter, "U.N. Agency to Help China Curb Population Growth," *New York Times*, March 16, 1980.

3. Nossiter, "U.N. Agency."

4. Nossiter, "U.N. Agency."

5. Office of Technology Assessment, *World Population and Fertility Planning Technologies: The Next 20 Years*, February 1982, www.fas.org/ota/reports/8235.pdf.

6. "Forced Abortions Claimed," *The Day*, May 9, 1980.

7. Victoria Graham, "Measures Taken in China to Stem Population Growth: Price Paid for Forbidden Child," *Sarasota Herald-Tribune*, August 10, 1980.

8. Connelly, *Fatal Misconception*, 343.

9. Nossiter, "U.N. Agency."

10. Nossiter, "U.N. Agency."

11. John S. Aird, *Slaughter of the Innocents: Coercive Birth Control in China* (Washington, D.C.: American Enterprise Institute Press, 1990), 8.

12. Nossiter, "U.N. Agency."

13. Hvistendahl, "Half the Sky."

14. Aird, *Slaughter*, 40.

15. Aird, *Slaughter*, 124.

16. Michele Vink, "Abortion and Birth Control in Canton, China," *Wall Street Journal*, November 30, 1981.

17. Steven Mosher, *Broken Earth: The Rural Chinese* (New York: Free Press, 1983), 225.

18. Mosher, *Broken Earth*, 225.

19. Steven Mosher, phone interview by author, February 3, 2011.

20. Mosher, *Broken Earth*, 226.

21. Christopher S. Wren, "Old Nemesis Haunts China on Birth Plan," *New York Times*, August 1, 1982, http://tinyurl.com/4vtf8pg.

22. Wren, "Old Nemesis."

23. Victoria Graham, "Wife Abuse Rampant in China: Birth of Girls Dreaded," *Daytona Beach Morning Journal*, November 6, 1982.

24. Aird, *Slaughter*, 14.

25. Sidney B. Westley and Minja Kim Choe, *How Does Son Preference Affect Populations in Asia?* Analysis from the East-West Center Series, no. 84 (Honolulu, HI: East-West Center, September 2007), 3; Aird, *Slaughter*, 40.

26. Connelly, *Fatal Misconception*, 347.

27. "Scholar to Fight Expulsion from Stanford," Associated Press, *Tri City Herald*, February 25, 1983, http://tinyurl.com/6zme6qc; Ross H. Munro, Ellie McGrath, and Donald Shapiro, "Education: Battle in the Scholarly World," *Time*, March 14, 1983, http://tinyurl.com/ydgfoxk.

28. Munro et al., "Education: Battle in the Scholarly World."

29. Connelly, *Fatal Misconception,* 350.

30. Bernard D. Nossiter, "Population Prizes from U.N. Assailed," *New York Times,* July 24, 1983, http://tinyurl.com/46zjsf6.

31. Loretta McLaughlin, "Mexico to Host Population Meeting: UN Conference in Crowded City Will Focus on Soaring World Problem," *Boston Globe,* July 22, 1984.

32. "U.S. Withholding U.N. Contribution," *Victoria Advocate,* February 7, 1985; "U.S. Cuts Off Funds Aimed for UNFPA," *Park City Daily News,* August 27, 1986.

33. Marguerite Sullivan, "Sociologists Study Abortion Laws," *Rock Hill Herald,* March 29, 1976; Attané and Guilmoto, *Watering,* 3.

34. Paul Lewis, "U.N. Population Plan for China a Test for U.S.," *New York Times,* March 12, 1989.

35. Rob Stein and Michael Shear, "Funding Restored to Groups That Perform Abortion, Other Care," *Washington Post,* January 24, 2009, http://tinyurl.com/a9s6pa.

36. Aird, *Slaughter,* 40.

37. Stanley K. Henshaw, Susheela Singh, and Taylor Haas, "Recent Trends in Abortion Rates Worldwide," *International Family Planning Perspectives,* March 1999, 47.

38. Whasoon Byun, interview by author, Seoul, December 15, 2010.

39. Charles F. Westoff, "Recent Trends in Abortion and Contraception in 12 Countries," *DHS Analytical Studies* 8 (February 2005): 1.

40. Nie, *Behind the Silence,* 135.

41. Nie, *Behind the Silence,* 138.

42. Institute for Social Development Studies, "New 'Common Sense': Family-Planning Policy and Sex Ratio in Viet Nam" (paper presented at the Fourth Asia Pacific Conference on Reproductive and Sexual Health and Rights, 2007), 8, www.unfpa.org/gender/docs/studies/vietnam.pdf.

43. Centre for Youth Development and Activities, *Reflections on the Campaign Against Sex Selection and Exploring Ways Forward* (Pune: Centre for Youth Development and Activities, 2007), 18.

44. Elaine Chow, "Made in China Deal: Half Off Abortions with Your Student ID," http://tinyurl.com/pk998s.

45. Nie, *Behind the Silence,* 105.

46. Nie, *Behind the Silence,* 98.

47. Vijaya Nidadavolu and Hillary Bracken, "Abortion and Sex Determination: Conflicting Messages in Information Materials in a District of Rajasthan, India," *Reproductive Health Matters,* May 2006, 160–171.

48. Centre for Youth Development and Activities, *Reflections on the Campaign,* 8.

49. In 2006 a study published in *Lancet* put the number of botched abortions worldwide at 68,000 a year. http://news.bbc.co.uk/2/hi/health/6176756.stm.

50. *The Missing Daughters of India* (brochure).

51. Dhanashri Brahme, interview by author, Delhi, June 30, 2009.

52. *Missing Daughters of India.*

53. "Beijing Declaration and Platform for Action," Fourth World Conference on Women, Beijing, China, September 4–15, 1995, www.uneca.org/acgd/gender/en_beijing.doc.

54. "UNFPA Guidance Note."

55. Sutapa Agrawal, Public Health Foundation of India, interview by author, Delhi, June 29, 2009.

56. Goldberg, *Means of Reproduction,* 185.

CHAPTER 11

1. "Bride Dumped at Matchmaking Agency," *The Star*, April 11, 2009, http://tinyurl.com/c74otd.

2. Imbalance in 1980s generation: Wen-shan Yang, interview by author, Taipei, December 31, 2009. Number of working age adults: "East & Southeast Asia: Taiwan," *CIA World Factbook*, http://tinyurl.com/2bslwk.

3. "Vietnamese Wife's Taiwan Dream Sours," *Taipei Times*, March 6, 2007, http://tinyurl.com/5v5y95g.

4. See agency websites: http://www.idealbride.sg; http://tinyurl.com/63jksj9; http://www.qq-99.com/en.

5. Norimitsu Onishi, "Marriage Brokers in Vietnam Cater to S. Korean Bachelors," *New York Times*, February 21, 2007, http://tinyurl.com/4rh9dvr.

6. Graeme Hugo and Nguyen Thi Hong Xoan, "Marriage Migration Between Vietnam and Taiwan: A View from Vietnam," in *Watering the Neighbour's Garden* (Paris: CICRED, 2007), 368.

7. Lee Jiyeon, "South Korean Foreign Bride Matches Often End in Tears," Reuters, May 29, 2008.

8. Martin Fackler, "Baby Boom of Mixed Children Tests South Korea," *New York Times,* November 28, 2009.

9. "Marriage Agency to Curb Abuse," AFP, January 8, 2009, http://tinyurl.com/45lvvnd. Also see rural marriage statistics in Hugo and Nguyen Thi, "Marriage Migration Between Vietnam and Taiwan," 367.

10. Michael Bristow, "Taiwan's Foreign Brides," BBC, December 25, 2002, http://tinyurl.com/4hyhcsh.

11. Marcia Guttentag and Paul F. Secord, *Too Many Women? The Sex Ratio Question* (Beverly Hills, CA: SAGE, 1983).

12. Zhu Chuzhu, interview by author, Xi'an, China, December 21, 2009.

13. Chai Bin Park and Nam-Hoon Cho, "Consequences of Son Preference in a Low-Fertility Society: Imbalance of the Sex Ratio at Birth in Korea," *Population and Development Review*, March 1995, 75.

14. "Sans Females, Men Go Gay in Mehsana," *Times of India,* July 15, 2008, http://tinyurl.com/59yv4x.

15. Hvistendahl, "Half the Sky."

16. Jiang Quanbao et al., "Son Preference and the Marriage Squeeze in China: An Integrated Analysis of the First Marriage and the Remarriage Market," in *Watering the Neighbour's Garden* (Paris: CICRED, 2007).

17. This is based on projections for 2020. Nicholas Eberstadt, quoted in "6.3 Brides for Seven Brothers," *Economist*, December 17, 1998, http://www.economist .com/node/179826.

18. Christophe Guilmoto, "Characteristics of Sex-Ratio Imbalance in India, and Future Scenarios" (paper presented at Fourth Asia Pacific Conference on Reproductive and Sexual Health and Rights, 2007), 11–12.

19. *Holding Up Half the Sky: Women's Rights in China's Changing Economy* (Washington, D.C.: U.S. Government Printing Office, 2003), 12.

20. Monica Das Gupta, "'Missing Girls' in Asia: Magnitudes, Implications, and Possible Responses" (panel discussion, American Enterprise Institute, Washington, D.C., September 17, 2008).

21. Graeme Hugo, phone interview by author, October 14, 2009.

22. Accessed December 15, 2009.

23. Yeong Sug-heo, Women Migrants Human Rights Center, interview by author, Seoul, December 16, 2009.

24. Lee Jiyeon, "South Korean Foreign Bride Matches."

25. Aruna Lee, "Korea's Desperate Housewives: Foreign Wives Find Korea a Bad Fit," *New America Media*, May 14, 2007, http://tinyurl.com/4cfqdvr.

26. Xoan Nguyen, interview by author, Ho Chi Minh City, December 17, 2009.

27. "YWCA of Taiwan," National Council of Women of Taiwan, http://tinyurl .com/4op,hzcs. *Handbook of Living Information for Foreign Spouses in Taiwan* (Ho Chi Minh City: Taipei Economic and Cultural Office), http://tinyurl.com/6jkdmxo.

28. He Huifeng, "Mainland Bachelors Seek Marital Bliss in Vietnam," *South China Morning Post*, March 31, 2010.

29. Gary S. Becker and Richard A. Posner, *Uncommon Sense: Economic Insights, from Marriage to Terrorism*, with Richard A. Posner (Chicago: University of Chicago, 2010), 33.

30. Also see Rhys Blakely, "Show Us Your Loo Before You Woo, Indian Men are Told," *Times* (London), March 26, 2009, http://tinyurl.com/dhdzgy.

31. Nguyen, interview by author.

32. *Why Virgin Bride*, video, Life Partner Matchmaker, http://tinyurl.com/ 4rvfl5p.

33. "Foreign Brides Rejuvenate Korea's Aging Society," Deutsche Presse-Agentur, October 28, 2009.

34. Christopher Shay, "After Murder, South Korea Rethinks Marriage Brokers," August 17, 2010, http://tinyurl.com/4z826l5.

35. "eBay Acts over Human Trafficking," Reuters, March 13, 2004, http://tinyurl .com/47ru3h8.

36. Hugo and Nguyen, "Marriage Migration," 379.

37. A Taiwanese broker's fee may reach $10,000. Peter Hung, interview by author, Taoyuan, Taiwan, January 3, 2009. In 2009 Vietnam's per capita income was

$1,052. U.S. Department of State Bureau of East Asian and Pacific Affairs, "Background Note: Vietnam," November 30, 2010, http://www.state.gov/r/pa/ei/bgn/4130.htm.

38. Tran Giang Linh, "Female Marriage-Based International Migration and Its Impacts on Sending Households" (presentation given at Institute for Social Development Studies seminar, Hanoi, May 9, 2008).

39. Valerie M. Hudson and Andrea M. den Boer, *Bare Branches: The Security Implications of Asia's Surplus Male Population* (Cambridge: MIT Press, 2005), 203.

40. "Vietnamese Women Wed Foreigners to Aid Family," Associated Press, August 10, 2008.

41. Hugo and Nguyen, "Marriage Migration," 374.

42. Tran, "Female Marriage-Based International Migration."

43. Hugo and Nguyen, "Marriage Migration," 384.

44. Tran, "Female Marriage-Based International Migration."

45. Tran, "Female Marriage-Based International Migration."

46. Tuoi Tre, "Sex Imbalance to Leave Vietnamese Men Single," *VietNews*, December 28, 2009, http://tinyurl.com/4t5hz4j.

47. "Vietnamese Girls Marrying Taiwanese Men: The harbouring of illusions," *Lao Dong*, February 5, 2001.

48. Hugo and Nguyen, "Marriage Migration," 385.

49. "Vietnamese Women," Associated Press.

50. "Wife Buyers Turn to Cambodia After Crackdown on Marriage Brokers in Vietnam," Associated Press, March 25, 2008, http://tinyurl.com/47jgx2g.

51. Tran, "Female Marriage-Based International Migration."

52. Xoan Nguyen and Xuyen Tran, "Vietnamese-Taiwanese Marriages," in *Asian Cross-border Marriage Migration,* ed. Wen-shan Yang and Melody Chiawen Lu (Amsterdam: Amsterdam University Press, 2010), 168. See also Louise Brown, *Sex Slaves: The Trafficking of Women in Asia* (UK: Virago, 2001), 53.

53. Lena Edlund, "Son Preference, Sex Ratios, and Marriage Patterns," *Journal of Political Economy*, December 1999, 1276.

CHAPTER 12

1. Mara Hvistendahl, "No Country for Young Men," *The New Republic,* July 9, 2008, http://tinyurl.com/48m844m.

2. This story was separately related to me by Tran in an interview (Hanoi, October 22, 2009) and by Doan Thuy Dung and Nguyen Quoc Nam at the International Organization for Migration (interview by author, Hanoi, October 21, 2009).

3. Ta Thu Giang, "Vietnamese Women Fall Prey to Traffickers," *Asia Times,* September 27, 2002, http://tinyurl.com/47k3jbx.

4. Hoang Thi To Linh, *Cross-Border Trafficking in Quang Ninh Province,* International Organization for Migration (paper distributed by Hanoi office), http://tinyurl.com/4okg7yx.

5. Erica J. Peters, "Colonial Cholon and Its 'Missing' Métisses, 1859–1919," *Intersections: Gender and Sexuality in Asia and the Pacific*, September 2009, http://tinyurl.com/4cg8a59.

6. Yi Wang, *Anti-Human Trafficking Program in Vietnam*, Oxfam Québec, August 2005, http://tinyurl.com/67zs6x7, 7.

7. Tuoi Tre, "China Is Biggest Trafficking Destination: Report," *VietNews*, February 22, 2010, http://tinyurl.com/4l2h8ok.

8. Hoang, "Cross-Border Trafficking."

9. Also see Kritaya Archavanitkul et al., *Combating the Trafficking in Children and Their Exploitation in Prostitution and Other Intolerable Forms of Child Labour in Mekong Basin Countries*, Southeast Asian Ministers of Education Organization, June 1998, http://tinyurl.com/4mfx3so.

10. Hoang, "Cross-Border Trafficking," 4.

11. Hoang, "Cross-Border Trafficking," 5.

12. Tiantian Zheng, *Red Lights: The Lives of Sex Workers in Postsocialist China* (Minneapolis: University of Minnesota Press, 2009), 52.

13. Nam You-Sun, "N. Korean Women up for Sale in China: Activist," AFP, May 12, 2010, http://tinyurl.com/4zl7h7m.

14. Hannah Beech, "Buy Freedom," *Time*, November 17, 2003, http://tinyurl.com/4j2qvom.

15. Lee Tae-hoon, "Female North Korean Defectors Priced at $1,500," *Korea Times*, May 5, 2010, http://tinyurl.com/32r3pj9.

16. Mark Lagon, "'Missing Girls' in Asia: Magnitudes, Implications, and Possible Responses" (panel discussion, American Enterprise Institute, Washington, D.C., September 17, 2008).

17. "China Faces Growing Gender Imbalance," BBC, January 11, 2010, http://news.bbc.co.uk/2/hi/8451289.stm.

18. Timothy J. Gilfoyle, "Prostitutes in History: From Parables of Pornography to Metaphors of Modernity," *American Historical Review*, February 1999, 131.

19. Gail Hershatter, *Dangerous Pleasures: Prostitution and Modernity in Twentieth-Century Shanghai* (Taipei: SMC Publishing, 1998), 40.

20. Avraham Y. Ebenstein and Ethan Jennings Sharygin, "The Consequences of the 'Missing Girls' of China," *World Bank Economic Review* 23, no. 3 (2009): 409–410.

21. John Kennedy, "China: Sex Workers Demand Legalization, Organizer Detained," August 1, 2010. http://tinyurl.com/27dkfd4.

22. Hseng Khio Fah, "China's Imbalanced Gender Ratio at Birth Causing Women Trafficking from Neighbors," *Shan Herald*, December 15, 2009.

23. Beech, "Buy Freedom."

24. *Gao v. Gonzales*, 04-1874-ag, 2nd Circuit Court of Appeals, 2006.

25. Zhang's story appears in Hvistendahl, "Half the Sky."

26. Hvistendahl, "Half the Sky."

27. Zhu Hui'e, International Labor Organization, interview by author, Kunming, China, August 28, 2008.

28. These are 2008 prices, and they reflect the bare minimum a man must pay for a wife. Elsewhere, brokers list prices up to ten times as high for women in "top condition." Hvistendahl, "Half the Sky."

29. Keith B. Richburg, "Chinese Border Town Emerges as New Front Line in Fight Against Human Trafficking," *Washington Post*, December 26, 2009, http://tinyurl.com/ye6u788.

30. Valerie M. Hudson and Andrea M. den Boer, *Bare Branches: The Security Implications of Asia's Surplus Male Population* (Cambridge: MIT Press, 2004), 214.

31. Ravinder Kaur, phone interview by author, June 15, 2009.

32. Ravinder Kaur, "Across-Region Marriages: Poverty, Female Migration, and the Sex Ratio," *Economic and Political Weekly*, June 19, 2004, 2601.

33. Doan Thuy Dung, International Organization for Migration, interview by author, Hanoi, October 21, 2009.

34. India's share of world total: "Child Marriage in India Endangers Maternal Health: UNICEF," AFP, January 15, 2009, http://tinyurl.com/4nzw9uc.

35. John F. Burns, "Though Illegal, Child Marriage Is Popular in Part of India," *New York Times*, May 11, 1998, http://tinyurl.com/4mtcqrg.

36. Hvistendahl, "Half the Sky."

37. Michael Sheridan, "Kidnappers Swoop on China's Girls," *Times* (London), May 31, 2009, http://tinyurl.com/4bzv72n; "China Sets Up Website to Recover Trafficked Children: Report," AFP, October 27, 2009.

38. Sushil Manav, "Men Fall Prey to 'Fake Wives' Racket," *Times of India*, May 27, 2008.

39. Mei Fong, "It's Cold Cash, Not Cold Feet, Motivating Runaway Brides in China," *Wall Street Journal*, June 5, 2009, http://online.wsj.com/article/SB12 4415971813687173.html.

40. Justin Lahart, "Preference for Sons in China May Lead to Bubbles in U.S.," *Wall Street Journal*, June 18, 2009, http://tinyurl.com/5w9q92d.

41. "2009 Official AIDS Report," *People's Daily*, November 22, 2009, http://tinyurl.com/6h4qzbm.

42. Ebenstein and Sharygin, "Consequences," 409.

43. Ebenstein and Sharygin, "Consequences," 412.

44. Joseph D. Tucker et al., "Surplus Men, Sex Work, and the Spread of HIV in China," *AIDS* 19, no. 6 (2005): 539–545. See also Joseph D. Tucker and Dudley L. Poston, eds., *Gender Policy and HIV in China: Catalyzing Policy Change* (Springer Science/Business, 2009). See also Joseph D. Tucker et al., "Syphilis and Social Upheaval in China," *New England Journal of Medicine*, May 6, 2010, 1658–1661.

CHAPTER 13

1. Marcia Guttentag and Paul F. Secord, *Too Many Women* (Beverly Hills: Sage, 1983), 116.

2. The flyer, which appeared at my Shanghai gym one day, directed interested participants to an event organized by a group called 1937 Club. The website for the group is 1937club.com.

3. Philip L. Walker, "A Bioarchaeological Perspective on the History of Violence," *Annual Review of Anthropology* 30 (2001): 587.

4. David Courtwright, *Violent Land* (Cambridge: Harvard University Press, 1996), 13.

5. Valerie M. Hudson and Andrea M. den Boer, *Bare Branches: The Security Implications of Asia's Surplus Male Population* (Cambridge: MIT Press, 2005), 193.

6. Christopher Mims, "Strange but True: Testosterone Alone Does Not Cause Violence," *Scientific American,* July 5, 2007, http://tinyurl.com/6fo2cne.

7. James M. Dabbs et al., "Testosterone, Crime, and Misbehavior Among 692 Male Prison Inmates," *Personality and Individual Differences*, May 1995; also see Mims, "Strange but True."

8. A. Salvador et al., "Correlating Testosterone and Fighting in Male Participants in Judo Contests," *Physiology and Behavior* 68 (1999): 205–209.

9. "Wrestler Chris Benoit Used Steroid Testosterone; Son Sedated Before Murders," FOXNews.com, July 17, 2007, http://tinyurl.com/ypzaco. "'Roid Rage' Questions Surround Benoit Murder-Suicide," CNN.com, June 27, 2007, http://tinyurl.com/4grpuew. Anahad O'Connor, "Wrestler in Apparent Murder-Suicide Had High Levels of Testosterone," *New York Times*, July 17, 2007, http://tinyurl.com/69ezktx.

10. Alan Booth et al., "Testosterone and Social Behavior," *Social Forces*, September 2006, 171.

11. Booth et al., "Testosterone and Social Behavior," 175.

12. Booth et al., "Testosterone and Social Behavior," 176.

13. J. M. Dabbs, "Testosterone, Smiling, and Facial Appearance," *Journal of Nonverbal Behavior* 21 (1997): 45–55.

14. James M. Dabbs and Robin Morris, "Testosterone, Social Class, and Antisocial Behavior in a Sample of 4,462 Men," *Psychological Science*, May 1990, 209.

15. "Marriage and Fatherhood Linked to Lower Testosterone Levels," *Science Daily*, October 11, 2007, http://tinyurl.com/49gz7rf.

16. Allan Mazur and Joel Michalek, "Marriage, Divorce, and Male Testosterone," *Social Forces*, September 1998, http://cogprints.org/632/1/Joel.html.

17. Mazur and Michalek, "Marriage," 327.

18. Rose McDermott et al., "Testosterone, Cortisol, and Aggression in a Simulated Crisis Game" (paper presented at the Hendricks Conference on Biology and Political Behavior, Lincoln, NE, October 13–14, 2006), 9, http://tinyurl.com/5wpndgm.

19. Booth et al., "Testosterone and Social Behavior," 175.

20. Martin Daly and Margo Wilson, "Killing the Competition: Female/Female and Male/Male Homicide," *Human Nature* 1 (1990): 83–109.

21. Robert Wright, *The Moral Animal* (New York: Vintage, 1994), 100.

22. This and the following passages are taken from Livy, *The Early History of Rome*, Books 1–4 (Harmondsworth, UK Penguin, 1973), 42–46.

23. Guttentag and Secord, *Too Many Women*, 42.

24. Guttentag and Secord, *Too Many Women*, 42.

25. Guttentag and Secord, *Too Many Women*, 40–47.

26. James L. Boone III, "Parental Investment and Elite Family Structure in Preindustrial States: A Case Study of Late Medieval-Early Modern Portuguese Geneaologies," *American Anthropologist*, December 1986, 872.

27. Boone, "Parental Investment," 860.

28. Lionel Tiger, "Osama Bin Laden's Man Trouble," *Slate*, September 28, 2001, http://www.slate.com/id/116236/.

29. United Nations Office on Drugs and Crime, "Homicide Statistics, Criminal Justice Sources: Latest Year Available (2003–2008)," http://tinyurl.com/47fpcy8.

30. United Nations Office on Drugs and Crime, "Homicide Statistics, Criminal Justice, and Public Health Sources: Trends (2003–2008)," http://tinyurl.com/5ttogu3.

31. Lois A. Fingerhut and Joel C. Kleinman, "International and Interstate Comparisons of Homicide Among Young Males," *JAMA*, June 27, 1990.

32. Courtwright, *Violent Land*, 69.

33. Courtwright, *Violent Land*, 58–59.

34. Richard Florida, "A Singles Map of the United States of America," *Boston Globe*, March 30, 2008, http://tinyurl.com/yvv9f8.

35. Courtwright, *Violent Land*, 69.

36. Courtwright, *Violent Land*, 94.

37. Courtwright, *Violent Land*, 77.

38. Courtwright, *Violent Land*, 81.

39. Courtwright, *Violent Land*, 137.

40. Courtwright, *Violent Land*, 64.

41. Courtwright, *Violent Land*, 65.

42. Malcolm Gladwell, *Outliers* (New York: Little Brown, 2008), 168–169.

43. Philip B. Kunhardt III, *Violence: An American Tradition*, prod. Sheila Nevins (HBO, 1995).

44. Courtwright, *Violent Land*, 74, 81.

45. Paul Trachtman, "Tombstone: History and Archaeology," *Smithsonian*, May 2006, http://tinyurl.com/4u89nd9.

46. Courtwright, *Violent Land*, 112.

47. Courtwright, *Violent Land*, 114.

48. Hinton Helper, *The Land of Gold* (Baltimore, MD: Henry Taylor, 1855), http://tinyurl.com/4j6bdqh.

49. Eliza Farnham, *California, In-Doors and Out* (Edward Dix, 1856), 386, http://tinyurl.com/4s9har9.

50. Ellen Carol DuBois, "Seneca Falls in Santa Cruz," *Common-Place,* January 2009, http://tinyurl.com/4gfupjj; J. S. Holliday, *Rush for Riches: Gold Fever and the Making of California* (Berkeley: University of California Press, 1999), 92.

51. Chris Enss, *Hearts West: True Stories of Mail Order Brides on the Frontier* (Guilford, CT: Twodot, 2005), xi.

52. Courtwright, *Violent Land.*

53. James Z. Lee and Wang Feng, *One Quarter of Humanity: Malthusian Mythology and Chinese Realities* (Cambridge: Harvard University Press, 2001), 51.

54. Lee and Wang, *One Quarter of Humanity,* 49.

55. Zhu, G., "A Preliminary Study of International Migration of the Chinese People," *China Journal of Population Science* 6, no. 4 (1994): 403–415; also see Courtwright, *Violent Land.*

56. Lee and Wang, *One Quarter of Humanity,* 71.

57. Elizabeth J. Perry, *Rebels and Revolutionaries in North China, 1845–1945* (Stanford: Stanford University Press, 1980), 277.

58. James L. Watson, "Self-Defense Corps, Violence, and the Bachelor Subculture in South China: Two Case Studies," in *Proceedings of the Second International Conference on Sinology, Section on Folklore and Culture* (Taipei: Academica Sinica, 1989), 209–221.

59. Claude Lévi-Strauss, Joachim Neugroschel, and Phoebe Hoss, *The View from Afar* (Chicago: University of Chicago Press, 1992), 46.

60. Perry, *Rebels and Revolutionaries,* 102.

61. Jonathan D. Spence, *The Search for Modern China* (New York: Norton, 1991), 185.

62. Perry, *Rebels,* 121.

63. Perry, *Rebels,* 108, 121.

64. Perry, *Rebels,* 65.

65. Perry, *Rebels,*112.

66. Spence, *God's Chinese Son* (New York: Norton, 1997).

67. Spence, *God's Chinese Son,* 62.

68. Spence, *God's Chinese Son,* 162.

69. Spence, *God's Chinese Son,* 55; Spence, *Search for Modern China,* 172–173.

70. Spence, *Search for Modern China,* 170.

71. Spence, *God's Chinese Son,* 211, 249.

72. Spence, *God's Chinese Son,* 305.

73. Spence, *God's Chinese Son,* 171.

74. Spence, *Search for Modern China,* 178.

75. Matthew H. Sommer, *Sex, Law, and Society in Late Imperial China* (Stanford: Stanford University Press, 2000), 12.

76. Hvistendahl, "No Country."

77. Danielle Laraque and Committee on Injury, Violence, and Poison Prevention, "Injury Risk of Nonpowder Guns," *Pediatrics,* November 2004, 1357–1361.

CHAPTER 14

1. Douglas Colligan, "Tipping the Balance of the Sexes," *New York,* November 7, 1977.

2. "China Schedules Probe into Japanese Sex Romp," Associated Press, November 20, 2003, http://tinyurl.com/6697w9r.

3. John Pomfret, "Wild Weekend's Hangover; Outrage Follows Japanese Tourists' Orgy with Chinese Prostitutes," *Washington Post,* October 3, 2003.

4. Peter Gries, *China's New Nationalism* (Berkeley: University of California Press, 2004).

5. Michael Tyler, "'I Stepped out of the Lift and into an Orgy,'" *Telegraph,* October 5, 2003, http://tinyurl.com/64uc65y.

6. Closing of hotel: "Japanese Orgy Trial Opens in China," CNN.com, December 12, 2003, http://tinyurl.com/4n7cuso.

7. "Masterminds of Japanese Orgy Get Life," *China Daily,* December 17, 2003, http://tinyurl.com/4vc9olr.

8. "China Jails 14 on Sex Party for Japanese," *New York Times,* December 18, 2003, http://tinyurl.com/4asr2bm.

9. "China Jails Orgy Organisers," BBC, December 17, 2003, http://tinyurl.com/4mjkgmy.

10. Japanese investigation: "Sex Party Trial in China Ends," Associated Press, December 14, 2003, http://tinyurl.com/4s95myr.

11. Mara Hvistendahl, "The Boxer Shorts Rebellion," *The New Republic,* March 26, 2008.

12. Hvistendahl, "Boxer Shorts"; "Chinese in Belgrade, Beijing Protest NATO Embassy Bombing," CNN, May 9, 1999, http://tinyurl.com/6yef9rx.

13. Zheng Wang, "National Humiliation, History Education, and the Politics of Historical Memory: Patriotic Education Campaign in China," *International Studies Quarterly* 52 (2008): 784, http://tinyurl.com/4rgtknh.

14. Hvistendahl, "Boxer Shorts."

15. "The Immoral Foreign Blogger," EastSouthWestNorth, August 28, 2008, http://tinyurl.com/4u48nxr.

16. Zhang Jeihai, "The Internet Search for the Immoral Foreigner," August 25, 2006, http://tinyurl.com/4nzdopl.

17. Hvistendahl, "Boxer Shorts."

18. Lena Edlund et al., *More Men, More Crime: Evidence from China's One-Child Policy,* Institute for the Study of Labor Discussion Paper Series (Bonn, Germany: 2007).

19. Jim Yardley, "Indian Women Find New Peace in Rail Commute," *New York Times,* September 15, 2009, http://tinyurl.com/mrlj2k.

20. Edlund et al., "More Men."

21. Edlund et al., "More Men."

22. Mary E. John et al., *Planning Families, Planning Gender* (Bangalore: Books for Change, 2008), 84.

23. Soutik Biswas, "India's 'Pink' Vigilante Women," BBC News, November 26, 2007, http://news.bbc.co.uk/2/hi/7068875.stm.

24. Biswas, "India's 'Pink' Vigilante Women."

25. Jean Dreze and Reetika Khera, "Crime, Gender, and Society in India: Insights from Homicide Data," *Population and Development Review*, June 2000, 347.

26. John et al., *Planning Families*, 77.

27. Avraham Y. Ebenstein and Ethan Jennings Sharygin, "The Consequences of the 'Missing Girls' of China," *World Bank Economic Review*, November 5, 2009, 417.

28. Ebenstein and Sharygin, "Consequences," 417.

29. Thérèse Hesketh, interview by author, London, November 25, 2008.

30. "China Youth Crime 'in Rapid Rise,'" BBC, December 5, 2007, http://tinyurl.com/yoc8jl.

31. John et al., *Planning Families*, 56.

32. Michael Wines, "Stunned China Looks Inward After School Attacks," *New York Times*, May 1, 2010, http://tinyurl.com/2fte7fe.

33. Michael Wines, "Attacker Stabs 28 Chinese Children," *New York Times*, April 29, 2010, http://tinyurl.com/38qajge.

34. "China Executes Killer of Eight School Children," BBC, April 28, 2010, http://news.bbc.co.uk/2/hi/8648077.stm.

35. Hudson and den Boer, *Bare Branches*, 202.

36. Tim Mason, "Women in Germany, 1925–1940: Family, Welfare and Work, Part I," *History Workshop*, Spring 1976, 77.

37. Hudson and den Boer, *Bare Branches*, 255.

38. Hudson and den Boer, *Bare Branches*, 257.

39. Ehrlich, *Population Bomb*, 48.

40. Therese Hesketh and Zhu Wei Xing, "Abnormal Sex Ratios in Human Populations: Causes and Consequences," *Proceedings of the National Academy of the Sciences*, September 5, 2006, www.pnas.org/content/103/36/13271.full.

41. Xiong Peiyun, "Aiguo ruhe zhuyi," *Southern Breeze*, 2008, http://tinyurl.com/4vo8q4v. See also China Digital Times, in "China's Nationalism, and How Not to Deal with It," May 10, 2008, http://tinyurl.com/6295g2.

42. Amelia Gentleman, "Indian Prime Minister Denounces Abortion of Females," *New York Times*, April 29, 2008, http://tinyurl.com/44n7dt.

43. Hvistendahl, "No Country."

44. Mara Hvistendahl, "Making Every Baby Girl Count," *Science*, February 27, 2009, 1164–1166.

45. Mara Hvistendahl, "Making Every Baby Girl Count."

46. Hvistendahl, "Has China Outgrown?"

47. Mara Hvistendahl, "Making Every Baby Girl Count," 1165.

48. "India Sex Selection Doctor Jailed," BBC, March 26, 2006, http://tinyurl.com/lyf69.

49. Carla Power, "But What If It's a Girl?" *New Statesman*, April 24, 2006, http://tinyurl.com/6gamvnk.

50. Sukhbir Siwach, "Haryana to Keep Track of Expectant Mothers," *Times of India*, December 10, 2010.

51. Wonacott, "India's Skewed Sex Ratio."

52. "Indian Colleges Ban Jeans to 'Protect' Girls," AFP, June 10, 2008, http://tinyurl.com/nktkoe.

53. Tulsi Patel, ed., introduction to *Sex-selective Abortion in India: Gender, Society, and New Reproductive Technologies* (New Delhi: Sage, 2007), 51.

54. This and the following quotes are taken from Amin Malouf, *The First Century After Beatrice* (London: Abacus, 1994).

55. "Missing Girls in Asia: Magnitudes, Implications, and Possible Responses" (paper presented to American Enterprise Institute symposium, Washington, D.C., September 17, 2008), http://www.aei.org/event/1796.

CHAPTER 15

1. Monica Das Gupta, Woojin Chung, and Li Shuzhuo, *Is There an Incipient Turnaround in Asia's "Missing Girls" Phenomenon?* World Bank Development Research Group, February 2009, 2.

2. Das Gupta, Chung, and Li, *Incipient Turnaround*, 9.

3. UNDP, *Asia-Pacific Human Development Report: Power, Voice, and Rights: A Turning Point for Gender Equality in Asia* (Colombo, Sri Lanka: Macmillan, 2010), 145. http://tinyurl.com/4gwmjjo. Also see Augusto Lopez-Claros and Saadia Zahidi, *Women's Empowerment: Measuring the Global Gender Gap* (Cologne/Geneva: World Economic Forum, 2005), 1, http://tinyurl.com/4zn8mtw.

4. Heeran Chun et al., "Understanding Women, Health, and Social Change: The Case of South Korea," *International Journal of Health Services* 36, no. 3 (2006): 575.

5. "Country Comparison: Total Fertility Rate," *CIA World Factbook 2010*, http://tinyurl.com/3yur88. Carl Haub, "Did South Korea's Population Policy Work Too Well?" Population Reference Bureau, http://tinyurl.com/48w2xf3.

6. Sidney B. Westley and Minja Kim Choe, *How Does Son Preference Affect Populations in Asia?* (Honolulu, HI: East-West Center, September 2007), 9.

7. Westley and Choe, *How Does Son Preference?* 9.

8. Heeran Chun, interview by author.

9. These projections were calculated using data from 1990, for boys then ages five to nine. Chai Bin Park and Nam-Hoon Cho, "Consequences of Son Preference in a Low-Fertility Society: Imbalance of the Sex Ratio at Birth in Korea," *Population and Development Review*, March 1995, 74.

10. Heeran Chun, email to author, November 28, 2010.

11. Park and Cho, *Consequences of Son Preference*, 80.

12. Westley and Choe, *Son Preference*, 6.

13. Kyung-Sup Chang, "The State and Families in South Korea's Compressed Fertility Transition: A Time for Policy Reversal?" *Journal of Population and Social Security (Population)*, supplement, 1(2003): 1, http://tinyurl.com/6dgagdu.

14. Doo-Sub Kim, interview by author.

15. Baik Eun-Jeong, Korean Medical Association, interview by author, December 17, 2009.

16. Therese Hesketh, Wei Xing Zhu, and Li Lu, "China's Excess Males, Sex Selective Abortion, and One Child Policy: Analysis of Data from 2005 National Intercensus Survey," *British Medical Journal*, April 9, 2009, http://tinyurl.com/4tb5wfw.

17. Some biographical details: Steven Mosher, phone interview by author, February 3, 2011.

18. U.S. Committee for the United Nations Population Fund, "Who Is Steven Mosher?" http://www.planetwire.org/files.fcgi/3750_StevenMosher.pdf.

19. Population Research Institute, "Our Mission," http://www.pop.org/about/our-mission-801.

20. Steven Mosher, "A New Front in the Abortion Wars: Banning Sex-Selection Abortions," *PRI Review*, November-December 2008, http://tinyurl.com/4ata5eo.

21. "Hadley Arkes: Senior Fellow," Ethics and Public Policy Center, Washington, D.C., http://tinyurl.com/4koj2rx.

22. Hadley Arkes, "Abortion Facts and Feelings," *First Things*, April 1994, 34–38, http://tinyurl.com/4jdy7os.

23. Richard E. Cohen and Brian Friel, "2009 Vote Ratings: Politics As Usual," *National Journal*, November 25, 2010, http://tinyurl.com/y8d66cv; http://tinyurl.com/4ba5tkh.

24. "Text of H.R. 1822 as Introduced in House," http://tinyurl.com/4fuc69k.

25. *Special Alert: New Civil Rights Legislation*, video, Population Research Institute, http://tinyurl.com/47z5loh.

26. The figures in Edlund's study reflect the practices of 230,000 families, only a fraction of whom aborted female fetuses. Lena Edlund, email to author, November 27, 2010.

27. "H.R. 1822: Susan B. Anthony and Frederick Douglass Prenatal Nondiscrimination Act of 2009," http://tinyurl.com/65lpccn.

28. "Text of H.R. 1822 as Introduced in House," http://tinyurl.com/4fuc69k.

29. Population Action International, *The Shape of Things to Come: Country Case Study South Korea*, http://tinyurl.com/6hwdled.

30. Cho Young-Youl, interview by author.

31. Florence Lowe-Lee, *Is Korea Ready for the Demographic Revolution? The World's Most Rapidly Aging Society with the Most Rapidly Declining Fertility Rate* (paper for Korea Economic Institute, 2009). http://www.keia.org/Publications/Exchange/04Exchange09.pdf.

32. Lowe-Lee, *Is Korea Ready?*

33. Population Action International, *Shape of Things to Come*.

34. Jaeyeon Woo, "Government Plays Matchmaker," *Wall Street Journal*, November 26, 2010, http://tinyurl.com/4jluro3.

35. Baik, interview by author.

36. Baik, interview by author.

37. Geun Tae Kim, "Korea: Quality Childcare," *OECD Observer*, http://tinyurl.com/66f443q.

38. John Sudworth, "South Koreans Told to Go Home and Make Babies," BBC, January 20, 2010, http://tinyurl.com/yfzgj3m.

39. Woo, "Government Plays Matchmaker."

40. Population Action International, *Shape of Things to Come.*

41. Hong and Tietze, "Survey of Abortion Providers."

42. "Continued Sentences for Abortion Crimes Are Unjust," Network for Pregnancy and Birth Decision Rights (Seoul), http://tinyurl.com/4af8cuh. Translation in "Resisting the Criminalization of Abortion in South Korea," http://tinyurl.com/5sg74dn.

43. John M. Glionna, "In South Korea, Abortion Foes Gain Ground," *Los Angeles Times,* November 29, 2009, http://tinyurl.com/y8vwmrl.

44. "Reaffirming Reproductive Rights," *Hankyoreh,* March 6, 2010, http://tinyurl.com/4hnbbka.

45. Sangwon Yoon, "'Abortion Republic' Makes an About Face," Associated Press, March 18, 2010, http://tinyurl.com/65a2efx.

46. David Plotz, "The Seoul of Clones," *Slate,* October 19, 2005, http://www.slate.com/id/2128361/.

EPILOGUE

1. "Swaying for Gender," BabyCenter.com, accessed April 2, 2009.

2. Jesse Invik, Suzanne Mills, and Tyler McCreary, "The Third Sex: Supporting the Struggles of Transgendered People," *Briarpatch*, November 2005, http://tinyurl.com/6daes9o.

3. "Sex Selection and Family Balancing," Fertility Institutes' website, http://www.fertility-docs.com/fertility_gender.phtml.

4. Claudia Kalb, "Brave New Babies," *Newsweek,* January 26, 2004, http://tinyurl.com/6grvhof.

5. Mimi Rohr, "Fertility Institutes: The Clinic that Helps Couples to Choose the Sex of Their Babies," Frédéric Neema Photography, http://tinyurl.com/65h64u4.

6. Debora L. Spar, *The Baby Business: How Money, Science, and Politics Drive the Commerce of Conception* (Boston: Harvard Business School Press, 2006), 127.

7. Etzioni, "Sex Control, Science, and Society," 1108.

8. Helen Bequaert Holmes, "Sex Preselection: Eugenics for Everyone," in *Biomedical Ethics Reviews: 1985,* ed. James M. Humber and Robert F. Almeder (Clifton, NJ: Humana Press, 1985), 43.

9. Landrum B. Shettles and David M. Rorvik, *How to Choose the Sex of Your Baby: The Method Best Supported by Scientific Evidence* (New York: Broadway Books, 2006), 51–52.

10. Shettles and Rorvik, *How to Choose the Sex of Your Baby,* 51–53; F. Økland, "Excerpt: *Will It Be a Boy? Sex-Determination According to Superstition and to Science,*" *Journal of the American Medical Association* 99, no. 7 (1932): 587.

11. Allen J. Wilcox, Clarice R. Weinberg, and Donna D. Baird, "Timing of Sexual Intercourse in Relation to Ovulation," *New England Journal of Medicine*, December 7, 1995, 1517–1521, http://tinyurl.com/48zsyl8.

12. The President's Council on Bioethics, "Choosing Sex of Children," *Population and Development Review*, December 2003, 754–755.

13. Vicki Mabrey, "Choosing the Sex," *60 Minutes*, prod. Miriam Weintraub, April 14, 2004.

14. "Half of Fertility Clinics Allow Parents to Pick Gender," Associated Press, September 20, 2006.

15. Meredith Wadman, "So You Want a Girl?" *Fortune*, February 19, 2001, http://tinyurl.com/5srhget.

16. Dena Braun, "Pruning the Family Tree," http://tinyurl.com/6agw5ob.

17. Amy Harmon, "Embryo Screening" (video), *New York Times*, September 1, 2006; Spar, *Baby Business*, 98–99.

18. Marcy Darnovsky, interview by author, Berkley, CA, April 29, 2010.

19. Spar, *Baby Business*, 100.

20. Robin Elise Weiss, "Girl or Boy? Sex Selection Techniques for Everyone Before Pregnancy," http://tinyurl.com/344c67.

21. Robin Elise Weiss, *Guarantee the Sex of Your Baby* (Berkeley, CA: Ulysses, 2007), 6.

22. Ruth Shalit Barrett, "Girl Crazy: Women Who Suffer from Gender Disappointment," *Elle*, October 9, 2009.

23. Huntington Reproductive Center figure: Lonny Shavelson, "Many Clinics Use Genetic Diagnosis to Choose Sex," NPR, December 20, 2006, http://tinyurl.com/4sqr85m; Genetics and IVF Institute figure: Liza Mundy, *Everything Conceivable: How Assisted Reproduction Is Changing Our World* (New York: Anchor, 2007), 318.

24. Hanna Rosin, "The End of Men," *The Atlantic*, July-August, 2010, http://tinyurl.com/2c4vnxs.

25. Sunita Puri, interview by author, San Francisco, May 1, 2010.

26. Mallory Stout, phone interview by author, May 5, 2010.

27. Abbie E. Goldberg, "Heterosexual, Lesbian, and Gay Preadoptive Parents' Preferences About Child Gender," Springer Science/Business Media, 2009.

28. Dena S. Davis, *Genetic Dilemmas: Reproductive Technology, Parental Choices, and Children's Futures* (New York: Routledge, 2001), 101.

29. Darnovsky, interview by author.

30. "Country Comparison: Total Fertility Rate," *CIA World Factbook 2010*, http://tinyurl.com/3yur88.

31. Casey B. Mulligan, "The More the Merrier: Population Growth Promotes Innovation," *New York Times*, September 23, 2009, http://tinyurl.com/mdfdxw.

32. "Sex Selection," BioPolicyWiki, http://tinyurl.com/46d8hfp.

33. "Sex Selection: Options for Regulation," Human Fertilisation Embryology Authority, November 12, 2003, http://www.hfea.gov.uk/docs/Final_sex_selection_main_report.pdf.

34. In 2008 the agency issued the clinic a public warning letter, citing incidences of employees neglecting to test semen for chlamydia and gonorrhea in cases involving surrogate mothers. Steinberg says he had tested the specimens in question on-site but didn't realize a recent change in FDA policy required him to use external labs. Food and Drug Administration, Department of Inspections, Compliance, Enforcement, and Criminal Investigations, Warning Letter to Jeffrey Steinberg MD Inc., d/b/a The Fertility Institutes, November 18, 2008, http://tinyurl.com/5wz43wa.

35. Ethics Committee of the American Society for Reproductive Medicine, "Preconception Gender Selection for Nonmedical Reasons," *Fertility and Sterility*, May 2001, http://tinyurl.com/4euesq4; President's Council on Bioethics, "Choosing Sex of Children," 755–756; Darnovsky, interview by author.

36. Darnovsky, interview by author.

37. Spar, *Baby Business*, 3; number of clinics: Stephanie Saul, "Birth of Octuplets Puts Focus on Fertility Industry and Risks," *New York Times*, February 11, 2009, http://tinyurl.com/4rburmv.

38. Mundy, *Everything Conceivable*, 315.

39. Kahlil Gibran, *The Prophet* (New Delhi: Sterling, 1945), 23.

40. Taras Kuzin, interview by author, via Skype, May 28, 2010.

41. Amy Harmon, "Couples Cull Embryos to Halt Heritage of Cancer," *New York Times*, September 3, 2006, http://tinyurl.com/4umf9dr.

42. Allen Goldberg, "Select a Baby's Health, Not Eye Color," *Los Angeles Times*, February 17, 2009, http://tinyurl.com/arfjdo.

INDEX

Mara Hvistendahl is a Beijing-based correspondent for *Science.* Her award-winning writing has also appeared in *Harper's, Scientific American, Popular Science,* the *Financial Times,* and *Foreign Policy.* Proficient in both Spanish and Chinese, she has spent half of the past decade in China, where she has reported on everything from archaeology to the space program. A former contributing editor at *Seed* magazine and journalism professor at Fudan University in Shanghai, Hvistendahl sits on the advisory board of Round Earth Media, an organization founded to promote international journalism. This is her first book.

PublicAffairs is a publishing house founded in 1997. It is a tribute to the standards, values, and flair of three persons who have served as mentors to countless reporters, writers, editors, and book people of all kinds, including me.

I. F. STONE, proprietor of *I. F. Stone's Weekly*, combined a commitment to the First Amendment with entrepreneurial zeal and reporting skill and became one of the great independent journalists in American history. At the age of eighty, Izzy published *The Trial of Socrates*, which was a national bestseller. He wrote the book after he taught himself ancient Greek.

BENJAMIN C. BRADLEE was for nearly thirty years the charismatic editorial leader of *The Washington Post*. It was Ben who gave the *Post* the range and courage to pursue such historic issues as Watergate. He supported his reporters with a tenacity that made them fearless and it is no accident that so many became authors of influential, best-selling books.

ROBERT L. BERNSTEIN, the chief executive of Random House for more than a quarter century, guided one of the nation's premier publishing houses. Bob was personally responsible for many books of political dissent and argument that challenged tyranny around the globe. He is also the founder and longtime chair of Human Rights Watch, one of the most respected human rights organizations in the world.

．　　　．　　　．

For fifty years, the banner of Public Affairs Press was carried by its owner Morris B. Schnapper, who published Gandhi, Nasser, Toynbee, Truman, and about 1,500 other authors. In 1983, Schnapper was described by *The Washington Post* as "a redoubtable gadfly." His legacy will endure in the books to come.

Peter Osnos, *Founder and Editor-at-Large*